Breaking Autism's Barriers

of related interest

Raising a Child with Autism
A Guide to Applied Behavior Analysis for Parents
Shira Richman
ISBN 1 85302 910 6

Asperger's Syndrome
A Guide for Parents and Professionals
Tony Attwood
ISBN 1 85302 577 1

Our Journey Through High Functioning Autism
and Asperger Syndrome
A Roadmap
Edited by Linda Andron
ISBN 1 85302 947 5

Diet Intervention and Autism
Implementing the Gluten Free and Casein Free Diet
for Autistic Children and Adults
A Practical Guide for Parents
Marilyn Le Breton
ISBN 1 85302 935 1

The Self-Help Guide for Special Kids and their Parents
Joan Matthews and James Williams
ISBN 1 85302 914 9

I am Special
Introducing Children and Young People to their
Autistic Spectrum Disorder
Peter Vermeulen
ISBN 1 85302 916 5

Behavioural Concerns and Autistic Spectrum Disorders
Explanations and Strategies for Change
John Clements and Ewa Zarkowska
ISBN 1 85302 742 1

Finding Out About Asperger's Syndrome,
High Functioning Autism and PDD
Gunilla Gerland
ISBN 1 85302 840 1

Breaking Autism's Barriers

A Father's Story

Bill Davis

as told to Wendy Goldband Schunick

Jessica Kingsley Publishers
London and Philadelphia

First published in the United Kingdom in 2001 by
Jessica Kingsley Publishers Ltd,
116 Pentonville Road,
London N1 9JB, England
and
325 Chestnut Street,
Philadelphia, PA 19106, USA.

www.jkp.com

Library of Congress Cataloging in Publication Data
A CIP catalog record for this book is available from the Library of Congress

British Library Cataloguing in Publication Data
A CIP catalogue record for this book is available from the British Library

ISBN 1 85302 979 3

Printed and Bound in Great Britain by
Athenaeum Press, Gateshead, Tyne and Wear

Contents

Introduction   Tattooed For Life   11

Part I – The Beginning

1	Marriage	19
2	Infancy	27
3	Warning Signs	29
4	Genius Savant?	38
5	The Insolvable Puzzle	43
6	Finding Help	51
7	Diagnosis	54
8	Early Intervention	58
9	He Kissed Me!	62

Part II – Finding Appropriate Education

1	Starting School	67
2	Starting An In-Home Program	73
3	Wanted: Therapists	77
4	Hiring Rutgers University	84
5	Fighting For Funds	87
6	How To Handle Your IEP	92

Part III – Daily Life

1	Frantic!	105
2	The Pain Is Numbing	113
3	Aggression	120
4	Discrete Trial	125
5	Running On Empty	136
6	Behavior Control	140
7	Communicating Without Words	147
8	He Spoke!	152
9	Potty Training	162
10	Adventures In Eating	168
11	Teeth	175
12	Gymnastics	178

Part IV – Advocacy and Education

1	The Battle For Safety	185
2	Fighting For A Public Preschool Program	201
3	Helping Other Families	207
4	Telling The World	221
5	The Mainstreaming Myth	235
6	Kindergarten	245
7	Future Schooling	252

Part V – Learning To Cope

1	Socialization	259
2	Laughing And Feeling Joy	265
3	Music	272
4	Honkers	278
5	Making Ends Meet	281
6	Total Involvement	287
7	The Stress Of Daily Life	294
8	Secretin, A Potential New Weapon	301
9	Steps To Take	305
10	Sibling Impact	313
11	Jessica's Own Story	328
12	Vacations?	336
13	Friends And Family Support	343
14	Institutionalization	347

Part VI – Inspiration

1	Feeling Sorry For Yourself	353
2	Jae's Ingenious Programs	358
3	The Human Spirit	364
4	The Future Of Autism	370
5	Loving Your Child	377
6	Chris Today	383
7	Chris' Future	392
	Epilogue	399

To Alana and Justin
The two most beautiful people in my life.

To my parents
I love you. Thanks for always being there.

To Cathy
You elevate the word 'friendship' to a level never reached by most.

Wendy

I dedicate this book to my wife for her love, devotion,
selflessness, and creativity;
To Jessica for her sacrifice and humor;
To Danielle for hanging in there;
To my Mom for her sense of family and generosity;
To Wendy for her patience and expertise;
To Bill Stillman for his sensitivity and sense of direction;
To Dr. Landa for her knowledge;
To Charlie Jr. for his gift;
And to my beautiful boy, Chris, for his strength, bravery, and heart.
And for teaching me what unconditional love really is.

Bill

Introduction

Tattooed For Life

'A'... My nerve endings screamed with pain. 'U'... Every touch of the needle felt like an assault as it tattooed the letters across my chest. A massive biker sporting his own tattoos and earrings walked in wearing his helmet. Staring at me he asked, 'What's that, man?'

Not in the most jovial of moods, I answered quickly, 'It spells autism. It's a neurobiological disorder that my son has.'

'I understand, man. You want to feel his pain and let everybody know it exists, and like work with him and everything.'

He was right on the money. Just as those letters assaulted my chest, the disorder had assaulted my son. When people see the word 'autism' sprawled across my chest it's pretty hard for them to turn away. Inevitably it leads to discussion about the disorder, and that's exactly what I want. I am putting it in their faces, telling them, 'Open your eyes and look. There are kids out there like my son, who exist and are being ignored and forgotten. They deserve your attention. The courage I had to get this tattoo was nowhere near the courage these children have to fight autism.'

I also have a Chinese symbol tattooed on my neck that means bravery. The neck, being very thin-skinned, is another painful spot for a tattoo. But its prominence lets me tell the whole world how brave my son is. He has spent his whole life slaying this dragon called autism, and I could never find a greater hero.

The fight my son's been through and the fight my entire family has been through gives me great pride. I believe what we've experienced and accomplished can help many others. In fact, I know that we already have changed people's lives for the better. Families have called me on the phone to tell me they got through everything with their child because of us. Policemen have stopped me and said, 'Thank you so much for training us.'

People everywhere kept telling me to write this book, but I thought no one would be interested until one very moving moment in my life. While working as a bartender at Scooters Bar one Saturday night a group of eight came in for a birthday party. There were two kids, probably in their twenties, who each had autism and Down syndrome. Both were 'stimming,' a characteristic of autism that often involves shaking hands and heads, and moving all about in odd ways. Then the birthday boy walked in. He too had autism and was stimming wildly. Just wild! He had constant facial ticking. His fingers were waving. He kept touching and hitting his mouth and other people, and just couldn't sit still. As far as I could tell he was completely nonverbal. Surprisingly, everybody was giving him books for birthday presents. I found out later he reads, attends college, and has a brilliant mind. I walked over. 'Hi, I don't mean to intrude. My name is Bill Davis and I have a son with autism.'

Everybody stopped, 'Bill Davis? We read articles about you. Oh, my God!' And they all jumped around hugging each other.

'Happy birthday,' I said. The boy kind of looked at me and turned away, stimming.

I then gave him a Scooters t-shirt. 'Oh, that's so nice of you,' the mother said. 'He loves Scooters. He comes in sometimes with his dad.'

Suddenly the boy began typing on his keyboard. 'Wait a minute,' said the mother, 'He wants to type something.'

The kid typed, 'Mr. Bill, I've read your articles. Thank you for training the police. Good luck in Baltimore.' There had been an article talking about our making a future move to Baltimore. 'I know it's a hard road.'

I was crying. This was a guy with autism telling me thanks. He then typed, 'Do you think I'm smart?'

'Yes. I think you're very smart.'

'Then give your child a voice if he needs it. Let him type like I do if necessary, but give him a voice.' We hugged, he shook my hand, and for that brief moment all the stimming stopped.

Here was a guy who everybody looked at as an outcast, especially when he was hitting himself, but yet he was able to express so poignantly that he was a thinking, feeling human being who deserved to be helped. His thank you made me realize just how important my advocacy work was. I knew I was doing the right thing.

I've worked hard to give my son Chris a voice. We know that he communicates in every way, whether it be speaking, gesture, sign, or picture icons. And we listen to him. Eventually he'll either speak fluently or type. I can't wait for the day that he is able to talk to us like this guy and tell us all the secrets of his life that we're not privy to right now.

So I decided to write this story for Chris, for my family, and for all the others touched by autism. I want parents to read this book and realize there's somebody out there experiencing all the same triumphs and tragedies. Every time they feel down, I hope they can pick this book up and say, 'If they can do it, I can do it. I can be strong too.' I hope I can open up somebody's eyes and give them some understanding of autism.

I certainly hope professionals also gain a little understanding of what parents and children go through. They need to come off their pedestal when they talk only of budgets. These are not simply children to be babysat. They are human beings who want to learn and who want a friend. Professionals need to realize that their policy decisions can harmfully affect these children for years.

Hopelessly throwing their hands up in defeat to the bureaucracy is not acceptable either. I want apathetic government officials to say, 'My God, look what I've done all these years. I've neglected the people I'm supposed to be fighting for because I'm too wrapped up in making decisions based on my job security.' They need to stand up and shout that the system stinks, and then they need to change it.

There are people who have to learn from this. Everybody who ever stared should learn and understand what it's like to deal with a disorder like autism. Maybe they'll become a little more sensitive to those around them who are different. Parents should learn to tell their kids about disabilities.

If one pediatrician reads this and says, 'I'd better go out and take a couple of seminars,' then my job is done. If an educator says, 'Tomorrow I'm fighting for more services,' or if a policeman says, 'Let's get some training in here,' or if a parent says, 'We have to get more involved and I have to stand up for my son,' then I think my efforts are very, very worthwhile. I've helped the people where I live. Now I'd like to reach out to a broader audience.

While speaking at Franklin and Marshall College I showed a film. 'This is Chris a day ago. He's counting and busy with activities. Let me tell you about Chris four years ago. This child one day had no language, drank from a bottle, wouldn't look at us, wouldn't talk to us, wouldn't come out of the corner, spun around, waved his hands, played with his fingers twenty hours a day, kept falling down, and went limp at the touch. He was angry, aggressive, wouldn't leave the apartment, wouldn't look at food, threw up. Oh, my God. I once made a sandwich with bologna and from across the room he threw up. Horrible. And look at Chris today. It was a long fight, but Chris is the one who dug down deep.'

The biggest gift that we have is the human spirit. My son's strength is testimony to that spirit. I hope people will be inspired by him and be moved to find their own strength from within when dealing with adversity.

The Davis family – Bill, Jessica, Chris and Jae – in 1995

PART I

The Beginning

1

Marriage

'I see what our son sees and you feel what he feels. We make a very good team' – *Jae Davis*

My wife Jae was on one of her advocacy calls to a Mennonite family living in the boondocks of Pennsylvania. They needed help with their son who had autism. So she took our daughter, Jessica, and the two of them drove off to this unknown farm family an hour away. 'Call me when you get there,' I nervously requested feeling concerned about her driving off to some mysterious destination.

Two hours went by. No call. I called the Mennonite family. No answer. Four hours later I still hadn't heard from my wife and still no answer at the farm! Where was she? Were they in an accident? Did these people do something to her? I called the local police. 'Sorry, you have to wait longer before we begin a search.'

'I'm not waiting! My wife left here hours ago!' If *they* wouldn't do anything, then I would. I called the farm's local police station and every state trooper barrack on Jae's route, gave them her license number, and asked them to look for her. It was now six o'clock in the evening and no call from either my wife or the police. I felt terror running through my veins, and found myself calling every hospital along the route, checking for accidents.

Back on the phone again with the troopers I could hear their two-way radio conversations in the background. 'The car is here. I see the car. There's activity in the home. We're approaching the house...'

'Mr. Davis, we've located the car. It's at the house... We're going in! We're going in!'

For those next few seconds my brain went numb. I saw only black in front of me...

'Sir, your wife and daughter are fine.'

The police went in and found Jae and Jessica just sitting there with the farm woman! Apparently when Jae arrived the husband immediately took them out to lunch, and then they went to the church where their son was taught so she could observe his program. The church was in the back woods and had no phone. They didn't get back to the house until six o'clock.

About two years later when Jesse's bike was stolen a woman cop showed up to take the report. 'You're that guy who's so in love with his wife.'

'What do you mean?'

'I was on the other end of the phone when you reported her missing. You were in such a panic that I said to everybody, "Look what that guy's going through. He really loves his wife." It was really touching.'

It's true. I have a very deep love for my wife. But our marriage is certainly not a traditional one, not anymore. We have a good relationship, but we have had no time for any type of intimacy in four years. It's impossible. We don't have the time, not since our son Chris was diagnosed with autism. If we find two minutes, we're tired. We never get a chance to be romantic. We don't even go out to eat. In spite of it all, though, our relationship is strong.

When I think of Jae, I immediately think of our bond. We've had a very interesting life together that has changed drastically. Yet our connection is strong and we obviously were very much meant for each other.

After we were married we became the proud parents of a beautiful baby girl, Jessica. I was now the father of two girls, Danielle, from my first marriage, and Jessica. Everything was great. By the time Jesse was five, we were very settled in our relationship. Jae was starting back to work as a nail tech and I was getting more involved with hotel-restaurant management. We had decided not to have any more children when suddenly Jae discovered she was pregnant! Nervous about her age, she had an amniocentesis at Hershey Hospital. A week later a little blue card arrived in the mail announcing, 'You have a healthy male.'

'Oh, a little boy. I'm going to run with him and play ball with him.' I had all the typical expectations that go with a man about to father a son. When our boy was born, I was elated. Christopher was a wonderful baby and we loved him. Life was good.

Then Chris' behavior started to change, and our marriage naturally changed along with it. We worked furiously to find out what was wrong with Chris and get a diagnosis. Then we needed to find proper schooling and therapy. Before long, the majority of our time was taken up with development of an in-home therapy program.

We were always very close as a family, but now Chris' autism became a common cause. We all grew very strong and molded into one. Each of us became working parts of a whole.

I was doing a lot of reading and making a lot of phone calls to find help, and Jae gravitated toward developing the therapy. We didn't have time to think. She needed all sorts of things and I would go get them. If she had a problem in the therapy, I'd read about it and offer a suggestion. If she needed funding I would read the law and get it. We always complemented each other, but never to this degree. And we were working at such an advanced level of education. It was an amazing experience! We didn't have college degrees, but here we were talking and working with Rutgers University and Johns Hopkins!

We had boundless energy and just went all the time. I'd sit down on the couch, fall asleep for ten minutes, and then jump up. 'I'm up. I'm going to work. Tomorrow I'll make more calls.'

Once everything was in place we thought things would calm down, but then we began to realize that helping Chris would be a lifetime effort. There's always a new theory, a new program, a new way. We found we had to constantly observe and be there. So we had a choice: Either jump into the program completely or settle. And we weren't willing to settle. But the more we weren't willing to settle, the more our marriage took a back seat to helping Chris.

Before Chris' autism we used to sit down, have a drink, and watch a movie at night. Now Jae was on the computer creating her program for the next day and I was doing research. 'Come on,' I'd say, 'You're doing too much work.'

'No, I have to finish this. This is what I have to do.'

Our days were planned around what we were doing for Chris, and we were passing like ships in the night. But somehow there was an understanding that as much as this wasn't a healthy marriage lifestyle, it would not affect our bond because we were doing it together.

Strange as it sounds, a customer from the bar actually affected how I handled my marriage. He had a son with a horrible lingering, degenerative disease. The mother stayed twenty-four hours a day with the son during his many hospital stays until finally he died. A horrible death.

'For years every time he was hospitalized my wife stayed by my son's side,' the customer told me. 'My one regret is while she was always with our son and researching medical books, I felt I needed warmth and attention that I wasn't getting from her. So what did I do? I got a girlfriend. It was the most selfish, low down thing I could have done. I allowed myself the companionship when I should have bit the bullet.'

Looking for a girlfriend was not something that occurred to me. But what this guy said really stuck in my head. It's easy to see how someone might allow that to happen in such a difficult situation. Even in my own life it was not uncommon for our conversations to sound cold. 'Jae, I haven't seen you in four days.'

'Too bad. I'm doing this program.'

But conversations like this are no excuse for abandoning a marriage. So maybe our relationship takes a lot more hard work than it would with a typical child. Too bad. I made a decision: No matter how lonely or difficult life gets, I will never look elsewhere for companionship. There was no better companion than my own wife, and even though we weren't able to give each other the time together, I had immeasurable admiration for all she was doing.

Anything you read about autism almost always says that the parents' marriage suffers more than anything. A lot of people separate. Men especially seem to have trouble. I think men suddenly feel they are not head of the family anymore.

Originally life centered around them. 'Here I come. I'm home with my money.' But when the disorder hits, the mother usually takes hold of the disabled child and is the one who goes to the therapies and the meetings. She suddenly becomes the fighter and central figure in the family. I think a lot of guys become jealous because she's usurping their position. But, yet, they won't join their wives in the fight. They don't dig down deep into their hearts and learn to go to an IEP or talk and read about what their son needs. They won't read the MDE and CER. They would rather fight in the traditional male way. 'I want him to have the best! I'll earn the money while you go and make sure it happens.'

All of a sudden, the mother asks, 'What did you do today?'

'I went to work. I'm tired.'

'Really? I went to Philadelphia and we got a diagnosis. Then I came back and did six hours of occupational therapy. Afterwards I traveled to York for our child's speech and language. I then argued with an official about getting him two years of in-home programming. Next I'm giving him a therapeutic massage. And you're tired? Too bad.'

Now the guy has no ground to stand on. 'Where's my dinner?'

'Make your own dinner.'

Then the husband goes in for his final kill. 'How do you think you got all this therapy?! *I* paid for it.'

I've known guys to walk out on their family, and I've known guys to blame their wives genetically. All they can cling to is the old caveman mentality. 'I'm a dad and dads are strong! This is what we do.'

So I made a promise to myself that a fragile male ego was not going to run my life. I would never stray from my marriage or be unsupportive of or abusive to my wife. You would never hear me say, 'I'm being neglected and I need the warmth…' or 'Our marriage is nothing. We never see each other and I'm walking out.' Bullshit.

If I was going to believe in what I was doing and allow my wife to take hold of her growth and help my son, then I was going to have to step out of traditional roles and complement her. I needed to admit to her publicly and privately that she was absolutely brilliant. I've often told her, 'I can't believe the things you do! You're absolutely amazing.' And she is. She was the one who was doing so much for our son and I was humbled before her. Believe me, I've had my immature moments. I'll sit there and whine, 'I'm really tired and you're up there drawing pictures. Can't you stop?' But then I realize how selfish I'm behaving and stop.

Fighting together for Chris, we've both evolved together. We've done everything as a working unit. When I write she corrects and rewrites. When I speak she gives me suggestions. Sometimes I'll observe something in therapy and she'll correct it. We always give each other the time we need. I need three hours today to do data sheets and she needs me to take Chris out and have him back at four. We're a very cooperative team.

The motto of our house has become, 'Hey, if you want the laundry done, do the laundry. If you want a meal, make a meal. Everybody chip in.' There's no traditional mother getting up, making the beds, and waiting for the husband with dinner on the table. It's catch as catch can. We can't do it any other way and that's just a fact of life. There's no apologizing.

Occasionally, just from being overtired, we break down. By the time the kids are in bed and we've done the paperwork it's one in the morning and we still have to prepare for a speech class at nine the next day. Naturally we're falling apart. We're always tired and feeling under the weather. How much can you stay up?

It's an understatement to say that intimacy has diminished. We kind of grab it when we can. And we laugh at it. We laugh at a lot of stuff. I'll say, 'Ready to make love now?' And we'll laugh. It's become funny. We keep reminding ourselves of our answer. If we weren't so tired and it wasn't three in the morning we'd love to be together. But can we go to sleep now, *please*?! We know the feelings are there, but we also know that right now it's not going to happen. Candlelit dinners and romantic evenings aren't part of the equation.

For now there are other ways to make love. Talking to each other is one way. I love when Jae and I have some energy left to sit and review the day. The most enjoyment we have is when we get the kids to bed a little early and rent a movie and sit together. Other than that, we enjoy a walk every once in a while. Summertime is nice because we can go out a little more and catch a walk in the field.

Just relaxing at the end of the evening is a treat for us. It's nice to know Jae has nothing to do until we wake up again and we can actually sit and laugh at something. There are times we go to bed and we're just so overtired that we get silly and laugh uncontrollably. Those are the moments with my wife that I hold close.

One day I was leaving to take Chris to school in Baltimore and Jae said, 'Be careful driving.' And she looked at me and started to cry. She kissed me. It was the first time we had warmth between each other in a long time. I looked in her eyes and saw such love from her. And I knew why she was crying. She misses the intimacy. She misses being able to say, 'Let's go out and have a cup of coffee. Let's spend fifteen minutes together.' I went out and bought her flowers. I just wanted to let her know that I love her too. Seeing that love in her eyes was like falling in love with her all over again.

I'm very dependent on Jae for a lot of things. She does an awful lot for me and I get a lot of my strength from her. She put every article printed about us, everything I have ever written, and every t-shirt printed for our benefits all over the wall above my desk along with our kids' pictures. She is truly my greatest inspiration.

2

Infancy

Chris was a fairly normal, developing baby – very loving and very bright. There was nothing about him that would throw you off. Maybe I was a little blinded by my love, but I already had two other children and truly did not see any differences between them.

Chris recognized all stimuli. He looked directly at us and used to lie on our chests and coo and cuddle. He had developed some language – Daddy, Mommy, clap-clap. He played a little bit. And he always liked to eat. He sat in a highchair and ate with utensils. In fact, he had a voracious appetite. I remember before he had teeth we were all eating pizza and he got so mad that he growled at us. 'Look,' I said proudly, 'that's a real boy. He wants to eat that pizza!'

I guess there were signs of Chris's autism we might have zeroed in on, but we didn't know enough about it at the time. For example, I remember hearing a

Chris as a baby

noise from his room one night. I went up and found him in the corner of the crib without his blanket. He had vomited and all he did was crawl away from it and go to sleep. What does a typical child do when he throws up? He cries. But Chris just dealt with it. They always just deal with it.

3

Warning Signs

When Chris was about one-and-a-half I started to notice he had a few peculiarities; nothing that would send you running to the doctor, though. At first glance he was a normally developing little guy. I really wasn't blinding myself. Believe me, I'm the first one to say something's wrong with my child. But there was really no reason for us to suspect anything major was wrong with him. He was always very charming and affectionate!

I believed that what I did notice were nothing more than unusual personality traits. For instance, he didn't have the same normal fears most children have. Separation anxiety was never an issue for Chris. He would wander through a crowd of people and never look back, completely unconcerned about where we were. We used to joke about it. 'Look at this guy. He doesn't care about anything.' Of course, not sensing danger was an early sign that he had autism.

He also started becoming more of a loner. He wouldn't look at other kids and seemed to lose interest in his toys. His language development also seemed a little slow.

One particularly peculiar behavior was that Chris clung to me way past the point of normalcy. I used to come home from work in the summertime and go right out and play ball with Jesse. It was something she loved to do with me when she was younger. But Chris would hang onto me and not let go. He was like a little extra package. I literally had him in one arm while I ran, played catch, or kicked the soccer ball. I would walk around with him in the house too. This lasted for a period of months when he was a toddler. Whenever I was around, Chris clung to me to the point where it became a joke. And I loved it! Here was my boy clinging to me. He wouldn't let me go!

Later I read that a lot of children with autism will cling to a parent. And I don't mean holding on to the parent's pants shyly. It's not what parents imagine when they say, 'Mine clung to me too.' We're not talking about that. We're talking about the fact that I *could not* put him down! Now I realize that was another symptom of his autism.

Slowly but surely, Chris' behavior eroded. His language wasn't coming around as quickly as we were used to with Jessica, and it began to make us sit up and take notice. He only had a couple words when we believed he should have more so we tried urging him to speak. I remember taking great pains to talk more to him.

In some ways I guess it was unfortunate that we were such doting parents because we easily gave in to him when he wanted something rather than forcing him to ask for it verbally. If he wanted a bottle and started getting frustrated, we would give it to him rather than hold out till he asked for it. We'd punish ourselves thinking that maybe we weren't doing him any good, but it's hard when you see your child get so frustrated.

Oddly enough, in contradiction to his slow language development Chris began to exhibit a lot of qualities that were amazingly smart! He was about two years old when he began building beautiful objects with blocks! We actually photographed and drew designs of his structures because they were so fantastic. He also played with big plastic letters and numbers a lot. I remember watching him one day while Jessica and my wife were taking a shower. He wasn't more than two and he had never really spoken. As I watched, he set up A through Z with his plastic letters. I was shocked. We had no idea he knew the alphabet yet. 'Oh, my God! Jae! Jessica! Come down here!'

'We're in the shower!'

'No, get down here now!'

So they came running down. 'Look!' I exclaimed.

Mockingly they said to me, '*You* did that.'

'No! Chris did the alphabet! Not me!'

'Oh, please.' Jae walked over in her towel and messed it all up. Chris got mad and Jae said to him, 'Go ahead. Do it again.'

And he started once again to put ABC right in order. Their mouths dropped open. He took each letter and very slowly showed it to Jae with a sly smile. He understood she didn't believe me. When he got to Y he looked at Jae, took the letter, held it up and showed her with a superior look on his face. Then he tossed it into place. He did the same thing with the Z. He shot us a big smile, picked it up, waved it, tossed it down, and walked away. He knew he had done something pretty great. Our son appeared to be a rapidly developing toddler, perhaps even above normal.

One day Chris was in his highchair, eating and watching Sesame Street on television. They announced, 'We're going to do our alphabet now,' and Chris attentively sat up straight. I remember saying to myself, there's nothing wrong with this guy. Look at him. Those little oddities we've noticed are nothing.

'Chris,' I beckoned, 'they're going to do the alphabet. You can do the alphabet.'

Then the little Sesame Street character said, 'Repeat after me. A.'

Chris looked and said, 'Bah.'

Next the character said, 'B.'

'Bah.'

'C.'

'Bah.'

Chris repeated that sound twenty-six times. He could not say those letters. Clearly upset, he looked at me and put his head down.

From that point he stopped speaking. 'Jae,' I said, 'he knows. There's something wrong with him and he knows.' And he wouldn't speak again.

I'll never forget that. This guy knew the alphabet! He knew how to do it. He showed me he knew how to do it! When that character said 'We're going to say our alphabet' he perked up and smiled because he understood what she said. True, he spoke only minimal words like 'bye-bye' and 'clap-clap.' But suddenly he lost the ability to speak completely. It was the first time Chris realized what he stored in his head could not come out. It was a devastating day for all of us, including Chris.

Almost overnight he stopped eating. He crawled into the corner of the apartment and wouldn't go out. He wouldn't look at us. He went limp at the touch. He wouldn't kiss us. He wouldn't hug us. He cried and screamed and threw tantrums. He finger-played and flapped his hands. He stared at the fan for eight hours at a time. He started spinning things.

In fact, spinning objects was Chris' only form of play. He chose only the toys that reflected light and could spin. There was a disco-type ball that he'd spin all the time. And he spun a gyro-scope-type object that took on a spiral design as it turned. He also made me spin tops for hours.

The staring he did was really scary. You know how you see particles of dust in the air? He would just stare into the dust from a fan and go off into a trance.

I always took walks with Chris and continued even when he was behaving so bizarrely. But as time went on I began to notice that he was tripping. Somehow he would walk and mis-step. I really thought there might be something wrong neurologically because his clumsiness was unexplainable. He never did that before! I kept thinking to myself that something terrible was going on with my son, but I didn't know what.

From tripping on his feet he went to toe walking, a typical trait of autism. One day we were walking in the mall and he started walking on his toes. Just like that. He looked so peculiar it was almost embarrassing to me. 'Jae, my God,' I said to my wife. 'What's he doing?' We both agreed something was wrong. Something was going on here.

Then he started eating the wood on the table! He was grinding his teeth into the plaster of the walls. He ate a hole in the drapes! He ate his clothing. He ate ants, nails, mud. Chris was out of control before age three. We were told he had something called 'pica,' which meant eating inappropriate objects, believed to stem from a lack of minerals and elements. To say we were alarmed is an understatement.

Things were rough. He'd eat the corner of the table right off. We'd just watch him constantly. But I don't think we ever yelled at him. This was not behavior that you yelled at. Instead we would physically stop him from eating. 'Come here. You can't do that.' We'd take the material out of his mouth and just keep him away from it. We taped the corners of the table and we taped where the walls come together to stop him from eating the plaster. We put the drapes up. We never left his side.

Then came the scariest night of my life. While doing our regular nightly check on the kids we found Chris just sitting up and staring into space. Trance-like, he would not react to us whatsoever. 'Quick! Call the ambulance!' I brought him downstairs and tried getting him to respond, 'Chris! Chris!' I was desperately trying to hide my fear from my wife, but she collapsed and was frozen in the chair. Here was her child sitting in a trance.

A policeman arrived first. He was snapping his fingers and clapping his hands, but Chris would not come out of it. I could see how scared the officer got! Seeing him panic only terrified me that much more. Chris could not be aroused.

Then, out of nowhere Chris started to laugh! By the time the ambulance came, he had snapped out of the trance, laughed, then took his bottle and started to eat. The paramedics checked his vital signs and examined him, but found nothing wrong. We took him to the hospital, but they too said he was fine. Not one medical professional was able to tell us that this was probably a day seizure, a trance common to people with autism.

It just so happens that Chris received his DPT (Diptheria, Pertussis and Tetanus) inoculation right about the time he had this day seizure. There's no scientific evidence, but a lot of parents believe the amount and combination of the DPT vaccine may be causing a reaction that precipitates the onset of autism if you're genetically predisposed. I don't believe this was the case with Chris. After all, he was exhibiting some symptoms even before this episode.

The day after Chris' seizure I took him to the pediatrician for a complete check. 'Probably a nightmare,' the doctor said.

'Look, it wasn't a nightmare. There's something wrong. There are all these things going on. I've been doing a lot of reading, and I think my son has autism.'

'Give him some time. Don't rush to give him objects he wants. Let him ask for them first.'

'Look, you know what? No. There's something wrong.'

My wife and I later discussed the pediatrician's assessment and scheduled another meeting with him. 'Look,' I said, 'I don't agree with you. I've been doing a little bit of reading and I've been watching my child. I'm telling you there's too much degeneration. There's something wrong.'

'What do you think?'

'We have been reading lots of books and we think he has autism. He fits everything that is listed: Lack of friends, lack of social play, spinning objects, spinning around the room, rocking, not eating, not sitting, not attending. He looks like he doesn't hear us.'

'Well,' he said, 'OK, I think you should give him six months.'

'No. Absolutely not!' We were frantic to get Chris help immediately. 'We've got to do this now.'

So we set out on a burdensome journey of psychiatrists, neurologists, MRIs and hearing tests. We scheduled things very quickly, but it still took a few months to follow through with all the appointments. Jae traveled from clinic to clinic, paying huge sums of money. I was bartending and had no insurance so we had to pay for everything out of our own pockets. Among our bills was fifteen hundred dollars for the MRI, four hundred dollars for the psychiatrist, and two thousand dollars for the neurologist. Unfortunately, if we had stepped back and got an insurance card first many of these bills would have been covered, but we were not about to wait.

We were scared and nervous, but we were confident in our naïveté that we were doing what was necessary to pursue the road to help. We really thought we would quickly confirm that he had autism, get help, and everything would be fine.

We went to a psychiatrist who tried to get into Christopher's 'inner self.' At this point Chris wasn't even three years old. 'Chris, what is in you?'

I don't think so. Goodbye.

Chris had an EEG and an MRI. He had to be put under for the MRI. We went to a neurologist who said we'd better get him a hearing test because he appeared deaf. Children with autism can appear deaf and deaf children sometimes have autistic-like qualities until they get settled in their communication skills. It's not unusual to see a deaf child flap his hands the way a child with autism flaps.

We couldn't get a regular hearing test because Chris wouldn't put the earphones in his ears and he couldn't respond. So they put him to sleep and looked at his brainwaves while introducing sound. The test showed that Chris' hearing was fine.

We were in tears most of the time because we'd see our baby go off for all these tests. It was grueling. Nobody knew anything.

Nobody could find anything. Nobody could tell us what was wrong with our son. There was no one to give us any direction. There was not even a definitive test for autism, only a checklist of symptoms. And nobody really wanted to say he had the disorder.

The only thing the neurologist said to us was, 'Do you have a book on autism?' So obviously he suspected autism was the problem, but still he would not commit to a diagnosis. It was clear to us that there was not a lot out there for this disorder. No doctors, no experts, no special clinics, nothing. At least, there were none that we knew about. The specialists essentially admitted they didn't know much about autism, and we found ourselves with no one to give us advice.

There's a saying that goes, 'If you take your son to a bunch of tests and nothing's wrong, he has autism.' The physicians first have to discount everything else before they can make the diagnosis. In other words if he's not deaf, his brainwaves don't show anything, and they can't find anything else then he's got autism.

While we struggled to find a doctor who could help, Chris continued to get worse. I was reading a book one day while watching him outside in a sandbox. He was just taking grains of sand and watching them. Coincidentally, the book had a checklist for autism and one of the items was staring at little objects. As an example it actually described taking grains of sand and staring into space with them! 'They're describing my son. This is definite,' I thought.

After a while Chris wouldn't look at us. He stopped kissing. He stopped hugging. The worse he got, the more he wanted no one to touch him. It seemed overnight to me, but I guess it happened gradually. Desperate to keep him in our world with us, I started sitting with him for six to eight hours at a time. I would talk and read to him. Very intuitively we stroked and rubbed him. And once he allowed us to rub him, we hugged him.

In my own way I was desensitizing him. Sometimes I would push against him and say, 'Come on, bud, let's do this.' He'd try and I'd say, 'Boy, you're strong.' Then he'd smile. We would run and I'd say, 'Good running!' I was actually doing a therapy called Discrete Trial Instruction without knowing it. 'Let's roll down the hill! Watch Daddy!' I'd take him, we'd do it a little bit, and I'd say, 'That was great!' Then we'd do it a little more.

I was determined not to lose my son to this disorder. 'He's still my son,' I thought, 'and I want to play with him. Maybe in the beginning it's going to be very little, and maybe he's going to shun my touch, but I'm going to take him for a walk and I'm going to roll down a hill with him, and that's what I'm going to do!'

On a daily basis life was very, very hard. But it was kind of odd because we just sort of fell into it. It was as if our lives were never any different and we made a conscious decision that this was the way it was going to be. After all, we had no idea at this point if anything could be done to help Christopher. My attitude was, 'This is it. So I'd better get used to it. It's not so terrible.'

Ours lives were totally immersed in looking for help and working with Chris any way we could. We were ragged, and everybody around us was ragged. But somehow we held it together. The laundry was done and the place was clean.

We had tremendous amounts of energy in the beginning. Jae got up at six in the morning and went on till three the next morning. I was worrying about bringing in enough money to support the family and all the medical expenses and worked from two in the afternoon till one the next morning. And then the two of us would sit and talk about what was going on.

I would get up early the next day to be with my kids, especially Chris, but also to make phone calls and read. We read any information we could get our hands on. I felt that if I didn't put in a few hours of research each day then I was failing. I remember constantly whipping myself: 'Get up!'

4

Genius Savant?

The public often believes people with autism are savants, much like the star character in the movie *Rainman*. The general impression is that people with autism have one genius trait like math or music in a life otherwise devoid of intelligence. I'd like to say right now that more than half of the people with autism have mild to moderate mental retardation and only a small percentage have savant or 'splinter' skills. They are human beings who learn in different ways than those who are traditionally taught and they have major communication problems, but that does not mean their minds are not working. They may see the world in different ways than we do, but they are not stupid. Splinter skills just happen to be very obvious ways that demonstrate how differently a person with autism views the world.

My son, Chris, has some amazing splinter skills. His ability to spell is one of them we witnessed when he was a toddler. At a very early age we used to sing the alphabet song to him and he liked to lay block letters on the floor in alphabetical sequence. One day he was putting the letters in order and when he reached the end he put X, Y, N, Z. We looked at him and said, 'Chris, N doesn't come after Y.' He looked back at us with a smile as if to say no kidding and then flippantly took the N away. Apparently he knew it was wrong, but was trying to show us that we were singing it incorrectly. In other words, the way we sang the words 'X, Y, and Z' sounded like we were saying 'X, Y, N, Z.'

Chris also liked to spell corporate logos before he was even three years old. His first logo was SONY WONDER. Using foam puzzle pieces he quickly expanded his repertoire of company names while running errands or watching TV. For instance, using an inverted R, he spelled both TOYSRUS® and KIDSRUS®. Some of his other logos were spelled with the words lined up exactly as he saw them, but without letter spaces.

BURGER	CTW	BURGER
KING	SESAMESTREET	KING
		KIDSCLUB

Then there were other namess like NICKNITE, FBIWARNING, WARNERHOMEVIDEO, and REPUBLICPICTURES. By age four Chris was spelling from memory all the titles of movie videos he'd watched: FOZZIE'SMUPPETSCRAPBOOK, GONZOPRE-SENTSMUPPETWIERDSTUFF, CHILDRENSSONGSAND-STORIES, ROWLFSRHAPSODIES, COUNTRYMUSIC, ROCK-MUSIC, MUPPETTREASURES, TELETUBBIES, WISHBONE, BARNEY.

Once he went to Kids R Us® and ran around the store for twenty minutes so he could look at all the signs posted. When he came home he went right to the scrabble letters and spelled KIDS R US. Then he looked at me and spelled in the following order: BOYS R US, GIRLS R US, GUYS R US, GALS R US, TOTS R US, TYKES R US, BABES R US, SHOES R US. These were all the signs in Kids R Us as they went around the store in complete order!

This child could remember any words he saw! He once spelled the words 'Richard Hunt.' 'Who's Richard Hunt?' I asked. Jae didn't know either. Well, we were watching a Muppet movie later and happened to notice that the twentieth character printed on the credits was Richard Hunt. For some reason that caught his eye and he remembered it! I found myself looking at him in amazement. His ability to spell and remember words was truly incredible.

When we first got him on computer we gave him coloring programs. But we quickly decided to take him to the word page and let him type because of his love for spelling. He immediately typed the alphabet. 'Chris, that's great!' Next he typed numbers up to thirty. 'You're great!' Then we left him to experiment. Suddenly I heard Jessica yell, 'Oh, my God!' We came running in to find Chris spelling the alphabet backwards as fast as he could type! Z, Y, X... I can't even do that!

How much he understands what he spells is another story. A lot of these people have the ability to read very early on, but not to comprehend. So Chris can spell anything he sees, but he probably does not know what the words mean in many cases.

My son also has tremendous design abilities. He loves expressing himself with color. It's how he remembers characters, for instance. Big Bird is drawn as a big yellow circle. Elmo is drawn as a small red oval. When he watches a movie he freeze-frames it and studies the scene for fifteen minutes. Then he'll go over and draw the colors of everything that he sees. He can't draw the picture exactly, but he has all the characters and their colors in the right positions.

I have to do a lot of the more intricate coloring for him, but he is completely in control of which colors are used and where they go. If it's not right, he disapproves of the work.

I think the funniest thing he ever did was have me color a picture in Barney's Coloring Book. He gave me a crayon and pointed to a banner on the page. So I started coloring the banner, but he immediately grabbed my hand and gave me another crayon. I figured he must have made a mistake. So I started coloring again, but once more he grabbed my hand. 'Chris, what color?' Then he gave me another crayon. I happened to look down and spotted the cover of the book buried in back of the couch. It had a picture of the same banner we were now drawing. The banner was a rainbow and that was what Chris remembered and was making me draw. He memorized each color of the rainbow and stopped me at the exact points where the colors changed!

Thank goodness I had the sense to go along with what he was telling me, even though I didn't understand at first. It would have been easy to stifle his creativity just by saying, 'Stop grabbing my hand!' or 'Settle on one color!' It's just another example of how people with autism have a lot going on in their heads, but the average person doesn't understand them. People tend to discount what autistics are doing rather than watch closely to grasp the meaning of their communication. All this guy was trying to do was make a rainbow.

Chris also designs the most amazing 3D objects with things like buttons and toy shapes. It takes him hours. One night I came home late and found Jae copying down every little section of a huge multi-shaped object on the floor. 'What are you doing? What is this?' I asked. Then I stood back and saw what Chris had done. He created a huge dinosaur out of the tiniest objects. It was almost as big as the whole living room!

He doesn't really like to build with blocks. He prefers creating with small household objects like buttons. He'll put a big yellow thing here, behind it a figure three that peeks out, behind that a button that falls off to the side, and behind that a loose strip that connects to a thing up here. He likes making structures that fade into the background. Now I'm not saying he's designing the Empire State Building, but these are definitely designs, probably of buildings and other things he sees outside.

He once lined up dinosaurs on a table and then very intently adjusted each of the heads. Jae called me over to see. 'Come here. Get down on his level.' When I got down, I saw that the dinosaurs were placed in a 3D formation. He designed it so that each dinosaur just peeked out. They were put in a way that made them seem as if they were coming at you. He just loves to do this type of building.

Chris has such a wonderful ability to look at things and recreate them. I would love it if he grew up to design, paint, or build because I think it would be so rewarding for him. These splinter skills are miraculous gifts that would be a shame to waste. So I hope we can encourage him and guide him to use them in a way that he finds fulfilling.

5

The Insolvable Puzzle

'We're going to school,' the father said to his son.

The son, who had autism, started violently throwing things around and banging his body. Then he ran over to the computer and typed, 'Please take me to school. I want to go to school.'

'OK. Let's go.'

The boy started punching his dad.

'But I thought you just typed that you want to go to school!'

The boy ran back to the computer and typed again, 'Please take me to school!'

'OK. Here's your coat.' With that, the son threw even more punches at his father.

What was going on here? What's the lesson to be learned? Answer: The boy's brain wanted to go to school, but the autism wouldn't let him cooperate physically. Even though he could type the words, 'Take me to school,' his body wouldn't listen to his brain. Why not? No one knows. The disorder is a puzzle.

In fact, the symbol for the Autism Society is a ribbon designed as a multi-colored jigsaw puzzle. There's one particular design with a boy drawn behind the puzzle who's nicknamed Puzzle Boy. It's a bit of joke, but that's basically what autism is – a puzzle nobody can put together. For fifty years the theory was that autism was a psychological disorder. Now that theory's been put aside, but it has not been successfully replaced with any one new answer.

Experts don't know why autism develops or even if people have it at birth. There are all kinds of theories about antibiotics, vaccines, viruses, and genetic predisposition, but nothing's been proven. I believe autism is genetic, but who knows why or to what degree? The disorder affects all social strata and ethnicities. There could be twins in desert Africa with autism and there could be a very rich American child who developed it at age seven. It's baffling.

There are so many things going on with autism that the medical world has a very difficult time pinpointing its cause. Autism is considered a spectrum disorder because it has a wide range of behaviors. Of course that makes it even more of a mystery, but I must admit I like the fact that people with autism are very individual. As a parent, however, you can't prepare yourself for specific behaviors. There's no way of knowing what you're in for.

Some kids have seizures. Some don't. Some kids speak. Some kids can't. One poor boy self-stimulates all the time. Another one can verbally introduce himself, but has terrible social problems. One has a degenerative neurological disorder and is fading and another is very bright, but nonverbal. And then there's a child who can't eat much because he's allergic to everything and the allergies bring on symptoms. Some have mental retardation and some are savants. There are kids who are blind and deaf with autism. There are kids with Asperger's Syndrome, kids with high IQs, kids with low IQs, kids who hit themselves, kids who gouge themselves, kids who play piano from the age of three. Who can make sense of all that?

One of the reasons this disorder never gets diagnosed properly or dealt with is that there are no hard facts. There's no definitive physical test – only a checklist that looks for things like not playing with toys, not developing language, not looking at people, not having friends, walking on toes and flapping hands. Professionals aren't always comfortable telling parents their child has autism on the basis of such a checklist. They are trained to rely on hard data for diagnoses, not behavioral manifestations. They want to use blood tests, EEGs, and brainwaves. Where's that identifying bacteria or gene marker?

It is true that all these kids seem to have a lot in common. They are often lactose intolerant and have a lot of stomach problems. They get a lot of ear infections when they're very young. But what about the children with autism who don't get ear infections and the children without autism who do get them? It's not so simple to narrow their symptoms down into one easily identifiable group.

All types of physical things are going on and they're all going on at once. Researchers can't seem to pinpoint which problem came first and which is the most important. Most believe that it's almost like these kids are missing something and trying to make up for it. There's a theory that the neurons misfire and are unable to send the brain's messages. There seems to be a lack of hormones, especially serotonin, and there seems to be a lack of enzymes that produce the hormones. The stomach often has high peptides that can interfere with lucidity and cause upset stomachs. I once read somewhere that cells in the brains of people with autism actually exploded. So it seems people with the disorder are getting a bunch of miscues.

Researchers can't yet say, 'I see the brain stem on the film. That's it. That's where autism comes from.' Maybe one kid has a lot of cells in the wrong place and that's why he behaves one way. Maybe another kid's hormones are behaving in a particular way, and all he needs is a hormone injection to be helped. The other kid, however, can't be helped with the same hormone injection because that's not what's wrong with him. Autism is such a complex mishmash of things. I think one day researchers will start to put the autism puzzle together, but it will take intensive study of body chemicals, hormones and genetics.

When a child's symptoms are hand flapping and no friends, a typical doctor's response might be, 'Lots of kids don't have friends when they're young.' But we're not talking about a mother who says her son is a loner. We're talking about a child who has absolutely no social contacts and doesn't seek warmth, not even hugs. If you touched my son he would go limp. He and others with autism don't know how to receive physical affection.

When we took Chris to his pediatrician following months of troubling behaviors and a seizure, all the doctor said was, 'Wait. He'll probably talk.' Then he sent Chris to a psychiatrist – a complete waste of time. Nothing Chris had would be cured by psychological counseling. More pediatricians need to learn the signs of autism.

Physicians must learn how to step forward and say, 'I think your child might have autism. Take him for a diagnosis.' Why didn't my pediatrician do that? Why wasn't he able to say, 'Look, this all adds up to the possibility of autism. Go to Johns Hopkins *right* now and get a diagnosis so you can get to work on helping Chris.'

These pediatricians need to admit they have a gap in their knowledge and should try to upgrade their education. When I called my son's doctor to discuss a theory about the DPT shot causing Chris' autism, he just said he didn't know about it and hung up. He didn't say, 'I'm going to do research' or 'That's terrible.' I felt angry, but I was even more disappointed that he was not giving us help. And what I don't understand now is, where's his remorse? Why didn't this guy ever call me up and say, 'You know I was an ass. But I took a course and now I know better.'

In the meantime, families like us are left with no clear path to follow. We just struggle with the disorder day by day and keep trying all kinds of things. It's not unusual to hear conversations like the following:

'I gave him a glass of orange juice.'

'I didn't give him orange juice.'

'Mine eats only gluten-free bread.'

'We have no chemicals in the house, no perfume.'

But none of these parental attempts at experimental cures have proven to be a panacea. Behaviors like aggression and pain deferment continue to rear themselves. And those who suffer from the disorder intuitively try to find their own ways of coping.

People will remark that autism sufferers have a peculiar way of doing things. For instance, toe walking is a frequently seen behavior. But I don't think it's peculiar. I think it's brilliant! Autism often leads to balance and spatial issues so those with the disorder try to right themselves by walking on their toes. Why do they spin? Because it makes them feel better. Spinning and toe walking put people with autism into comfort zones. They are acting to make themselves right with the world.

Kids with autism have what experts say is an inappropriate attachment to objects. But I don't think so. They may be carrying the object to feel balanced and secure. They often use others as a tool to handle things that are upsetting to their senses. 'I can't make myself touch that sandwich so I'm smart enough to use you.'

I can say anything receptively to Chris. 'Chris, please go in the room and get the blue chair.' He understands me, but he can't speak that well. So he'll shy away from conversations because he knows he can't dive in and say, 'How are you today?' Instead he goes around it differently. But he tries very hard in his own way to fit in as much as possible.

Children with autism often seem to be in a state of confusion. You never know how they will react. For instance, I brought Chris into the bathroom when we got to school the other day and he went through a series of incredible changes in two minutes! Happy when we first arrived, I took him for our usual potty-run. But he said, 'No potty,' and started to walk out. He seemed to be confused about it being the end of the day.

I said, 'No, honey. We have to go to school.' And he got upset. We walked into the bathroom again and he started to cry. Then he took off his pants, didn't do anything, flushed the toilet, pulled up his pants, and was laughing. He started to hug me and jump and wrestle. But then suddenly he started crying again, and began rubbing his eyes with the tips of his fingers. I stopped him and he started laughing again. For the next twenty minutes he wanted me to throw him in the air and then happily went into class laughing and hugging me. Who can possibly predict or understand such wild emotional fluctuations?

You never know what's going to happen. You try to look for stability in your life, but these kids can be assaulted by the slightest thing one moment and then not be bothered by anything the next moment. It's impossible to tell when they're tuned out. Sometimes you can drop a garbage can in back of them, and they won't react to it. Sometimes they won't react to their name. They could walk right in front of a screeching, honking car and not have a care. Yet, I've seen a car drive by Chris and he was so shaken that his whole body went limp.

One time after a long day at Kennedy Krieger Center for Autism at Johns Hopkins we walked in the hot streets of Baltimore and everything was affecting him. He was having trouble with the heat. Then a bus went by and he jumped. A man came by and he jumped. He was holding on to me for dear life! He looked like a wolf boy in the city for the first time: Feral-like. I felt so bad for him. He just couldn't gain composure. So we went back to the hotel and stayed there the rest of the day. We turned the air conditioning on, lay in bed and watched TV. It was the only thing we could do. He just couldn't cope with all the stimuli.

To help people with autism cope, they are sometimes medicated. Dr. Temple Grandin, a renowned female author with autism, told my wife that the only time she'd recommend medication is during puberty. If it wasn't for her medication she doesn't think she could have gotten through it. So if we see Chris is really having trouble during adolescence, it might be a consideration.

Diet is another way parents try to help their children's autism. Gluten-free and lactose-free diets are supposed to help lower the peptides as well as increase lucidity and language. But Chris refused food for so long that we're happy he's eating at all. So we hate to limit the little food he does now enjoy.

A hormone now believed to help autism is secretin. I believe it aids in the production of serotonin. Interestingly, savants have more serotonin on one side of the brain which may be responsible for their amazing abilities. We just increased Chris' secretin dosage and noticed his receptive language has had incredible improvement. I can tell him, 'Hey Chris, you forgot your shoes. Go upstairs,' and he'll go get them. But I don't know if it's the secretin or if he would have started to increase his language receptivity anyway. Scientists really need a double-blind study to test the hormone.

Alternative health treatments are always available, but you've got to be careful with them. When we were first researching autism we saw a site on the Internet that said, 'Send one hundred dollars for an adobe brick.' They claimed all the kids in Arizona who ate adobe brick were cured of autism. Some people claim swimming with the dolphins and riding horses are cures. One kid went to Disneyland and began to speak so everybody rushed to Disneyland. But you never know why that boy spoke then. It could have just been the coincidental time when something clicked for him or maybe the marvel of Disneyland propelled him. Who knows? I've never been one to play the lottery. I'm not going to put food on the table if I depend on that winning ticket every day. So you've got to go out everyday and do your work rather than rely on miracle cures. If a large number of studies suddenly came in and said putting an egg on your head cures autism, I would try. But a few studies here and there aren't enough for us to try something unusual.

A lot of theories believed to help kids with autism all have one thing in common – the notion that you should spend a lot of time with the child. I believe it's the time more than the actual therapy program that is making the biggest difference for these kids. Spending time with them eventually gets them to listen, which eventually leads to learning. As a parent who's struggling with what route to take with a child with autism this is important to remember. It's not nearly as crucial to keep a bunch of data and paperwork as it is just to pay attention to your child. Until researchers come up with anything better, I believe time spent together is the most essential element in treating a child with autism.

6

Finding Help

Jae and I were desperately looking for answers to Chris' behavior. We read everything we could get our hands on, and were certain from our readings that he had autism. He fit every criterion to the max. No doctors would confirm it, but we knew in our hearts.

I was very frustrated that I was not doing enough immediately to help my son but, looking back, I intuitively did the right things. I kept him attending by spending one-on-one time with him as much as possible. I also had him do what is now called sensory integration, and I took him for walks. But I still was very worried and frustrated that I was not doing what was necessary.

I was on the phone for hours every day calling everyone I could think of who might have answers. First I called older people who were involved in a defunct support group. One man I spoke to had a forty-year-old son with autism. 'My son is now in an institution,' he told me, 'and you're going to have to spend a lot of money and he's probably going to become violent.' With that remark I hung up the phone.

I called everybody from lawyers to doctors. Many would tell me, 'I don't know what to tell you. We don't do anything for autism and we don't know who to refer you to.'

If names were mentioned in scholarly books or journals I tracked them down at their universities. 'Hi. This is Bill. I just read your article. Tell me about…' Most were willing to speak to me and I gathered a lot of information. I even went on the Internet and gathered ideas from other parents who had experience. Only five years ago there weren't that many autism resources out there. Now there are a lot more websites, books and press. Unfortunately with all that, ninety per cent of the public still knows nothing more than what it's seen in the movie *Rain Man*.

Our biggest hurdle was to find the right service agencies. I called every one listed and they knew nothing and gave me nothing. As a matter of fact, I was only a neophyte, yet I knew more than the people I was calling.

One woman said to me, 'Maybe you're not making the right calls.'

I responded, 'If that's true then why isn't somebody telling me where to make those right calls?'

How come the state didn't say, 'There's a great place over here' or 'Why don't you call there?' Parents of children with autism don't know what to do. If you have a mentally retarded son you call MHMR (Mental Health and Mental Retardation). One call answers all your questions. Where do I put him in class? Where do I get this? Where do I get that? Not with autism! I was told all the time, 'We don't handle that. We don't know.'

It's the worst feeling. I thought there'd be a million people to help my kid. I heard of disabled people getting help all my life and thought there were lots of agencies and available money. But all I heard was, 'We don't do that here.'

'Next month.'

'Six months from now.'

'No. We don't have any.'

I was shocked. Shocked! I expected everybody to say, 'Come on! Here's the place where you go! Here's all the help for your child.' Not true, especially with autism.

Finally somebody said, 'Our IU unit, Intermediate Unit, should have something.'

Ready for bureaucracy? The system in Pennsylvania says that between age zero and two if you're disabled the state is responsible. Between three and five the IU, Intermediate Unit, is responsible for the education of special needs children. From age five and on your school district is responsible for you. It's a stupid system because it's not seamless and at every new stage you have to start over.

Well, when we first called the IU we were told we needed an MDE, a Multi-Disciplinary Evaluation, done by their team in order to enroll Chris in their special education class. But that couldn't be done until after Chris had a formal diagnosis. All the research we had done and doctors we had visited with Chris meant nothing. It was not acceptable proof that he had autism. I couldn't understand. Why would I lie about a thing like that? Autism is not exactly something you wish on your child. His symptoms were obvious. But they insisted we get a formal diagnosis anyway or he could not get services. Like everyone else, however, the IU would not advise us where to get such a formal diagnosis. So our search for help continued.

Not one professional we found would take the lead in diagnosing our son. Obviously, there had to be knowledgeable people out there. We just had to find them. Finally, Jae led the way and got the first formal diagnosis from Seashore House at Children's Hospital in Philadelphia.

7

Diagnosis

It took about half a year to get Chris diagnosed from the time he had his seizure. We went to Children's Seashore House, a part of Children's Hospital in Philadelphia, and using a lot of standardized tests they concluded that Chris had autism. No great surprise there. But then they dropped the bomb. In all probability, they concluded, he was also mentally retarded and would never have language!

I'll never forget when Jae called me at work. 'They've diagnosed Chris with autism, mental retardation and language disorders.'

Now they were hitting me with other stuff!

'That's OK,' she said, 'We'll continue to go forward.'

'Well, what does it mean that he's mentally retarded?'

'I don't think he's mentally retarded, Bill. Look at him. He's bright. His eyes are bright. He wants to learn. He's got a lot of processing problems, but we've just got to find a way to reach him.'

I went back to work. I wish I could say to you we broke down, but we actually laughed a lot! I know that sounds terrible, but it was kind of like, 'OK, what else do you want to dump on us?'

Like everything else, we took it in stride. Our attitude has always been, 'Whatever this child can do with his life, whatever happens is fine. We will take care of him. That doesn't mean we can cure him or that he will be president of IBM. But if he grows up and he's a great poet or he simply stays at home and takes his walks with us, that's fine.'

This news didn't mean we were going to give up. How do you give up on a four year old? I would just have to think of alternative ways to communicate with him, that's all. We were going to keep going and try as hard as we could. Sure, every once in a while we'd break down and cry, but you never heard us cry out and say, 'Oh, God. This is terrible.'

We really believed in our hearts that our son was a bright guy. We knew he had language and processing problems, but he was too aware to have mental retardation. He was showing too many signs of complex thought. If he did have mental retardation we would be OK with that. I just felt that he didn't.

We decided to get a more complete diagnosis from a place we thought had more advanced experience with autism than Seashore House. Does he have brainwaves that are off? Does he have seizures? What about his language difficulties? We wanted a more detailed diagnosis with more direction.

So a few months later we went to The Kennedy Krieger Institute Center for Autism and Related Disabilities at Johns Hopkins in Baltimore. The whole family went, including my daughter. We felt it was a family problem that we all had to go through together, and Jessica went everywhere with us.

We walked in and the woman told me it would cost nineteen hundred dollars. Unfortunately, I wasn't thinking clearly and gave her Chris' Access insurance card. The Access card, however, is for Pennsylvania only. It does not cover medical expenses in Baltimore.

'Sir, I know you were told something over the phone, but we didn't realize you were out of state.'

'What are you telling me?'

'We won't go on with this unless you pay us.'

Luckily we had a checkbook and I wrote a check. Then we found out that neither the neurologist nor the head of speech and language were there that day. The only people available to do a diagnosis were a psychologist and the intern. 'I'm paying nineteen hundred dollars to get an intern and one psychologist?' I asked. I really wanted to walk out, but decided to go through with it since we had already driven the hour and a half to be there.

Chris was a wreck. Taking him into a strange building was a horrible ordeal and he did not want to go inside. Once there, they had him work with blocks and my wife showed them reports, diagnoses, medical things and pictures of what he had designed. Jessica and I saw the psychiatrist who gave us a checklist for autism. If there were twenty items on that list, Chris did nineteen and a half.

'Jessica, could you leave the room?' requested the psychiatrist.

She left. 'I really feel that Jessica is too involved with your son's disorder and you're taking away her childhood,' the psychiatrist admonished me.

'What are you talking about? My daughter comes home, she rides her bike, and she plays with friends.'

'Well, I grew up with a disabled brother and I know what I'm talking about.'

'You know what? You have problems? Don't put them on me.' I walked out of his office. Then I went back to the speech and language assessment where we weren't being told anything.

'Where do we go from here?'

'We don't know.'

All my buttons were pushed now. I had just begun fighting Pennsylvania for in-home funding because I was not satisfied with the IU class Chris recently started, and was really in desperate need of guidance. I was counting on the Kennedy Krieger diagnosis. 'I have this big IEP coming up, and I need you to write that he needs an in-home program. I need you to give us direction! Where's the diagnosis? When will he see a neurologist?'

'I can't do this diagnosis immediately...'

That was it. I called the head of the program, Dr. Rebecca Landa, and I started screaming at her about my experience.

'You know what?' she said. 'You're right.'

So we came back and saw the neurologist who wanted three hundred dollars more. They ended up putting together only a very basic diagnosis. It wasn't at all what we wanted.

Again I called and complained to Dr. Landa. She listened to what I had to say and we started to exchange ideas. It wasn't long before she straightened things out and started to develop her program even more. We actually became friends and forged a relationship that's continued ever since. In fact, we ended up hiring them later to help us develop an in-home program for Chris.

8

Early Intervention

The biggest mistake parents often make is after they get an autism diagnosis for their child. Their reaction is: 'I found out he has autism. Where does he go from here? Where am I supposed to take him now?' But until they learn the answers, they do nothing.

Finding good professional help for your child is a tremendous challenge and can take many, many months. But a child with autism can't wait until that happens. Parents need to start working with their son or daughter immediately! They can't wait until a school or therapy program is found. Every day that passes is another day their child slips further away. They must start working with their child themselves until they find a program!

I love these parents who say, 'He's going to the IU next year.'

'And what are you doing now?'

'Nothing. We don't know anything to do.'

You need to do everything you can immediately! And do what your heart tells you if you know nothing else. Sit next to him. Talk to him. Take him outside. Love him. Don't let him sit there and waste away. Start bringing your child into the world! I believe that it doesn't matter what you say or teach. The fact that your child sits for six hours a day while you make him look, listen and work those ear and eye muscles will help bring him into your world. Early intervention is the key, and parental involvement is critical for it to work.

Early intervention is the single most important concept in treating autism. You have to get to work early, and the earlier the better – even if it's just spending time, even if you don't know anything, the earlier the better. The brain is malleable; you can work with it. If my pediatrician was more knowledgeable or if I had more information at my fingertips, I would have definitely started working with Chris at two years old rather than full force at three-and-a-half.

Early intervention doesn't mean starting at school age. It means you intervene as early as possible. The longer you wait, the more severe the child gets and the harder it is to make a comeback. You see them retreat more into their own world. Their stimming becomes worse. They might become self-injurious or very aggressive. It's hard to teach language to an eight-year-old child who's never spoken before. It's also extremely difficult to introduce him to food. I know children who have lost the ability to chew or swallow because they haven't eaten for so long. It's also nearly impossible to socially introduce a child who hasn't been around other children all his life. I know kids who won't go near other kids and live completely in their own world.

Twenty years ago nobody knew any better and families left children with autism unstimulated for years. Parents had no information or services available to them. But today we know better. We know not working with children who have autism is the worst thing you can do. I think if you are semi-intelligent and have some intuition and love, you'll figure out something to do with your child even if you can't find any professional help. I can't believe a parent would just sit there today and do nothing.

How bad a mistake can you make by trying to stimulate your child? I always think of the 'what's the worst that can happen' scenario? If something doesn't work, you'll stop doing it. But if you find something that does work, even just a little, then it was worth the effort.

I will also add that if you find a forty-year-old guy wasting away in an institution, that doesn't mean it's now too late to work with him. You probably can't expect huge strides, but I have heard stories of intervention with institutionalized autistic adults who were like absolute animals, scratching their skin off and unable to accept human touch. But when someone came along and started to intervene by helping them to accept rubs or hugs, they came around. Obviously these people aren't going to lead the most fulfilling lives. After all, they've been in an institution since they were two years old. But it shows you the human spirit, and the ability to develop even at a much later age if given the opportunity.

Helping people with autism is like helping a stroke victim. They forget how to speak so you have to re-teach them from the beginning. You don't expect a Shakespearean recitation, but if you start teaching stroke victims they learn! It's the same with autism. Children with the disorder do not have a psychological problem. There is a physical reason for their disability, and they can be helped.

Dr. Rebecca Landa, at Johns Hopkins Hospital, is conducting a baby-infant project where they observe siblings of kids with autism or kids who look like they might have autism because of certain attributes or family history. She looks for eye movements, responses, brainwaves and shapes of the brain. The purpose is to catch autism in infancy so intervention can begin before larger symptoms surface. This research is important because we know that behavioral intervention and sensory integration can reshape the child. These and other therapies work, but they have to begin early and with intensity!

There's always a solution for children with autism if you can't find immediate professional help. If you don't know anything about therapy, can't find a book, and have no money, well, you're going to hug him. You're going to make him look at you and you're going to play with him. I bet that's just as good as any professional therapy until you can find something else. You can't just throw up your hands and let your child rot.

9

He Kissed Me!

We took things slowly with Chris after the diagnosis. I spent hours sitting with him trying to get some response by talking, reading, or rubbing him. I even crawled around with him. Everything I did was at his level. So if he sat in the corner, I'd come and sit in the corner with him and just talk. Then I started to stroke his arm lightly.

Slowly he started to give me his arm to stroke while he was doing something else. It was like he was saying, 'I'm doing the best I can. You can rub my arm.' I soon found tickling was great.

We reached a point where he was somewhat comfortable with me even though he wasn't looking directly at me that much. I started patting him a little bit and then that pat turned into a pat on the back. And that turned into a little rub on the head and finally he hugged me! I remember sitting for hours one day and sticking my lips out at him. 'OK, Chris, just look at Daddy and give him a kiss.'

He would turn away. 'OK, Chris, look at Daddy.'

Then he finally kissed me! He wiped it off right away, but he did it! He started enjoying these physical things I was doing with him, and he began to look at me and respond.

I thought to myself, 'First of all, he's a little boy and I believe little boys like to play and roughhouse. I don't care what disability he has, that's what I'm going to do.' So I started wrestling with him.

And I started rolling in the grass with him. He responded beautifully. Not only was he enjoying it, he was getting fit. This was a great plus because it's common for children with autism to have lax muscle tone and floppy reflexes. I would put his arms up and push against him and say, 'Go ahead. Push!' And when he resisted I'd say, 'That's good pushing!' The minute I felt a pressure I'd say, 'Great job! You are so strong!' He liked the feeling of his body going against mine. He was beginning to feel his own strength, and he'd smile and get more into it. I'd push against his hand and say, 'That's it! Come on!! You're wrestling now!! Oh, you won.' All of a sudden this guy was wrestling with me. He was pushing me back and laughing!

Today he kisses me and jumps on me all the time. We sleep in each other's arms and we bathe together. Now I know I can give him a kiss, leave the house, and come back to the same guy I left behind.

I learned later that there's a man named Higashi whose theory is to do eight hours a day of exercise with kids who have autism. He feels it not only fires the neurons but it gives them self-esteem. The activities are broken down into little parts and the kids have to pay attention in order to learn. So in a 'Simon Says' kind of way they're told, 'Do this.' Not only do they get physically fit; they're paying attention. They now have to 'do this.' Turns out I was doing a lot of that type of thing with Chris.

I always wanted him to be strong physically. I thought it was important. So when we wrestled I'd always say to him, 'You are the strongest guy.' And he'd smile. He knew it was something. When he would resist me, he was being rewarded for it. He got praise for it. So he would resist more.

They say these kids have flabby musculature and bad response time. So if that's the case should I let him languish in the corner and get worse? No. Instead I brought him out and said we're going to run up the hill. 'We're running! Look at us! We are fast. Let's do it again.' Do I think he's going to be the high school quarterback? No. Do I care? No. Just let him get the most out of his life by participating fully.

PART II
Finding Appropriate Education

1

Starting School

Once Children's Hospital in Philadelphia gave Chris his diagnosis we immediately called the IU to get him enrolled in school. Only now they told us, 'Chris needs a team to assess his requirements and prepare a Multi-Disciplinary Evaluation, an MDE. That can't be arranged for three months, and it takes two months to get the results. Once you get the results, you attend an IEP meeting to finalize Chris' Individual Educational Program. Then we find him proper class placement.'

'Wait! Wait! This child has a disorder. He needs to get started right away.'

'Sorry.'

'What are you, nuts? We have to get help for him! What would you like me to tell him a few years from now? That you were too busy doing paperwork so you delayed him by a year?'

Early lesson – bureaucracy rules, and unless you get some backing you're not getting anywhere. I called my local representative, Katie True. 'Look, I have this problem.'

Two days later representatives from the IU came to my house and all the evaluations were expedited.

I was ecstatic. We were finally getting help! At last we had an answer to what was wrong with Chris and were ready to roll up our sleeves and get to work. He was going to get the help he needed.

Little glitch…they don't have a class for autism. What do you mean you don't do anything for autism? What do you mean you don't have anybody who specializes in the disorder? My anger welled up and brought tears of fear and frustration for Chris! I never felt more upset. How could there be such a lack of services available to children with autism? Here I put in ten hours a day for a year trying to find help for my child and was coming away with nothing. There was no greater frustration.

An analogy to this would be if my child needed a wheelchair. 'What do you mean you don't fund wheelchairs? He can't walk! He must have one.' An incident like this would be scandalous.

Chris was placed in a multi-disabilities class with a lot of deaf children. The administrators thought that was a good idea. 'Chris doesn't speak either so he'll learn like they do.' I knew in my heart this was not right for him, but I kept quiet because I felt that at least he was going to school.

As soon as we were told about our son's class placement we immediately went and visited the classroom ourselves. The school was in a town about a half-hour away from us. It was a low-level building with a couple of classrooms, very official looking, very cold. We met the teacher and gave her a bunch of books and information about autism because she really didn't know much about it. As a matter of fact, she knew nothing. This was a mixed disability class with a lot of deaf children, a couple with seizure disorders, some with language problems, but none with autism.

We decided to go at this full force so we got the teacher and IU classroom whatever they needed. They had no carpet for the kids to sit on during circle time so Jae got a carpet donated from the local Carpet Mart. I went out and solicited a local car dealer to buy a used computer for the class. They had just a few books in the classroom, so my daughter offered to donate her books. The classroom was filled with hundreds of children's books donated by us. We even built a bookshelf that my daughter helped paint. We did a lot of drives for them and collected toys, equipment and furniture. True to form, they never said thank you for anything. But that's OK. We were happy he was going to school and happy to do anything we could to ensure that Chris got the best therapy.

We did a lot of preliminary preparation with Chris before he attended the IU. Just to get him to walk into the school was a big ordeal. We started a month in advance to introduce him slowly. Everyday we drove up to the building and then we'd go away. Then we'd drive up and take him out two steps. And then we'd drive up and go to the door. Finally we'd drive up and go in the lobby and down the hallway. It was fit after fit after fit! Chris was a hard person to deal with.

Then the IU told me he could take a bus to school so we wouldn't have to drive him. I was stunned. 'Are you nuts?' I said, 'What is wrong with everybody?' This was a three-year-old guy who was scared of getting out of the car, scared to leave the apartment and unable to communicate. But leave it to the state to suggest such an inappropriate idea.

Just picture how the bus trip would evolve. The IU holds class for children from all over Lancaster and Lebanon Counties. Let's say school started at ten. If Chris was first on the bus he would get picked up at seven-thirty. After traveling all over to pick up the other kids, Chris might have been riding the bus for two hours! That was not an unusual scenario. And then they'd do it all over again to go home. So if class ended at one, Chris would get home at three. And that's not exaggerating! Why would I even consider putting my son on that bus? I watched these kids come off the bus and sure enough, everybody stepped off crying, looking elsewhere and wearing no coats.

Most of these kids can't even talk! My daughter, Jesse, loves to take the bus because she gossips. But she's not on the bus for two hours, and can tell me if the bus driver yelled or drove off the route.

So I drove Chris everyday. And I stayed. It was such a struggle. First Chris fought against going in the building. Once inside he would cry and it took a while to get him settled. Then I'd sit and play with him a little bit or get him interested in something and try to fade out. Eventually, he'd go in a corner and look in a book or play with a block. But mostly he stayed in the corner and flapped his hands, a behavior kids with autism do when nobody knows how to bring them into the surrounding world.

He never played with the other kids and never really got any direction from a teacher. I never saw one person work with him, and certainly didn't feel I could leave. So I sat and watched.

If only somebody went up to him and said, 'OK, Christopher. Hi, Chris. Let's go over here.' But nobody was directing anything toward him. They'd try and coax him a little, but if he didn't respond, they'd leave him alone. There was a music teacher who came in and sang things to the kids like, 'What day is it today?' And the children would all point to the day. Chris, in the meantime, was off in the corner.

I wasn't comfortable at all to leave him in that kind of care in the kind of state he was in. From the bottom of my heart I knew this class was no good for him, but I had nothing else at that point and felt I should give it a try.

Maybe a visit to the school psychiatrist involved in Chris' original evaluation would help. 'You know, I'm beginning to get this sinking feeling about the class. What are you doing for Chris' autism? I see him doing nothing but crying and going off on his own in the corner. Nobody can reach him. I know that's not unusual for a kid with autism, but what are you doing for him?'

'Well, he's getting better socially. He sits now at circle time. At least he's sitting.'

'Well, that's a great accomplishment,' I answered sarcastically. 'You're supposed to be professionals. Can I see a plan?'

'No.' This was a member of the great team effort! Some team. Nobody knew anything.

Soon they were blaming me for my son's lack of progress. 'Mr. Davis, it would be better if you left because I think he's depending on you. He'll do better without you here.'

'No, he's not going to do better. This is a disorder. I'm not causing it. You want me out because I'm complaining. What are you doing for him?'

'We're trying to introduce him to the kids.'

'But what methodologies are you using specifically for autism?' They couldn't answer me. They just blamed their lack of progress on my presence.

I think they really just wanted me out of their hair because I was asking too many questions and demanding too much. I would go up to them and ask, 'What did you do today? I watched and he was in the corner! You didn't even go over to him.'

I remember there was once a woman substitute who apparently was not told that Chris had autism or even that he had language problems. Nothing. At that time, he drank ten bottles of formula a day and it was a big thing for him to hang onto them. So he had his bottle and the substitute wanted him to come and sit down. 'NO!' she yelled, 'Come over here!' I was watching from the outside. 'You have to come here! Come here! Hey! You have to sit over here... OK, give me this!' She went over and grabbed the bottle. Chris began to cry and go after the bottle which was exactly what she wanted him to do – follow her, sit down and get ready to leave. Outraged, I went in the room and proceeded to say a few choice things to her. This was no way to treat a child with severe autism!

When my wife came to pick us up I couldn't catch my breath. 'That idiot!' and told her what happened. Jae ran into the classroom and I went to the teacher in charge. 'If that woman sets foot inside this classroom again, I will go to whatever authority I need.' The teacher assured me that the substitute would not be back again. But the woman still stayed in the system – I believe she's now running one of the programs.

Not more than a couple months passed before I said, that's enough of the IU classroom for Chris. It was ridiculous. Luckily, we started our own therapy program at home a few weeks after Chris entered the IU system. Every spare minute we worked on the program. At first we thought it would be in addition to the IU class, but we found it so perfectly met his needs that we decided to pull him out of the IU altogether. There was no time for their nonsense. I think even if we hadn't started our own program, we would have taken him out of there. I wasn't going to torture him.

2

Starting An In-Home Program

Putting our in-home program in place was all-consuming. We sat eight hours a day every day making phone calls and researching. We didn't know where to go or how. We had never done research in our lives before this, and there were no easy answers about programming.

Jae quickly got her driver's license and started traveling everywhere for information. 'I'm going to New Jersey to research Rutgers University's autism program. I'm taking Chris to a clinic. There's a school in Delaware I want to see.' And things began to fall into place. My wife became such an expert in programming, therapy and research that people started asking what degree she had.

'My wife completed high school,' I beamed.

We studied everything we could get our hands on. Terminology and professional attitudes never intimidated us. When doctors, politicians, or even the head of Rutgers University said they were sorry, I would say, 'Excuse me. Let me tell you something. This is my son. If you don't respond to me I'm coming down to Rutgers and your life is going to change.' That was the attitude I took. There were a lot of fuck you's. 'Maybe you're not hearing me,' I'd say. 'Where do I go to get my son help? Don't fuck with my son.' I was not intimidated at all. As a matter of fact, the angrier I got the more effective I became in getting results.

When we realized the IU was not helping Chris, I began gathering legal information in preparation to do battle with the state. In order to leave the IU and go on our own with an in-home program we needed funding. I called lawyers throughout the country that I found named in journals, and I would say, 'Hi, Marty, I'm Bill Davis. I just read your article. Can you tell me...' They were all very nice to me.

We bought some therapy books and learned about a UCLA program called Lovaas that we felt would be perfect for our in-home program. Doctor Ivar O. Lovaas was famous for first using Applied Behavioral Analysis to reach children with autism. ABA is a system of taking tasks and breaking them down into smaller tasks. Prompts are used to get the child to perform each task, and immediate rewards are given when the task is performed successfully. Eventually, fewer and fewer prompts are used. It's really very instinctual. Lovaas got a bad rap because he was strict, but what people didn't know was that he helped a lot of older children with autism who had never been approached before. These were wild kids. Lovaas was very crude, but he got them to sit down and look at him! Getting them to attend was key. Once the kids attended, their eye muscles started to work.

The muscles connected to a lot of these kids' ears and eyes are lacking because they're not normally worked. Did you ever notice when you tell someone to look at you that their eyebrows go up? That's how you know they're paying attention. Typical kids have that. They listen. But not autistic kids. Try telling an autistic child to sit down and stay there. It's not so easy. What's going to keep them in that chair? Lovaas would say, 'You're going to sit five minutes and then you'll get a piece of candy.' He rewarded them for desirable behavior.

We called UCLA to set up a Lovaas program in our home. Consultants would actually come to us, set up a program and run it for a few weeks. Then they'd return every month and run a workshop for us. This would all cost us about sixty, seventy grand the first year, but we were willing to pay it. Unfortunately, they put us on a two year waiting list. What did they expect us to do in the meantime? Let him rot?

Our only alternative was to set up a therapy program on our own. So we tried our best to work with Chris at home using instinct and what we read. But we just couldn't seem to get our in-home program to gel.

It was Christmas time when Jesse, Chris and I went to the mall to buy gifts for my wife. We ran into Bonnie, a girl who once worked for me at the Hilton and lifeguarded at our pool, who now was home from college. 'How's the baby, Mr. Davis?' she asked in this kind of goofy Valley Girl voice.

'You know, Bonnie, we're pretty sure Chris is autistic and we've been trying some therapy on our own.'

'Oh, my brother's friend works with autistics.'

I jumped. 'What?! Are you kidding me? Where is she?'

'New York.'

'Oh, well.'

'But she's here this weekend.'

'Bonnie, you don't understand! I can't find anyone. I can't do anything. I'm running into walls. Can you call her?'

And sure enough Ruth Donlin, an expert behavioral analyst and therapist, came to our home free of charge, and has been a close family friend ever since. During her first visit she came in and went right to Chris. She talked very little. 'I'm going to approach your son and he's going to display many more characteristics and symptoms of autism while trying to avoid me. This means more hand-flapping, rocking and screaming. He's *not* going to like me invading his space and he's going to try not to pay attention to me at all costs. Please don't get concerned.'

And sure enough she went right in his face. She looked right at him, got down on her hands and knees, and said, 'Hi, Chris! Look at me.' He turned away and put his fingers in front of his face because somebody was trying to get at him, a familiar autistic reaction. It's like come on, get out of here!

But she kept giving him commands and doing things. Jae hit me and said, 'She's on his level! That's what I want. This will work for him.' Ruth kept pressing and eventually Chris was listening to her. I'll never forget it; when she was leaving, he smiled and looked at her. This was the first time he smiled since the disorder hit! And I believe it was because she reached him and he knew.

Ruth Donlin described the Rutgers program she used as Discrete Trial Instruction, and left us some literature. Jae started reading everything she could about it. This and other programs that we read about were all pretty close to Lovaas, but Jae decided to develop our in-home program based on the Rutgers model. Suddenly she metamorphosed into a professor.

No exaggeration! I came home one day and there was no bed in the room where we slept. There was no bedroom at all. She hadn't told me what she was doing and just went out and set up this therapy room replete with thousands of dollars worth of equipment, a camera, computers and a monitoring system to enable viewing from downstairs. 'What did you do?' I asked Jae.

'I am starting this session.' She set up her own Discrete Trial program!

'OK,' she said, 'You have two assignments. Get Rutgers to come to our home every few weeks, oversee the program, and make corrections – just like UCLA's Lovaas program, except they won't live with us. And we need people to do the therapy. I can't do this six to eight hours a day myself. Plus, I'm his mom and I'm too involved to be his therapist.'

'Get who? I don't know who to get.'

'Start making some calls.'

3

Wanted: Therapists

Where could I possibly find therapists? Up until now no one could even give me the simplest direction concerning autism. But I picked up that phone and I dialed. I called all kinds of agencies and local organizations. People were horrible to me. They had no idea what I was talking about. 'I'll pay them,' I said.

'No, we don't have anybody. What do you think, we're an employment agency?'

Then I got an idea. What about using college students studying special ed or psychology? I called Franklin and Marshall College, located in our hometown of Lancaster. I thought surely they'd laugh at me, and embarrassedly spoke to the head of the psychology department. 'Look, I have set up this program for my son. It's called Discrete Trial and Rutgers is going to consult and run workshops for us. What we need are people to train who will conduct the therapy.' I was making this up as I went along. I didn't even know for sure at this point if Rutgers would agree to help us.

'Do they get paid?'

'Yes.'

'How much?'

'I'll get back to you on that.' So I made some calls and asked what therapists are paid and was told twenty-five dollars an hour! Most of them get around ten an hour, but I heard twenty-five so I called the F&M official back and said twenty five. We found out afterwards that a lot of interns are not paid at all, but we were learning as we went along. Idiot that I am! I committed to paying therapists out of my pocket for twenty-five dollars an hour, thirty hours a week!

Naturally he said, 'OK.'

'Maybe they can get college credits,' I suggested.

'Yes. We could work that out. I'm turning you over to the guy who runs the intern programs, Roger Godin, because this would be considered his jurisdiction.'

Roger was very receptive and it took only a few weeks to get the F&M therapists from the time Jae set up our therapy room. Then I called Millersville, the other big college in the community, and set up an internship program there. Students actually started to apply. I was shocked!

One of our first interns was a girl named Aurora Gonzalez. She was on the Deans List and captain of the basketball team. She spread the word and more people started to show up! I couldn't believe it. My wife was interviewing and I was paying them.

Our internship venture was off and running. I got the undergrads, trained them, paid them, and they earned college credits. We had Rutgers come and give workshops, and we used the monitor to tape the interns so we could watch and correct them.

The internship program has been running now about four years. F&M is wonderful! I have a booth at their intern fair every year where the students come over and look through a book showing what we do. At the last intern fair we were the most popular booth. We're a big deal because the students get hands-on work, Rutgers workshops, Johns Hopkins workshops, go to conferences, get accepted into great graduate schools, and even get hired at Johns Hopkins Kennedy Krieger Institute Center for Autism. Of course, getting paid for earning college credits is not a bad incentive either.

The program has turned out to be very successful both for us and for the students. The therapists, some graduate and some under-graduate students, are all quite smart. If they're really interested they'll stay with us for a couple years, and usually work out beauti-fully. Of course we sometimes get the ones at the intern fair who say, 'I heard about the program and want to participate,' and never show up. And we've had some girls come just to participate in our Rutgers workshop. They put it on their resume and never show up again.

Occasionally we get someone with what I call the Jerry Lewis superman mentality. 'Throw your braces away! You're going to walk!' I've gotten very good at spotting it. They have this attitude that they're the one who's going to make the landmark change in your child. Their work is not about the child anymore. It's about them.

When Chris was just beginning to speak we had a therapist like that. One day he was drinking his bottle and this girl came in and said, 'Say hi, Chris.' He was on the floor and did not respond, so she grabbed the bottle out of his mouth and insisted, 'Say hello.' My mother, who happened to be there to witness the scene, grabbed the girl and started screaming at her. Even she knew how easily Chris could shut down and perhaps never utter another word. Naturally, we fired the therapist. But we became very protective of both the program and who was with our son.

Fortunately, most of our therapists are protective too. If we get a girl who's not doing what she should for the program she is outed immediately. The girls will come and say to her, 'You're not doing your data. I don't think you know what you're doing.' *They* yell at her. We once had a girl who was faking the data because she didn't understand it. She was only there for the credit, and the other girls hated her because she was potentially ruining the program. Finally, we filmed her and confronted her. 'Yeah,' she admitted. 'I don't know what I'm doing.'

Many of the girls we trained, however, have stayed in the field. Some of them have even gone on to excellent jobs at Kennedy Krieger's Center for Autism at Johns Hopkins. In fact, my wife jokingly complains that Kennedy grabs her best therapists. When Dr. Landa, the director, comes to see how our program is doing she inevitably asks that dreaded question, 'What about that one?'

And I say, 'Oh, boy, here we go. Another therapist lost.' Actually, we're very proud of the program and the fact that highly respected professionals think so well of what we're doing and the therapists we've trained. In fact, a current therapist named Jenny Nielsen has been asked to join Dr. Landa this summer to aid in research.

Generally, the therapists stay a couple years, become very involved, and feel we are a family to them. When they leave it's pretty hard for Chris. Does he think it's his fault? Does he think, 'Did I do this? Is it something I said?' But summer vacations and graduations come, and we've had to learn how to introduce new therapists so Chris understands and the program doesn't suffer. Over all though, I'd say Chris and the intern program have fared very well. Each has helped the other gain great success. I am very proud of both.

I went to Franklin and Marshall and worked with Christopher as a therapist for two-and-a-half years. I was a psychology major and the Davises trained me in the Discrete Trial therapy. It took about three months to learn, but then there were a lot of other little things to get a grasp on too. Bill and Jae are very careful about who's with their son so they observed me quite closely using a video camera in the therapy room. I was a little intimidated at first, but I really grew to love working with Chris.

I'm in law school now to learn special needs law. Bill inspired me with all his funding fights with the state. They had to go through such a process to get it. Working with them inspired me to go into this field.

Kim Egger, therapist

I was a psychology student looking for an internship and heard that Bill Davis was looking for some therapists to work over the summer with his son. When I heard his son had autism, I didn't know what to expect. I had the TV image in my mind of some child off in the corner not talking to anybody, not paying attention to anybody; just some little boy not in touch with reality. But when I met Chris he was full of life. Even though he was crying and trying to push me out the door, I took it as a good sign because it meant that he interacted with people. I knew we'd have something together.

I was trained in a lot of Discrete Trial programs. For each program there's different objects, different words, and different placements that you have to use. There was a lot to memorize.

Chris has changed a lot over the last two years. He is more social and will actually take you by the hand and pull you over to whatever he's doing if he wants to play with you. He's also talking now. When I first started he wasn't saying anything. Once in a great while he'd say 'bye-bye' because he wanted you to go. Then he started repeating the alphabet and numbers with his sister, Jessica, but only to her. There had to be some huge motivating factor for him to talk to someone else. So he's really started to come out now. I think he's feeling comfortable with what he knows and more confident in himself.

I think Bill is very humble and he's very giving. He's humble in the sense that he doesn't expect praise for what he's doing. He just takes raising his children as the normal course of his life.

Melissa Bennett, therapist

I always had an interest in special needs and heard about the internship position at my school, F&M. I trained over the summer and then officially started working regularly at the end of August. It's kind of overwhelming at first; all that Discrete Trial, sixty some programs to learn. It's like, oh my goodness, how am I ever going to learn all this? But they're such sweet and patient teachers.

And the set up! You walk in and what Jae has done is incredible. The whole system! You just look around this fairly small room and it's packed with supplies and books and all sorts of binders for data. They keep records of pretty much everything Chris does.

Now the program has changed a lot. When I first started they were only using Discrete Trial. We'd call him to the table, have a work session, and then he got to go play while we set up the next program. We'd call him back and do the same routine for all three hours. Just recently, they switched to a format that's a lot closer to what you would find in any school. We still run the Discrete Trial work sessions at the table, but they're alternated with other types of sessions. One of them is art. He paints on an easel, does coloring, makes beaded necklaces. There are sensory programs, story time, music and free play. It's a lot more social. During free play we bowl, throw the ball back and forth, use puppets, or do whatever he chooses. At snack time the other therapist and I sit around the table with Chris and converse. 'Do you want a cookie? Yes, I want a cookie. Do you want a soda?' There's s lot more social interaction.

This summer I'm going to do work at Hopkins with Dr. Landa. I'll be assisting in the Achievements summer program where Chris attends. The Davises definitely inspired me. I knew I wanted to work in special needs, but now I know I want to work in autism. I'll probably go into clinical psychology or a neuroscience program with a specialty in autism. They've definitely been a big inspiration in my life. I'm lucky I found them when I did.

Jenny Nielsen, therapist

4

Hiring Rutgers University

Setting out to hire Rutgers University Douglass Developmental Disabilities Center as our consultant was not as easy as setting up the internship program with Franklin and Marshall. My initial telephone calls to the university were not even returned. I left a lot of voicemails with their Center but they were all left unanswered. So finally I called and left the following message, 'I'm gonna tell you something. This is my son and you're not responding to me! I've got the whole day set aside for you. If I don't get a fucking phone call… I'm coming down and I will be on your university steps and I will tell everybody that you don't care!'

Guess what? I got a call the next day. 'Mr. Davis, you have to understand we're…'

'I want somebody to come up.'

'Mr. Davis, it's fifteen hundred dollars for four hours plus traveling time and meals.'

I said, 'Fine. When is he coming?'

So we set a date two weeks later for someone to come and look over our program. Meanwhile Jae and I had begun therapy, set up a room and monitoring system, and started working with new therapists from Franklin and Marshall College.

Setting up our therapy room was no easy feat either. It was not just the table and monitoring equipment that we needed. The therapy programs required lots of materials. For instance, one program taught color as a concept. We would have an orange, red and green object on the table. Chris would then have an orange object and we'd tell him, 'Put with same.' If he sat and looked at us, we'd do a hand-over-hand movement and help him put his orange object to the other orange object. 'Good boy!'

Another program would be sound discrimination. We'd have a bunch of instruments under the table and he'd have the same instruments in front of him. Then underneath the table we'd play a tambourine. 'What sound?' And he'd look and pick up his tambourine. Unbelievable! He was paying attention! He was picking it out of the air. That was the object of the program – try anything to get him to pay attention.

The catch was that these types of programs needed lots of materials. So Jae had me out shopping for all the different categories in all the different programs. 'I need nine thousand orange plates,' she'd tell me. And I would run around trying to fill all her requests.

Before we hired Rutgers we were doing all this on our own, but it was a battle and a lot of it wasn't understood. Although we did have some results they were painful and they were very short. My son used to regress and fold up if the program went wrong. He would crawl in the corner. He would stop eating. 'OK,' we'd say, 'We've got to start over.' And we would search back in the data and redo things.

When Matthew Bowman, the behavioral analyst from Rutgers University, was scheduled to come for a visit, I was a wreck worrying about what he'd think of our program. A very intellectual looking guy with pamphlets appeared at the door and I nervously introduced him to our five new therapists. We went upstairs to the therapy room. 'Is this all right?' I asked.

He responded, 'Who did this?'

'Oh no,' I thought, but answered aloud, 'My wife.'

'It's unbelievable! I've never been in a home like this.' He was impressed!

We started our session, and he showed us how to correctly do Discrete Trial Instruction. He also watched the films we made of the therapists working with Chris and looked at our data.

At one point he went over to Chris. 'Chris, come here,' commanded Matt. Chris didn't respond. Matt got up, took him, told him again to come here, and sat him down.

'This is what you do,' he instructed us. 'You have to physically prompt him if he doesn't listen.' And he gave Chris a piece of candy. 'Awesome work, Chris!'

At the end of the session Matt repeated again, 'Chris, come here.' And Chris sat down! I never saw anything like it. Chris never paid attention to anybody. He certainly never followed a command. It was a struggle every minute with us. He would cry and kick. But this was the first time we learned of this 'come here' command to get him to sit and pay attention. He actually complied quietly and listened. It was a defining moment in my life. I knew this was the right way to go for my son.

5

Fighting For Funds

After deciding to pull Chris out of the IU I called for a new IEP to request funding for our in-home program. 'I'm not satisfied,' I said. 'You're not doing anything for my son's autism. You're not attacking it and you don't have any plans. You don't have anybody who knows anything. I want an IEP and I'm going to present something to you.'

I came to the IEP meeting guns blazing! 'We've started a program and I want you to pay for it because it is the most appropriate education there is for him. *You* don't have an appropriate education for him.'

And they didn't. They had no classroom geared for kids with autism so they couldn't fight me. The only point they brought up was, 'What about social aspects? He's not going to be with kids if he's all alone at home.'

I answered. 'Number one – this is a social disorder. So what are you talking about? If I put him in with a bunch of kids, is he going to become social? It's like putting a kid in a wheelchair in a race. Is he going to get up and run now? Number two – I take him to a swimming program and other local programs. Plus my daughter's friends come to our home all the time and he plays with them too. That's what we're doing socially.' Then I showed them a list I prepared of every place I took him where there was socialization with other kids. They had nothing to say.

Next the speech teacher from the IU started to discuss Chris' language progress. 'Well, my evaluation of Chris...'

And I interrupted, 'Your evaluation of Chris, what? You never saw him. You never brought him to any language.'

'I was in the room once observing him.'

'So you're going to give me an evaluation because you went in the room one time! For how many minutes?'

'Fifteen minutes.'

'Get out!' This was so typical of the IU. Here was a speech and language teacher who knew nothing about autism. She didn't even know how to approach my son. Yet she was the one giving an evaluation.

The law says you must give an appropriate education for each disability and this IU unit clearly was not. The key word is 'appropriate.' If you say, 'I want the best,' or 'I want a specific therapy,' the state will fight you. The word is 'appropriate.' That's what you go to court with if necessary. I had them! They didn't have an appropriate education for Chris, but *I* did and I could prove it.

I prepared my case by intensively studying educational law. I went to the IEP with stacks of paperwork from cases I downloaded from the Internet. So every time they said something I countered with 'Wait!' And I'd go through my papers and say, 'No. The law does not say that. It says...' They couldn't believe it.

My tactic was first to use scientific literature to prove that our ABA, Applied Behavioral Analysis, program worked. I provided statistics from Rutgers and Lovaas and data that I took everyday. 'See here? Here's our first day. Chris couldn't do this skill. Now look. Two months later Chris can do that skill plus some others. Here's a series of trials for proof.'

'Where do you get these therapists?'

'My therapists are students from Franklin and Marshall College. There's no law that says therapists have to have a degree.'

I really believed in what I was petitioning. What are you going to do with an autistic child like Chris who isn't speaking, who can't be with other children, and who can't even sit down? There's almost no choice but to give him in-home programming. Chris couldn't fit into a classroom and there was no program for him outside so we developed one of our own. It was an intensive program in which we did forty hours a week, seven days a week, six hours a day with two therapists at all times. There was no better education available for Chris.

Experts believe a child who's not attending, who really is wild and out there, really needs an in-home program in the beginning because you're sitting with him one-on-one. Most of the research data shows that many children with autism need in-home, intensive programming. Therefore it's the appropriate education. It's tantamount to saying my child needs a wheelchair. There's no way around that fact, so he's provided with the wheelchair. Chris was barely venturing out of the house, he wouldn't go into other buildings, and he couldn't participate in generalized group activities. So an in-home program is what he needed.

Autism therapy is intense. It's forty hours a week of one-on-one therapy. Workshops need to be held, data must be kept and lots of equipment needs to be purchased, all for this one kid! And that forty hours a week of therapy takes many hours a week of planning. And then there's meetings that must be held with the therapists. And what if he shuts down? Then you've got to figure out the problem and revise the program.

Parents must realize early on that the public education systems or the IU systems for the most part are not set up like that to help the child with autism. The educational administrators kind of gloss over what they provide and try to make nice with the parents. It's kind of like bringing your broken car to a garage and the repairman says, 'I'm not a mechanic, but I'm going to clean your car. It'll look nice. You'll put it in the garage and it'll sit and look OK.'

'Well, the transmission's broken.'

'I can't fix transmissions, but I'll shine the chrome for you.'

That's the same attitude a lot of the educational systems have for teaching children with autism. So it's unlikely that autistic children will get the full services and education they need any time soon. First awareness has to happen. Twenty years from now people may become aware of the huge amount of work it takes to treat autism and dig down deep in their pockets to fund it. The research will tie in with the funding, and the teachers will meet the researchers. Until that time parents are going to have to do a lot themselves.

There's plenty of money. But the states allocate it for other things. I think the system stinks. And I'm not the only one. After filing one of my many complaints with the governor's office, a staff member called and agreed with me. 'Off the record, the system stinks,' she said, 'and there's nothing I can do about it. You're a hundred per cent right.'

When it comes to hard work and small results, state funding doesn't exist. If a child in braces gets funded for physical therapy and he walks, then that money was well spent. If you give my child fifty thousand dollars worth of speech and language and all he says is 'cup,' no one thinks that investment was worthwhile. Fifty thousand dollars is a big advance! But his one word doesn't suit those controlling the purse strings, and it certainly won't get money allocated in the budget. Imagine the scenario when asked to account for the funds. 'What did you do with that money?'

'Chris now says "bye".'

'What are you crazy? We gave you fifty thousand dollars so this kid could say bye? We're not getting a lot of bang for our buck here, pal. Forget it! We want to see that kid perform Shakespeare!'

And how do they tell six other families with different disabilities that they are using large sums of money only for this one child?

What happens when the Down Syndrome parent says, 'Excuse me. My son is in the class with ten other Down Syndrome kids with one teacher and an aide, and you're telling me you're giving Chris Davis forty hours a week at home?!'

Setting up our own in-home program was a big step for both us and Lancaster. It was clear they did not want to fund us. They never even suggested it in spite of the fact that they were already funding another family. Despite the state's secrecy, I was able to trace the family and speak to them. They were very happy with their funding, but kept very hush-hush because they were probably afraid they'd lose the money.

What an act of cruelty for the state not to be more honest with us! How about saying, 'By the way, you're mentioning a home program. That's great because Mr. Jones has one and his son is steamrolling ahead.' You would think that as educators they would let me know a home program is what a lot of these children need. Instead they didn't even mention it. Withholding information like that is the same as not telling a child who needs a brace that there's a better, more expensive one.

The father of the child with the in-home program was a lawyer. He said to me, 'I spit people like this out for breakfast. I can get anything I want from them.'

And I said, 'Well, I'll get what I want too.'

And that's what I did. I turned off my tape recorder that had been on during the IEP and said to the IU administrator, 'There's a news article coming out about Chris. I will make you look like a monster if I don't get funded. I will tell the world that Lancaster is not giving appropriate education to disabled children. Now what's it going to be?'

'Mr. Davis, we will give you your money.'

'May I put my tape recorder back on?'

'Yes, you may.'

6

How To Handle Your IEP

The world of special needs is a confusing maze of rules, regulations, theories and treatments. To get the money and services your child deserves requires breaking through a great deal of bureaucracy. I once attended a seminar on autism that made a joke of all the terminology. Whenever you used an acronym without explaining it, you had to throw a quarter in a jar. Unfortunately, it's not a joke when you have to deal with this system effectively.

As the parent of a child with special needs, a fact of life you must understand is your child's IEP or Individualized Education Program. It is a written document that sets the educational goals and specific services your child will receive by the state for the coming year. The document's outcome is determined at your IEP meeting. An IEP meeting is held every year, but parents can demand another one any time they wish. If you are not happy with the way your child's program is going, you are entitled to request changes at an IEP meeting.

The meeting is between professionals, parents and the disabled child if he is able to speak for himself. It is based on the MDE, the Multidisciplinary Evaluation, and results in the CER, which is the Comprehensive Evaluation Report, a specific listing of all services you're going to receive.

One reason for an annual IEP is that the law wants to know whether your child's still disabled and continues to need special services. For Chris, that's pretty stupid considering autism is a lifelong disability. But, OK, the original concept was to keep the child's progress going, reassess him, and update his goals. Maybe he needs more services; maybe he needs fewer. Maybe he needs eight hours a day or maybe he needs a summer program. His educational goals plus other services that relate to his disability are all discussed. Perhaps the child now needs speech and language, occupational therapy and the use of a computer device to help him speak.

The professionals at your IEP meeting can say anything they want. They can say they have a great public educational program and refuse to pay for your in-home program. Then it's left to you to prove that their program isn't appropriate for your child and that your program is. And that's not very simple.

You'll find the most obtuse language and detailed terms in your IEP. The law requires all kinds of procedures to be described in the most minute and technical form. For instance, you say, 'I want my son potty trained.' They will write up goals like, 'He will eliminate sixty per cent of the time according to schedule as...' This language has a tendency to blur everything and make it difficult for the average parent to understand.

So first off, protect yourself by hiring a lawyer. There are agencies out there in every state that give free legal advice to people with disabilities. In my case it was the Philadelphia Center for Educational Law. I filed Chris right away with them over the telephone. 'Hi, I'm Bill Davis. My son Christopher is autistic. I need some advice.'

The IEP was originally conceived so that parents would have power in making decisions about their disabled children. It's meant to be a tool for parents to voice their opinions. But I believe the original concept has become distorted. IEPs and the professionals who write them survive on budget allocations. The end result is stagnation. I've found very few educators at these meetings who say they're going to give my son everything he needs. Instead they say, 'How about two hours of speech instead of twelve?' They try to give whatever fits in with their budget plan.

There's an old story about an insurance company that reimburses the state for speech and language services. It calls the IEP administrators two weeks before an IEP and says, 'We're now allowing for three half-hour sessions of speech a week for kids with autism.' So at the IEP the administrators say, 'We reviewed your child's MDE and we think he needs three half-hour sessions of speech.'

'Good. Where is he going to get it?'

'Down at this clinic. It's all paid for by the insurance.'

'Wonderful. Thank you.'

Then the insurance company calls six months later and says, 'We've changed our policy and can't afford to pay for the speech anymore. We have to reduce it to one half-hour a week.'

So your IEP administrators call you in and say, 'We've reviewed all the data and we think your child only needs one half-hour a week of speech.'

You're sitting there saying, 'Why does he only need one half-hour a week?' But what you don't realize is they're not basing the decision on educational philosophy. They're basing it strictly on finances. That's the trouble with these IEP professionals today. Everything is based on budget. And they lie. Why can't they at least give you the courtesy of being honest and say, 'We can't afford it. We're not going to get you the money.'

Kids with autism are not a priority. Let's say my son had a heart problem and the doctor knew he needed major valve surgery performed by a specialist. What if the doctor said to himself, 'This kid only has a small chance. Let's just give him a minor bypass, and that's what we'll tell him he needs.' How horrendous! You'd throttle the guy.

But that's exactly what they do to my son. 'Chris only needs a speech teacher once a week.' It's common knowledge he needs more, but they always want him to settle for something less.

'What, are you nuts? The child can't speak. What are you talking about?'

'That's what he needs.'

At least say to me you don't want to pay for my child's speech therapy, not that he doesn't need it. Don't insult me with a line like, 'We feel that one meeting a week with our language teacher would be a such a boon for Chris.'

The system has evolved into a scenario where professionals rule and parents are scared. The professionals show little interest in the parents' opinions and then go on to describe what they already had planned. 'OK, we've drawn up our goals and here's what your child is going to get.' Parents have been told to make friends with their IEP administrators and not to rock the boat. So they don't ask a lot of questions or insist on certain services.

Think of a single mother with very little education. She's got three kids, their father has left, she's on disability payments, and she's got a kid with autism. She goes into an IEP meeting and they tell her, 'Mrs. Smith, I am the head of the IU. Your son will be put into this classroom.'

And she nods yes, then meekly says, 'You know, my son really isn't talking.'

'Please, Mrs. Smith, next year we will address that.'

'Oh. I'm sorry. It's just that I heard about a certain therapy.'

'We don't do that here. It's not our policy.'

'Oh, I'm sorry.'

What the bureaucrats have very successfully done is taken the power system, the system that is supposed to work for the parents, and turned it into their own. They've lopsided the whole thing. Their thinking is, 'We're in charge here. We will tell you where you are going and we're not telling you a thing more unless you ask about it. Yes, there are a lot of services out there, but we're not going to integrate them because you didn't ask for them specifically. Too bad. We don't have to spend the money and we don't need a qualified teacher because you didn't demand one. Good. We can stay easily within our budget. Bye-bye.'

Here's how that mother is likely to be appeased. 'Is Jimmy brushing his teeth?'

'No. He can't do that.'

'By the end of this year we will have him brushing his teeth.'

'Oh, thank you.'

What they don't tell her is that by the end of this year Jimmy could be reading if they did it right. Jimmy could be talking. Jimmy could be eating correctly. Jimmy could hug his mom. But they'll take something like brushing teeth, a motor skill, and make that the big thing they teach.

'We'll teach him how to comb his hair.'

'Aaah! That's wonderful! He never combed his hair before. I can't get him to do that.'

'We'll get him to do that.'

So they shoot for these small goals and the parents are delighted. Well, *I'm* not delighted. My IEP administrators would say to me, 'Who do you want present at your IEP?'

'I'd like the governor.' Of course they didn't call him, but my point was that this is important. Somebody should listen.

'What goal do you want for your son?'

'I want him to speak. I want him to attend college when he's older.'

'Well, we mean short-term.'

'Short-term? I want him to speak! Why do you keep asking me? That's what he needs.'

You're going to have to fight for what you believe in at your IEP. I don't mean emotionally. 'I believe in the best for my child,' won't cut it. No. You need to be specific. 'I believe in forty hours of

Discrete Trial, three hours a week of speech therapy, occupational therapy one hour a week, gymnastics two hours a week and a specially programmed computer.'

I've developed a kind of mindset for going into an IEP that I believe all parents of autistic children should have. Decide what you want and don't be afraid. Don't be afraid to anger anybody. Don't try and make friends. I simply don't believe in that attitude. I'm not saying you should go in mad, but go in knowing that ninety per cent of the people you meet are not there to give you what you want.

They're there to give you what the insurance company said they'd pay for or what the district leader said they're going to do. A lot of decisions are based on cost effectiveness and who is available. You've got to understand that. So when they say to you, 'We have a speech teacher. She normally sees the children one half-hour a week,' that's how much they can afford, not necessarily what's best for your child. Don't go in expecting them to say, 'We've reviewed it and he needs two hours a week.' Expect them to give you the least amount possible and be prepared to fight.

How do you prepare? First you need knowledge to empower yourself. That's the most important thing. You must read and read and read, and write and write and write, and collect your data. And that's got to be your job for a while. You must have knowledge about your kid's disability, knowledge of the law, and knowledge of services. Read the laws. Read the legal journals with disability articles. And be sure to have complete knowledge of your child. Look at him. What does he need? If he only does well in a one-on-one situation then that's what he needs! Remember, what they're telling you isn't necessarily true for your child.

Research all that's out there. When you know your child needs a certain service, do not waver. Simply go in and tell them. If your district is not doing a type of program or therapy that's good for your child, then ask for it. Don't be afraid of setting lofty goals.

Having him paint a picture is nice, but what about learning to speak?

Once you decide what you want, collect data and facts to back it up. Be prepared if they ask, 'Why does he need forty hours a week? We don't do forty hours a week. We do twenty.'

You can then respond, 'Lovaas, a renowned autism expert, and all the surrounding data say he needs forty hours a week.' You have to really know your stuff. You have to study educational law. Get a copy of the state educational laws and really learn them. So if they say to you, 'You're not entitled to that,' you can say, 'Hey, wait a minute. Number 541 says that I am.' You've really got to study.

One of the reasons Discrete Trial Instruction is so good in the very beginning is because it is all data-based. I went to my IEP with Chris' data and said, 'Is my child doing well? Let me show you. Let me show you our program. Here he started out on day one doing twenty per cent and now he's doing seventy-five per cent.' It's all written down.

Keep data all the time! You can't go into a courtroom or before an administrator asking for funds and say, 'He's doing very well. I feel in my heart he's improving.'

When that administrator says, 'Show me,' you have to have proof.

'I'll show you. Look at our data. He couldn't do the alphabet. He only got A thru D three months ago. Now look at the data for this week. He got A thru F.'

If you haven't begun Discrete Trial, then maybe you want to ask for it and prove that it's successful.

When you have all your facts and data as back-up, you can simply say, 'I have worked with my child and this is what I want for him. I have research and data. So there's no use discussing anything but how to get this. I'm not here to battle with you because there's no battle. This is what he needs. If he were deaf, wouldn't he need sign? Yes. Would you say to me we don't do sign here? No. Well, don't say to me "we don't do Discrete Trial here." Don't tell me that. I don't want to hear budget mentioned. I don't want to hear policy mentioned. This is a living being that we're talking about.'

I developed an opening ploy for parents at IEPs that I think works particularly well. Go in and say, 'I don't know everybody here in the room. Let's go around the room and introduce ourselves. Please tell me your degrees that specialize in autism along with your hands-on experience.' You will find that their mouths open.

'Well, I'm the school psychologist.'

'And you're here because of my son so you must have a great knowledge of autism. What is it?'

'I went to the seminar held at Rutgers recently.'

'You went to the seminar at Rutgers? How long was it?'

'Three hours.'

'Three hours and you're going to tell me what's good for my son?'

Then the next one introduces himself. 'I'm the speech patholo-gist. I've been doing this for ten years.'

'How many children with autism have you seen?'

'I've seen two.'

'Two? How many hours did you give them?'

'They had a half-hour a week.'

'A half-hour a week? And they don't speak, do they?'

'No.'

'Oh, so you think a half-hour is enough?'

'No. That's what I was told.'

As you can see, this exposure of credentials immediately sets you in a power position and shows them that they are not in a position to tell you what you're supposed to get. It is very rare to find somebody who says, 'I graduated from Johns Hopkins with my Masters in autism. I trained at the South Carolina Institute of TEACCH.' If someone does say that, thank goodness. Then you've probably got somebody who knows what your child truly needs.

The key thing to remember in an IEP is the word 'appropriate.' Your child deserves a Free Appropriate Public Education – FAPE. That's the legal term used. Your job is to show that the services they are providing are not appropriate for your child and the services you are asking for are.

Don't use emotion or lines like 'This is the best for him' or 'I think this is good for him' or 'I want him to have the best.' Ask instead, 'How are you teaching him speech?'

You might hear an answer like 'Well, I take him for a half-hour each week and I sit him in the corner...'

'That's not appropriate,' you can respond, 'and I'll show you why. It says here that children with autism need at least two to three hours of intensive speech a day by a trained professional. A half-hour is not appropriate. I want full speech services and I'm not faltering from that line.' If they say we don't have a speech department then say, 'Get me one. Send me somewhere. Pay for it. Too bad. Let someone come to my house.'

You've got a bunch of tired bureaucrats who constantly work through red tape just to get through the day. So when you say, 'I want this particular set-up,' they're going to fight you. They want the status quo.

'This is not what we do here,' they'll say. They've also learned to be wary of people who try to take advantage of the system. I know one disgraceful family who sued for money to buy a boat because their kid loved water.

One of the IU administrators who started with me four years ago told me recently, 'Before you, I had never been confronted by a parent who told me what to do. Quite frankly, I was upset. And then I realized that you were just fighting to get the best for your son.'

Don't expect the IEP administrators to telephone you and say, 'By the way, we just found some great therapy for your child, and we're going to give it to him.' Don't expect them to say, 'We went on a trip and looked all around for the best therapy and we're setting it up for you next year.' That's what you think should happen, but they're not going to do it.

Remember, you cannot fight for your child through emotion. I've hired experts from Rutgers to appear with me when I thought I needed them. When you come with somebody who has extensive credentials they listen. It cost me four, five hundred dollars, but it was worth it.

If you're starting a home-based program with a behavioral management group, hire one of them to come in with you. 'Here's the person who's running my program. Here's the therapist. He's going to tell you why my son needs this.'

You have to make up your mind. People sometimes fight for the fight. That's where they're wrong. 'Inclusion above everything. I want my child in kindergarten with all the other children no matter what the services.' I don't believe in that. That's just fighting for fighting's sake.

Choose the right battles. For instance, fight for properly trained teachers. Tell them, 'There's one thing I will not tolerate. You need trained teachers. Not teachers who attended one course. They should be graduates of respected autism programs and have hands-on experience with children who have autism.'

When teachers say to me, 'I've been in special education for six years and recently attended a Progress in Partnership Autism Conference,' that's not good enough.

I've told them, 'I don't want to hurt your feelings, but a fifteen-hour conference and no hands-on experience does not make you qualified to teach my son. So tell me, if my son has an episode, how do you work with him and redirect him? You don't know what an SD means? Let's forget it then. You're just not able to teach my son effectively.'

While battling for what you think your child deserves don't forget to use a very effective weapon – publicity. Go to the newspapers and get human interest stories written about how hard it is to get appropriate services. Go to your local state representative and tell him, 'I want you to call the special ed unit and tell them you support me in my fight for my child.' I called up Senator Arlen Specter and many other representatives, and they made calls for me! Once IEP administrators know you have a little power and are willing to go out there and get an article written, they respond.

If your IEP still doesn't work out the way you want, don't give up. You have not exhausted all your options. First you should know that there's a 'stay-put' law if you still disagree with your IEP. Parents are always worried that everything will be taken away if they argue, but services can't be removed. Your child continues to get the same services until the argument is resolved.

Remember that signing your IEP doesn't mean you agree with the decision. It just documents that you were in attendance. I suggest if you are not in agreement that you sign it and put in parentheses 'do not agree.' Then there's no twisting of your words.

Mediation should be your next step. If you can't agree on the number of hours of service your child needs, a professional arbitrator will try and arrange a compromise. If a compromise cannot be reached you can go to court. There you argue before a judge exactly what you've been arguing in mediation – appropriate education.

When we were fighting at our IEP meetings I would say to my wife, 'Jae, there's no other way. If this is what he needs then what am I'm worried about? What's the worst that can happen? We'll go to court because I'm not bending.'

And I would say to the IEP administrators, 'You're not understanding me. Maybe I can make it simple for you. There's NOTHING TO TALK ABOUT! I want this for my son. Don't mention money to me. I don't work for you. I don't care what money you have. And don't tell me what hard work it is and you've never seen it before. Go and get it. Otherwise we go to court. So either you say yes and we discuss the details or else I sue you. What would you like to do?' There's no varying. There's no place for compromise.

PART III
Daily Living

1

Frantic!

The first couple of years living with Chris' autism was like walking a tightrope. He would often shut down in the beginning. It was very scary. He would either withdraw, stop eating, stop drinking the bottle, or sit in the corner. We still don't know why. Was it something in his learning program? Was something simply just bothering him? From age two-and-a-half to four-and-a-half I wanted to be around him all the time. I hated going to work because I felt like I was taking a chance when I left. Will he stop doing another activity while I'm gone? Will I lose him?

We lived in constant worry about what was going to happen next. One day he'd sleep. One day he wouldn't. One day he'd scream. One day he'd cry. He'd go into laughing fits. He'd have a new self-stim everyday. It was a time of great unknowns.

Everyday was a battle. We spent our lives trying to make his life OK, and my poor daughter often took the brunt of it. She was told all the time to be quiet, don't do that, shut up, sit down or you're going to upset him!

Jae and I were constantly at each other's throats, threatening and yelling at each other. 'Why did you take the banana and put it on the side when YOU KNOW HE WANTS IT IN FRONT?!!?!' It was terrible. 'GET OUT! You don't know what you're doing!' Then

Chris would cry because we were arguing. 'That's it! Everybody out of the house!' Please, it was tough! It was really tough!!

One time he came down and shut off the TV. We had no idea why, but no TV was allowed on in the house. If he heard it upstairs he'd run down like a maniac with fear in his eyes and turn it off. We don't know why or what affected him, but we had to have the TV off. So we didn't watch for two months. Then one day I put it on quietly. He came down, looked at it, and let it stay on. Those types of things happened all the time.

What would happen if we let Chris get upset? Why worry and go to such great lengths? Getting upset is actually a very soft description of what happened if things didn't go Chris' way. His whole day could be thrown off. It was a frightening prospect – not because we were concerned about *our* day, but he had such an overreaction to things.

I know parents whose child was attached to an Ace of Spades and it had to be sitting on the chair when he came down at nine o'clock or that was it. He went crazy!

And that was very similar to the way Chris behaved. I felt if I made the wrong move or took him to the wrong place he would tantrum, act aggressive or become violent. It was not uncommon for Chris to head-butt. He would lash out at you and come up at your chin with his head. At the very least if something upset him he'd either stop responding, cry, or be out of sorts all day. He would just shut down.

Sometimes while driving to the grocery store I would pass the mall and Chris wanted to go there instead. Well, that was it! Crying, stomping, hitting his head. He kept that up for a long time.

And these tantrums could be for something as simple as stopping at a red light. Absolutely. He would go crazy in the car when we stopped so we'd try and speed up. If a car got in my way, I'd crazily get out and tell the driver to move.

My wife tried working this and other problems out by developing a program of flash cards to explain things to him. 'It's red. See this. We have to stop now. Wait…'

Going out to do anything with Chris, especially at the beginning, was frenetic! I was a maniac. Just a trip to the store was an ordeal. If someone got loud he'd jump and I'd yell at the person. 'Get out! Get out of the store!'

'What are you talking about?'

'Shut your mouth!' It was horrible. We were horrible. We went around like maniacs because everything affected this poor guy.

If I had to run errands and take Chris with me here's how it would go. 'Let's go to the store and get Chris' bagel. But it's got to be the right bagel and when we go I have to park on the left side of the street. OK, I found a parking space on the left side. Now take him in the store. Wait a minute! There's that woman with the yellow dress. He hates the yellow dress! Turn the other way!' Next I'd say to myself, 'I have to stop and get gas, but I have to stop the car and he doesn't like when the car stops… Now I want to take him out and go into another store and we're parked on the thruway…'

That's the way we thought all the time. Chris used to throw tantrums when we shopped and we couldn't get him in or out of the buildings. He simply went limp and became such dead weight that I'd have to use all my strength to pick him up and move him. It's gotten a little easier, but oh, God…

He was just a mess. We were a mess. I thought OK, this is going to be our life. We're going to have to take care of him. I honestly thought at the time that he would NEVER get out of the state he was in. I would leave the house crying because I worried about what might happen while I was at work. 'He just said the alphabet, but if a therapist does something wrong he might shut down. What if he becomes violent?'

The aggression was terribly scary. He would just come at you and was especially a master at going for your throat. Therapists would sit across the table from Chris and he'd suddenly clench his teeth, start to shake, and LEAP for them! He'd grab the girls by their throats! He was very strong and they were frightened to death. You'd see the fear in their eyes. He looked like a caged animal at times throwing tantrums, crying, kicking, or running back and forth. At night he'd move his bowels in his diaper and throw his feces or rub them in his face and hair. The behaviors were endless.

I've always taken Chris on a lot of walks with me, but one time he had a little fall and scraped himself. Chris was very tactile and for some reason his knee and shin areas were extra sensitive, so he refused to walk and wouldn't stop crying or touching the cut. I tried putting Band-Aids on, but he wouldn't let me. We ended up putting him in sweatpants for days, even when he went to sleep, until the cut disappeared. He still insisted on checking it, though, and every time he'd check he'd cry when he saw the scrape. For some reason he just couldn't deal with it.

After this episode I started holding his hand when we walked. And if he started to fall, I'd catch him and pick him up because I certainly didn't want to go through that again with him. It was so disconcerting to know that such a minor incident could ruin his life for days!

Eating around Chris was another problem. If he smelled my sandwich he gagged and refused to eat the rest of the day. We were so concerned he would stop eating that we were very careful not to have our food around him.

When Chris was sick with a cold he didn't know what was happening and we couldn't explain it to him. It was horrible. He'd stop eating, lose weight, look pale, and get dried out. All we could do was get him to drink water.

Noises were a problem too. We couldn't vacuum the house! He was frightened to death of the vacuum. So we tried to desensitize him by showing a card with a vacuum cleaner running and then play the noise of the vacuum. Then we'd show him the vacuum and say, 'Look, we're going to go rum, rum. It's going to go on. So you come downstairs, but we're going to do this.' He slowly became less and less afraid. It's the same thing as rubbing his back. The more we did it, the more he became desensitized. But it had to be done all the time!

When we were first toilet training, a therapist took Chris to the bathroom and he quickly wanted to get off the potty. The therapist insisted he try for five more seconds. He did not go back in the bathroom for four months after that! We couldn't get him to go near it! I was so upset that I fired the therapist. 'You don't push him to do anything!' You couldn't.

It was always frightening when I look back. One wrong turn and maybe he would never speak. Or he'd never do therapy or class work again. It always seemed like he took all these steps forward and then could immediately lose them. He'd shut down or develop a new stim. Or he'd lose one stim and develop another.

I'll never forget when Chris started saying the alphabet on our walks. I was so afraid if he didn't recite that alphabet every two minutes, I'd lose him or he'd never say the alphabet again. I kept prompting him continually. 'Chris, A... B...' I did it so much. I think he hated it. And then I hated myself for doing it so much. But I didn't know what to do. It was very hard.

He used to be attached to an object one day and then suddenly lose the attachment. But while he had the attachment he insisted on bringing it everywhere. There was a time he was attached to pictures of the Honkers from Sesame Street. He knew every one. He'd have to bring every picture wherever he went. If he was missing one, forget about it. He wouldn't leave the house. He'd frantically search all over the house, turning over couches. He would take fifty pictures with him in the car, and when it was time to get out he wanted to take them. If he was going to gym class he wouldn't put them down. So we tried to coax him. Let's say he took a couple of rubber lizards. 'OK, we're going to gym class. Put lizards in car.'

'Honey, put lizards down.'

And he cried and flailed. 'No.'

Gradually he put them down. He began to understand.

We started making a special place by the door where he could leave his objects. 'Put puppet there. It will be there when you come back. Come on. Let's do this. We can get out the door. Come on, we can do this. Great job! Look at that!'

Then we'd come back, 'See, he's right here.'

We did the same thing in the car. 'When we get back to the car, that lizard will be here.'

It was a difficult process and took a while. Everything takes a while.

I really lived my life in a frantic state. Once while on vacation in Ocean City we were sitting quietly for the first time in four days and eating breakfast. Chris was staring in fascination at a fan when a woman came and sat at the counter right in front of that fan! Chris started screaming and pounding. I ran up and threw ten dollars down. 'Move!!'

She looked and started to ask what I was doing? But I yelled, 'GET UP!! I'll buy you breakfast! Move!'

'OK! OK!'

'Look, I'm sorry, but my son's looking at that fan! Get out of the way!' She thought I was crazy. But it taught me a big lesson. I remember that incident because it made me realize I could not go through life making everybody move out of the way. Chris was going to have to understand that.

I originally told myself, 'This is our life. That's it. Sorry. We're going to have to follow this guy around twenty-four hours a day and do every little thing for him.' I always pictured myself clearing the path like when you chase a baby around. 'Wait, there's an electrical cord over there.' I was doing that all the time. But we realized we had to stop. It wasn't to make *our* lives easier, but to stand up for *him*.

Believe me, it was hard telling a boy who had trouble staying still, 'You're going to have to lie in your bed. You can't run around and jump and throw things. I'm going to put you back in bed each time.' But we remained vigilant, and after a while life got easier and easier. Lo and behold, I turned around one day and had this changed guy. 'OK, it's bath time. It's bed time.' He was going along. It's still not easy. But once they catch on and you establish certain things you can teach them so much.

It was impossible not to worry all the time about something setting my son off. I was always saying, 'Chris, look at me. Look at me.' We'd take a walk and I'd talk to him non-stop for fear he might go off into a trance. I thought if I saw him start looking off into the distance I would immediately snap him back. 'Chris! Daddy's here. Look at Daddy. Look at Daddy!'

Leaving him alone in his room was even scary. I thought I might go up and find him lost to the disorder. Still today, if twenty minutes go by and he hasn't come down to join us I'll go upstairs and say, 'Come on. Shut your movie off. We're going downstairs.'

I think it's natural behavior when parents learn their child has autism to behave the way we did. And I don't even know if that's bad. I think you have to create a very safe environment in the beginning. We may have gone a little overboard. We still do to a certain extent, but I won't allow people running around my house disturbing his tranquility. That doesn't mean my daughter can't play music and sing. She always has friends over. There's even noise from the vacuum.

Before if Chris disliked something, it could have been six months before he recovered. Now when he's taught something new it's like, bang, he gets it! And if he doesn't like it, he's able to handle himself without breaking down. When I think back to those earlier days he's almost unrecognizable.

Now if we say, 'Chris, you can't sit there,' he might voice dissatisfaction, but he'll sit someplace else. If he falls off the rings in gymnastics and tumbles down he'll be upset, but he'll get back up. Maybe not till the next day, but he'll still get back up on those rings.

That's what I really love to see. It's the best feeling in the world to know that now if something goes wrong my son will be OK. I no longer feel frantic about losing him.

2

The Pain Is Numbing

I'll never forget a family whose daughter with autism was extremely self-injurious. She would bleed from hurting herself. They'd put her in the shower to wash the blood off and she'd hit her head against the shower wall! They actually ran out of towels while cleaning off the blood. The mother had a breakdown and they had to put the daughter in an institution.

An aide once took her to the bathroom on a field trip and the girl went over to the sink and just banged her head until it opened. Once after being given the wrong medication she put her fingers in her eyes! Horrible. She's had to be constantly medicated and wear protective clothing and a helmet. The father visits her on weekends and some days she says, 'Hi, Dad. So nice of you to come.' Other days she says, 'You fuck, I'll kill you!'

Once the father said to me that he read a book by a woman with autism who wrote she never felt pain. The injuries actually numbed her to the world like self-medication. To me it was the saddest thing. But he was delighted because this notion helped him go through life. 'My daughter's not being hurt. She doesn't feel pain.' She cracks her head open but she doesn't feel the pain! He wanted anything to grasp that made him feel his daughter wasn't hurting. I understood what he was going through.

There's a famous case where they strait-jacketed a kid because he was gouging his eyes and beating himself in the head so badly that he was giving himself concussions. Once while sitting in the strait-jacket he hit his head against his own knee so hard that he broke the kneecap and opened his head.

A lot of kids with autism are self-injurious. They seem to have either an inability to perceive pain or they defer the pain. It's not quite clear. And then sometimes they overreact to even the smallest of pains. When Chris stepped on brambles in bare feet he was not bothered, but when he scraped his shin he walked around upset and in pain for days. After oral surgery he never reacted. I've read cases where kids have broken their legs and didn't cry. You don't even see any sign of pain on their faces. It makes it difficult to know if they simply can't deal with it, are able to defer it, or if the neurons aren't giving them the pain message. Maybe it has to do with the lack of serotonin in certain parts of the brain and the abundance in other parts.

When Chris does gymnastics his hands get a little raw from the bars and he'll cry out. Then he angrily shakes and rubs his hands. Maybe it's the surface nerves that really affect him while deeper injuries don't. You just never know. We do know that we have to be very careful, though, because the brain just does not seem to be getting the proper messages and it's dangerous.

One of the great things about the recent writers who have autism is that they tell you what they felt and theorize why. Temple Grandin, the first to say she thinks in pictures, said that whenever her mother had her wear a woolen hat to school she would scream and bang her head against the car. The scratchiness of the wool was so overwhelming that she wanted to bang her head through the glass. Only nobody could understand that.

A lot of these self-injurious kids did not have early intervention. They especially did not get therapeutic touching and stroking. I'm not saying that it would have helped this girl who cracked her head open. I don't know. Maybe it wouldn't have. But when nothing's being done, as the years go by a child with autism keeps retreating further and further. After a while that person is hard to bring back. When somebody begins to open their own head at age twelve, it's pretty hard to handle at that point. Even if you start to medicate, the behavior can continue. This is usually the point a person is institutionalized.

No matter what the disorder, the human body and brain still demand stimulation. And if you can't get it, you're going to do something. When a typical person taps nervously because he's bored, he has the ability to say to himself, 'Snap out of it, you're annoying people.' But the autistic child doesn't have that ability. Tapping fingers become slapping thighs and slapping thighs become chest hitting. Chest hitting turns into head banging. I believe self-injurious behavior is a natural outgrowth of the need for stimulation. 'The less stimulation I get, the more my body demands I start to hurt myself.' When you see a child with terrible self-stimulatory behavior, stims, it's because they're fulfilling a need.

Living with autism must be a tremendously frustrating life. It's like going to China. Picture yourself in a strange city. People are walking by in different clothes and chattering in a language you can't understand. What do you do? How do you survive? It must be a very strange feeling.

A child with autism probably has the same strange feeling. He's out in the world starting to observe things and saying to himself, 'There's a hundred people in this supermarket all talking and exchanging money and doing things. And I am not part of this whatsoever. I can't figure out one thing they're doing and I don't know why they're doing it. I don't know what they're saying. I know I'm different and I can't even participate in this world if I wanted so I'm going to stay over here away from all the jabbering and stimulate myself.' It's what their bodies demand. There's too much coming at them and they retreat. They can't get stimulation from the world so they give it to themselves. Then you see them make all kinds of noises and bodily motions because they're falling into this horrific pattern of self-stimulation.

One reason I have taken the task to learn every nuance about my son is to know where and what stimulation he needs. That way I can stop him from becoming self-injurious. Why does a child with autism hit himself in the head? It's because he needs stimulation; it makes him feel better. But I have gotten Chris to the point where he will come to me for what he needs.

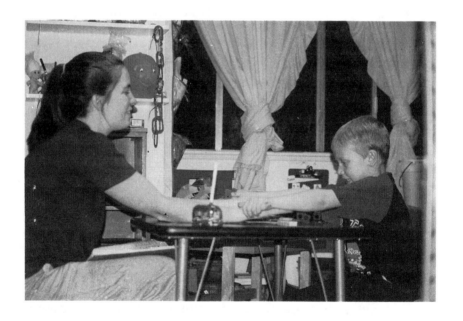

Chris in therapy, squeezing Jenny's arms. He does this out of excitement and frustration

A lot of people with autism like pressure to the brain and body. Temple Grandin speaks of the squeeze machine she created to satisfy her need for pressure. Where most children long for a pat, children with autism like deep pressure. It just makes them feel better. Chris used to squeeze himself all the time and likes deep pressure on his head. Pushing and deep pressure massage is very comforting. If kids with autism don't have the ability to get enough pressure, that's when they become self-injurious.

So I've tried to give pressure to Chris so that he would come to me instead of seeking it elsewhere. He'll take my hand, put it by his head, and I will just press on his forehead and he seems to be better. Or he'll come to us, lie down on his stomach, put my hand on his back, and I will press. In essence, I've become his squeeze machine so he doesn't hit his head against the wall or gouge his eyes. It's far better that he seek out the feeling from me or find other acceptable ways to give it to himself, rather than become self-injurious. One way or another he will seek it.

Why they don't come up with a Temple Grandin squeeze machine I don't know. I think some people have built their own. We bought a weighted vest for Chris called a Kelly Vest. You put it on and wear it like a weighted quilt, but we rarely use it anymore because it's not necessary. Just the other week, however, he was really having a tough time settling down to sleep so we put the vest on him and he pulled it right up under his neck and went to sleep. He needed that pressure. It kind of grounds them.

The vest cost us about two hundred dollars! The weights are the type you find in ankle weights. You could easily take a vest and put weights in it yourself rather than buy one.

Ironically, children with autism like pressure but don't want to be touched: 'I want to be hugged and I want pressure, but I don't like being touched.' For example, almost every autistic kid I see will extend his arm out so you will scratch it. Some of them look back as adults and say, 'The arm was like an outer extension of myself. I wanted you to scratch me and touch me, but by giving you my arm it wasn't really touching my body and I could deal with that.'

Realizing all these things, I started out stimulating Chris by rubbing his back just a little, touching him just a little, or hugging him just a little. I did this every day, hours a day, until the touching increased a little and he wanted even more. I was desensitizing him.

Chris still self-stimulates himself to a certain extent. At first he was doing a lot of finger playing, spinning and rocking. A couple times he banged his head and I would say, 'Ow! That hurts! Ow! That would hurt Daddy. Come on, let's go!' So I always tried to make clear that this was pain. This was not something that feels good. I really think that the degree of head banging is a progression. There are cases, however, that are so severe, you can't keep up with them and they end up just being medicated.

A lot of stims come and go. Chris hits his mouth now, an imitative behavior of a boy in his class. So we'll say to him, 'Come on. Let's do this,' and redirect him. We're always on top of him. We refuse to let these self-injurious behaviors progress.

We were very protective of Chris right from the beginning. I was always saying, 'Ow! Don't do that,' when he would behave dangerously toward himself. We were right on top of him all of the time teaching him that he mattered and should take care of himself and be gentle.

I think Chris had this inner self-preservation. The more we gave him a boost, the more he would improve. Whether he understood me or not, I would constantly talk to him. On our walks I'd always say, 'Here comes a car. We have to stop because we don't want to get hurt.'

Last night he was getting excited and instead of flapping his hands out in front, he now hits his chest. So I came over and rubbed his chest, 'We don't want to hurt your chest, Chrissie. You know we take care of ourselves, and you take it easy.' So he clapped his hands because clapping's an acceptable thing. We always taught him, 'Clap. Not that other behavior. Clap.' If you're out in public you don't want your kid ridiculed for his self-stims. Teach him instead to clap if he gets real excited. People will accept that. Chris has learned, and by switching from chest banging to clapping he tells me he understands. That's Chris. He takes care of himself. And we've helped him see that he is worth protecting.

3

Aggression

I know a family who once went on a trip and from the backseat of the car their boy with autism punched his father in the head, took the wheel and tried to steer the car off the road. On a number of occasions he also punched his mother and beat her. He threw a teacher through a glass door and punched a girl in school hard enough to break her jaw. He's a big kid who weighs about one hundred and eighty pounds with an air of mental retardation about him. You'd never think he looks mean, but at any minute he could just turn around and hurt you.

Another boy, featured in a film, came home for the weekend from an institution. 'Hi, Mom,' he greeted.

His mother jumped back. 'Don't touch me.'

She was so scared of him. He had been hurting her and handling her private parts for years.

'I learned. I sorry.'

In the movie he was interviewed. 'What do you do wrong?'

'I know I hurt my mother. And I touch her places. I don't mean it.'

In another film a kid with autism suddenly reached over, pulled the therapist's hair, and lifted her out of the seat. She was struggling to get him off. One minute you saw him co-operating in therapy. The next minute he was hurting her!

I remember very distinctly holding Christopher in my arms outside when a woman came up to us. This was the period when Chris clung to me and I couldn't put him down. The woman, taking her newborn out for sun, remarked how beautiful my son was. Acting like the proud father, I tried to engage Chris in communication and told him to look at the baby. Smack! He hit that baby right in the face! I was shocked. The baby had been asleep, not crying, not doing anything. My son just reached over and gave this baby a wallop in the face! I apologized and the woman walked off. I was lucky that's all she did. It sounds stupid now, but I actually thought Chris was just acting like a big lug, a real boy.

Another time Jessica was watching the boy next door who was a couple years younger than Chris. Chris was reading a book on the couch when the toddler came over, picked up one of his toys, brushed against his leg and, out of nowhere, and I mean out of nowhere, Chris shot a kick into this kid! The kid flew across the room and slammed off the wall! It was frightening. And Chris never changed expression. He never looked up from the book. Thank goodness the toddler was OK.

Did he find the unpredictability of children a threat? Perhaps. But unfortunately, children were not the only target of Chris' aggression. He has hit me in the nose with his head and taken me by the throat. He has come up and head-butted me so that I've fallen over and my whole head rings. He butted my daughter, Jesse, one time and really hurt her.

I've seen him sit across the table from therapists and get so mad at something that he clenches his fists, starts to shake, and grabs them by the throat! I'm telling you, you get scared. The reaction is so quick and the strength is so unbelievable. He goes right for the throat.

I've been told children with autism have innate abilities to hurt. Who taught this kid to head butt under the chin? Who taught him to go for the throat? It's very scary to live in fear of someone.

Unfortunately, aggression can be a fact of life for children with autism. But what happens when they're fifteen and weigh one hundred and eighty pounds? This is where legal trouble develops, and why you must become your child's legal guardian. If you're just a parent, your teen stands on his own if he's in trouble. Taking legal guardianship is one act all parents of children with autism should do. It prevents their adolescent from being put into the juvenile system if they do something wrong. If they stand as an independent adult they will suffer consequences as an independent adult even though their mental capacity is not the same. Laws also exist that protect children with autism while in school. For example, if your child's in class and suddenly becomes aggressive he can't be suspended or expelled if that aggressiveness is part of his disability.

Obviously, we hope Chris' aggression never comes to that. We haven't had an episode of aggressive behavior or frustration in a long time. He's really become very subdued. I think it's a combination of a whole list of strategies we take with him. We soothe him, use behavioral management techniques, use time-outs, don't reinforce unwanted behaviors, redirect behavior, administer secretin, help him find a variety of communication methods, teach him to be funny, teach him to be a kid, get physical, take him to gymnastics and teach him how to deal with frustration.

We make allowances as well. I know that if I push Chris too far or he's getting a little frustrated, I've got to realize it and back off. That's why I'll ask him, 'Do you want Daddy to go?'

'GO.'

'OK, you play.'

Chris has also learned to work through his anger with unaggressive physical motions. He'll now clench his body to get rid of frustration rather than cry for three hours or pounce. He doesn't get physically ill or ruin a whole day anymore. It was scary for a couple of years worrying whether or not he'd get upset. He'd pace, be mean, cry and lash out.

We've learned to give him a break from his therapy work and take him for a ride or a walk. It's important to observe how a child with autism is responding to an activity and then ask him if he needs a break. Look at his actions. You have to pay attention to him. There are times you have to say, 'It is very hard today. Let's go play,' or 'Open door. Go ahead. You can go.' You have to adjust to the child all the time. It's constant thinking on your feet. 'We can allow him this activity, but we can't allow him to watch TV because then he doesn't come back.'

Our symbol for taking a break is a child walking down the stairs, and he's learned to give it to us whenever he needs a breather. We taught him that choosing to break was not just an excuse for getting out of work, but was him making a reasonable decision. 'I am overwhelmed and I need a break. Stop! Go! Bye-bye.'

The kid in the film that attacked the therapist may have been very bored or frustrated and not known how to communicate. That is why I think it's crucial not only to give the child a break, but to give him some means of communication. It's good if you acknowledge that he needs a break, but still the child has no power. Allow *him* to tell you! Don't just make it your decision.

Part of Chris' lack of aggression is from knowing he has power over what happens to him. You have to give your child means to express himself. Put yourself in the child's position. For instance, he may be thinking, 'I have no way of telling you that the only thing bothering me is that pink pen right there. It is absolutely overwhelming me and I just want to get up and break that pen!'

So you have to be able to ask the right questions and give the child ways to communicate. It sounds easy, but it took years for us to learn and it's still not over. It'll never be over. But for Chris to be able to say no, stop, or 'give me a break' is an amazing feat.

Here's an example of teaching Chris to use communication as a means to power. The cats used to startle him and he used to get off his bed if they came on it. So I told him to tell the cats to go! 'Push them off the bed if you don't want them there. *You* have to stay on the bed. You're in charge.'

So he would say, 'Go.' He soon realized that he didn't have to rely on his dad to push the cats off anymore. *He* could actually stay on the bed and take control *himself*. Enabling communication lessened Chris' frustration level and gave him empowerment. I believe it's a necessary step in lessening aggression for all children with autism.

4

Discrete Trial

'I can't stand it! My son looks like a monkey in an experiment!' I took my fist and punched it right through the screen door. It was the third screen in a few months. I hated this Discrete Trial. I hated that Chris was upstairs in therapy six hours a day. I hated seeing him cry. I hated seeing him cajoled and moved around and pushed and pulled. I would sit downstairs and cry while I watched on the monitor. I can't even remember how many times I walked out of the house in tears. 'This child's not getting anywhere and I don't care,' I said at one point. 'I can't hurt him anymore. I'm going to stop this therapy even if there *is* a chance it might work.' I changed my mind every two hours about whether or not the program was working and if we should continue. Until he really started to zip through programs and learn things, I was embroiled in turmoil.

Discrete Trial Instruction is a program that systematically breaks down tasks into specific instructional parts. Using consistency and repetition, children with autism can achieve success and learn important skills with minimal frunstration. So how do you get a child with autism to drink from a cup? First, it may be, 'Do this.'

And you show him just to hold the cup. He may be afraid to extend his hand and touch that cup; you just don't know. There are a lot of things going on that you don't know, but they are physically not psychologically-based issues! This is an important point that people *have* to understand. The child's inability to extend his hand for that cup is not something he can get over through reasoning.

Another Discrete Trial lesson might be to teach a child how to brush his teeth. So first, 'Put your hand on the toothbrush.' That's done over and over until he's mastered it. 'OK, touch brush... Very good! Touch brush.' Once it's mastered he goes on to putting the brush up to his mouth, and so forth. Tiny steps like these are taught for everything.

The first skill we taught Chris was sitting at the table. 'Come here.' That meant come to the table, sit down, and pay attention. 'Go play.' That meant he'd finished doing his task and might get up and play.

Then there was category matching. How do you teach a child with autism that an animal's an animal? We used the command 'put with same' a lot. This is a big Discrete Trial program. We used it with colors. 'Here's orange, red, blue. You have blue. Put with same.' He'd put it anywhere. 'No. Blue is blue,' and we showed him so he began recognizing the same colors.

Sound discrimination was taught that way too. There was a tambourine, a bell and a flute on the table. Underneath on the therapist's side were the same instruments. She shook the tambourine under the table and asked Chris to do the same. That meant Chris had to pay attention, hear, say to himself, 'I know that sound comes from this,' and shake his tambourine.

Motor skills were another big program. There was a lot of 'do this.' Physical movements were very hard for him to get in the beginning. Over and over again like Simon Says we'd repeat, 'Do this.' Eventually he paid attention, listened and made a motor planning movement, but the simplest thing was so impossible for him. We showed him to raise his hands above his head and instead he would raise his hands forward. It was hard for him to get that. So Discrete Trial used a lot of physical prompting in order for him to get the movements.

There was also something called a 'no-no' prompt. The therapist would say, 'Do this,' and hold her arms up. Chris couldn't do it so she'd say, 'No.' I always hated that. You're supposed to say no nicely, but I hated it. And then she'd show him and put his hands up.

Chris cried a lot in the beginning of his Discrete Trial therapy. The therapists forced him to sit and attend, but he didn't want to sit down and would cry. It was heart wrenching for me and I had to leave the house. There were times I came back and said, 'That's it! Tear down everything. Get it out of the house! He's not taking anymore of this. *I'll* teach him. He'll just be with me. Too bad.'

My wife would say, 'No. He's got to learn. You've got to stop.'

There were a couple times while I watched on the monitor that he started yelling 'fuck you.' Shocked and feeling Discrete Trial was to blame I'd yell, 'Jae, that's it! Throw all this shit out! He's not doing this anymore.'

And she'd say, 'No! This is going to help him!'

What I kept saying to myself was, 'I don't care if he gets better. I can't do this to him anymore. I can't.' It was like having a child in the hospital hooked up to tubes and crying. Of course the hospital is doing him good, but it's agonizing to watch. You say, 'I don't want to do this to him anymore,' but deep down you know better. That's how I felt about Discrete Trial in the beginning.

The typical reaction of a kid with autism when you're bringing him out of his world is anger, crying and tantrums. I couldn't stand seeing him like that. I just wanted him left alone. If he wanted to sit in the corner, I wanted them to leave him alone and let him sit. If you think about it, though, I was really no different than any other parent. How do you react when you take your kid to kindergarten and she starts crying? Your instinct is to want to take her out. That's what I was like.

To get a better handle on what we were doing with Chris, I started reading more about the therapy and became somewhat of an expert on technical things like prompts. If we were having a little trouble or the girls weren't getting the therapeutic methods right, I would read the explanation and translate. 'Have everybody read this paragraph! Here's why you're doing it and how you do it.' Sure enough, they started to understand what they were doing and Chris started improving.

The monitor and camera quickly became important tools. First of all, we could see and hear what was going on and talk to the therapists. 'Andrea, you gave him that on the left side. Can you switch it to the right, please?'

Second, we had the ability to tape sessions, so our Rutgers consultant, Matt Bowman, could take the tapes, review them, and critique us. 'I reviewed the tape of Ms. Gomez and she's not doing this right,' or 'Guys, you missed the data.' The monitoring system turned out to be an invaluable tool.

For a few years, Matt Bowman's role was really as our behavioral analyst. Every month he analyzed all the data, the programs, Chris, Chris' progress and the therapists. First he'd view tapes of the therapists and then he'd visit once a month and have each therapist do a little bit at the table and correct them. He was really helpful. 'Melissa, you need to look up when you present the data to Chris.' At times he even told us that certain therapists had to go because they weren't capable of doing the job. Jae, however, didn't always agree with him and they would argue over a therapist's fate.

Matt regularly introduced new Discrete Trial programs. 'Chris is now going to learn about animals or color matching or sound discrimination.' If Chris mastered a program, Matt had us change it. He also had us change the room around at times to facilitate the instruction.

We had to learn so much – SDs (Discriminative Stimulus Instruction that controls a response), no-no prompts and so many other different terms. Literally, you have to graduate from Rutgers to understand it all. Matt was on the phone all the time with us, and Jae went to three Rutgers conferences to learn the jargon. She even took our daughter Jessica.

Despite the complexity of the theoretical philosophy, the programs were quite elemental in the beginning. Therapists would sit there and go, 'Do this… Good job.'

'Do this… Good job.'

'Do this… Good job.'

'Clap hands.' If Chris just looked blankly at the therapist she'd take his hands. 'Good job… Clap hands.' Then he'd do it on his own. 'Great job!'

To give Chris more praise while making things more interesting, Matt had us vary what we said. We weren't just looking at Chris and robotically saying 'good job.' We'd come up with all kinds of lines. 'You are awesome!' 'Good guy!' 'What a wonderful little man!' 'Fantastic job!' 'Wonderful!' We actually did it down the alphabet. It was as elemental as that.

One of the keys to Discrete Trial Instruction was rewarding desirable behavior. Verbally praising Chris for how well he did was one form of reward, but more incentive was necessary. Candy was a big reward at first. He ate so many sweets!

After a while we stopped the candy. How many M&Ms could he eat? And all that sugar! His teeth were a mess. Mostly though, we were starting to feel the candy reward was too much like Pavlov's dog. 'Here you go. Very good. Have a treat.' So Jae started thinking of new rewards, rewards that made him a more active participant in life.

We chose to reward him with hugs, tickling and poker chips. Anything that he responded to would be a reward. He liked to throw poker chips down the stairs and watch them go. So when he got five chips he'd go to the steps and throw them. He learned he wasn't just working for candy anymore, and his motivation stayed high.

One of the big rewards in Discrete Trial is you get to go away from the table. 'Go play' is the big term because the child knows he can go off by himself for a break. You might only do it for a couple seconds or a few minutes. You want to keep things flowing. As a matter of fact, the therapists used to do it so quickly when they wanted to get him used to the command that it annoyed me terribly.

So as part of this 'go play' reward, Chris was put on a token system. If he got three responses right he put a token in a special holder. After three tokens he turned them in to go play and could do whatever he wanted. Permission to leave the table was the biggest reward.

Rutgers devised a test for us about a year ago to determine which reward worked best. It took us days to run the trials. The test measured Chris' highest response to a stimulus for a reward. You offered him two things to see which one he chose. Then you'd do it another way and then another way with a different therapist. It took days. From this data you saw the most effective rewards for Chris. I think he liked the squiggly snake the best.

Slowly we increased how long Chris sat at the table and the number of things he did until he's now at the point where he sits at the table for a long time doing fifteen, twenty things. We also started doing lessons with task books. Chris opened the book and did what the page showed. On the first page it may have shown a picture of a puzzle. Chris went and got a puzzle, dumped it out, completed it and put it back. Next he'd turn the page and it may have been a picture of beads being strung, so he'd follow it and string the beads. Things were really advancing.

We started out with these very basic learning skills and advanced to working in a book to spelling to going to the window. 'What's the window? Touch the window.' We had him go to the bathroom using three step commands. 'Go to the bathroom. Get the towel. Get the red towel.' These things were amazing.

You could give him letters in the program and say spell watermelon and he'd spell it. This was different than his splinter skill simply to spell what he wanted on his own. In the program we'd give him ten letters and eight of them would spell the word. So we'd say, 'Spell watermelon,' and he'd pick out the letters. It certainly wasn't the traditional way of teaching with phonics, though.

That's why Discrete Trial Instruction works in the beginning. The traditional methods don't work for these kids. The saying goes, 'If they're not getting it, you're not teaching it correctly.' My son isn't stupid or incapable of learning. He and other children with autism just learn a different way, especially in the beginning. These are children who don't know what pragmatic language is and can't conceptualize. They are not part of our world, so why would you want to stick them in a classroom where they're going to be taught in traditional ways? Imagine a teacher asking the class, 'What day is it?' Are you crazy? These kids with autism have no idea what she's talking about!

Discrete Trial was so successful for Chris that my initial anger and fear of it changed to over-zealousness. I now got upset if a therapist did anything to impede his progress. I used to watch on the monitor and if there were two therapists talking to each other about their personal lives, I became incensed. 'You're wasting my child's time!'

I read that you must always attend to your child so if I saw him alone for ten minutes I would insist that somebody go over and make him look at their face. If therapists were slow in setting up the next program I'd storm up there. 'What are you doing? You're wasting his time.' If this therapy was succeeding then I wanted him to have more and more and more. If four hours were good then eight hours were better. I turned into a madman.

In spite of Chris' wonderful successes, he still never uttered a word. One day Matt Bowman came and said, 'I want to try something… Chris, say AHH.'

And Chris went, 'Ah.'

I fell off the couch! I'd never seen anything like it. My wife was upstairs in the therapy room crying. It was unbelievable. We knew he had the physical ability to speak, but this was the first time the guy made a sound in years.

Normally I would never go up to the therapy room because I always felt I was interfering, so I was downstairs watching the monitor. But I was cheering and screaming and yelling so loudly that they all started to laugh because they heard me. Matt Bowman and his Discrete Trial Instruction changed for us what was only hope that Chris might someday speak to absolute knowledge that he would.

Every month Matt would hold a workshop for us, but these workshops soon became public events. It was a big deal in Lancaster to fund somebody for an in-home program. They were spending a lot of money and naturally we were under very close scrutiny. So people from the IU started attending our Rutgers workshops. They were checking up on us, but they were also coming to improve their own knowledge-base.

We'd get phone call after phone call. 'I am so-and-so. I work for the IU. May I come and see the workshop?' At first I was uncomfortable. I'm a very private person, and suddenly I was opening my house to strangers. People I didn't know were marching in!

Then things really started getting hairy after a local news article was printed on autism. I called the reporter to compliment her article and then she decided to write a focus piece on us. At first we didn't want to do the story because we felt it was exploiting the disorder. But people kept telling us we'd be doing a public service by raising awareness. The reporter did a beautiful piece called 'Love Will Find A Way.' Parents called and wrote me letters after the story and we began to see that we needed to continue bringing public awareness. A TV station called and asked me to do 'Twelve-thirty Live,' a live show out of Lancaster, and I accepted.

Now reporters, cameras, PhDs, doctors, parents and state workers were all entering our home. It's very hard opening your home to ten, fifteen, twenty people a day. I couldn't even shower without making an announcement that people should stay out of the bathroom for a few minutes. We were in a panic all the time. I would hire people to clean the home and lay out platters of food. Jessica wasn't allowed to bring friends home. Thirty people would show up sometimes. There weren't even enough parking spaces and the neighbors would wonder what was going on.

We felt a lot of pressure in the beginning to really do well. People were watching everything we did and we wanted to show that the program was succeeding. The local government scrutinized everything we did. Representatives of the IU were always peering into something, whether it was data, research, program set-ups or videos. In-home programming was very new and I think they wanted to catch us. I don't think it was the money so much as the suspicion about our ability to run our own therapy. Could this child possibly be thriving? They sent somebody over every week. But we knew what we were doing and had the data to prove it.

They would say things to me like, 'I hear Chris lost weight.'

So I'd respond, 'How is it your business?' They were always playing a game with me and it aggravated me greatly. *They* didn't know how to initiate an autism program. *They* didn't know how to do anything!

I once threw a guy out of my house who came to evaluate Chris. He was pompously throwing out a lot of words from Applied Behavioral Analysis like SD and prompt, and had his nose in everything. So I said, 'What is your agenda? You have some agenda here. You're obviously snooping all over. What is it?'

'I studied a little bit about autism,' he replied, 'and now we're developing a program.'

'So where were you when my son was diagnosed if you're a member of this IU?'

'Well, we wanted to help you.'

'You wanted to help me, but you didn't come forward and say you knew all this.'

'We gave you money.'

Now he really set off a raw nerve. 'You gave me money? But did you come over and set up the program? Did you provide teachers? Did you provide any expertise? Get out!'

'Do you want me off the team?'

'You can be part of any team you want. You're just not coming in my house. You sit here and espouse all these terms to show me how educated you are, and yet you weren't there when my son needed help. I want you out of my house. I think you're after something, whether it's to find a hole in my program or something with Chris. This is very delicate and I don't want you here.'

We were very strong in what we were doing and the IU administrators started to see that they couldn't pick us apart. Word was out about us and people were impressed. 'Look what they've done,' they'd say about us with respect. We were even lauded by Dr. Mary Jane Weiss, the head of Rutgers Research and Training Division at Douglass Developmental Disabilities Center. No longer could the government bureaucrats pass us off as this nutty family. People were saying, 'Hey, this is beautiful.'

Today we're used to all the scrutiny. It's not unusual for congressmen, senators, educators, state legislators and reporters to come to the house on any given day. Kids come in and moms come in. People take pictures. It took a while, but we've calmed down and adjusted to this microscopic lifestyle. No longer do I worry if the house is clean or if there's food to serve. We're busy doing our work, and we know we're doing it well.

Even Chris has adjusted. He now loves showing off for visitors. That's his big thing. When Matt held workshops he would say to the observers, 'I'm going to try a puzzle.' And Chris would jump up, quickly put the puzzle together, and walk away. 'Well, I guess that's the end of that program,' Matt would respond.

It turns out that kids develop great ways of beating the program because they're so bright. Let's say you set up colored objects for them to touch. 'Touch blue. Touch red. Match with same.' Often a therapist would develop a pattern of asking and the kids eventually learn the order of the exercise. Or they might give physical cues for the right answer. So the kids sit bored and rotely touch the pattern without thinking. Every once in a while the therapist changed the order on Chris and he'd miss it because he wasn't paying attention. To check this problem, there is something called a 'master.' That's when you bring in a new therapist to repeat the program. She does it differently than the first therapist, so the child has to pay attention and think about the commands. If he gets it all right, then he has mastered the program.

As Chris progressed we started combining other programs like TEACCH from North Carolina, Lovaas and Greenspan because they seemed to teach more life skills. I was getting a sneaking suspicion that Discrete Trial Instruction by itself was not going to help Chris move on to another level of development. OK, Chris was stringing beads, but how is stringing beads a life skill? How is this going to get him a sandwich or help him cross the street? He did work from a book, but when he came downstairs he didn't do what I asked. I was really troubled over the way the lessons carried over into real life. Chris learned to brush his teeth, but could he do it in the bathroom on his own? Or was he just going to do it when presented with an icon at the table? These were things about Discrete Trial that were beginning to bother me. I wanted to see my son become more actively involved with the world around him.

5

Running On Empty

Suddenly Jae and I were haggard looking, old and tired. If you look at a picture of us five years ago, we had very young faces and were very well-kempt and groomed. Jae always looked young. Young, young, young, young, young. But now the stress ate away at us. I had tremendous bags under my eyes, chest pains, stomach problems and headaches that all still exist today. Jae started getting migraines. Our sleeping patterns were disturbed. We never got more than a few hours of sleep.

We truly ran on empty. There was never a rest. It wasn't like, 'Hey, the weekend's here! That's great. Now we can relax.' I felt like I was wasting time if I used it to take a nap. So instead, I'd make calls to this society and that society or I'd go to a meeting. From the inception of Chris' autistic symptoms, I was driven.

We did forty hours a week of Discrete Trial Instruction when we started our in-home program, and we soon incorporated our own ideas, speech and language therapy and physical exercise. Running in-home therapy meant designing programs, buying or making the materials, setting up equipment, scheduling therapists, recording data, reviewing data, reviewing bills, maintaining a tape library, filling out timesheets and fixing the computer. Plus I was working seven days a week at my bartending job. I remember Jae saying to me, 'I don't think you can keep up the pace.'

I responded, 'If anybody ever tells me that I'm not helping then I'll slow down. But until then I can't. I'll just keep doing this till I fall down.' She was worried that one day I would collapse. But she was living the same way I was. We weren't taking any care of ourselves. We were grabbing food indiscriminately, weren't exercising and were gaining lots of weight.

If Jessica woke up in the morning I'd say, 'Jess, Daddy's tired. Go back to bed or go watch TV.' I couldn't do that with Chris, though. So if Chris woke up and came over to me, I jumped out of bed. Many times he'd wake at six in the morning and Jae and I would look at each other, 'All right. Who's going to do it today?'

I'd get up, brush my teeth, sit with him and get him something to eat. Then I'd take him for a ride. About eleven o'clock I'd come back and say, 'Jae, please.' And she'd let me sleep for an hour while she took him. Then I'd get up and go to work.

When I returned home, Jae was exhausted so I'd put Chris to bed and she'd sleep for an hour. Then she'd get up about two in the morning and say, 'I have to do data on the computer.' Before you knew it, it was three, four o'clock in the morning. And we were up again at six.

Household chores started to fall by the wayside. How do we do the laundry? How do we make dinner? Our bedroom was the therapy room so Jae and I no longer had a bedroom. We slept on a futon in the living room. Things were getting dilapidated; the ceiling fell in. But we didn't care anymore. 'Just walk over it and leave me alone. I don't care. Sorry, I just don't have any time to do this.' Maintaining the house was not on my list of priorities anymore.

There was no time to shop for ourselves; I can remember wearing socks till they fell apart. And I always felt guilty about spending time or money on anything that wasn't for Chris. 'Money should be going to his needs and the time should be going to him too,' I told myself.

Chris' life, too, seemed to be nothing but therapy. It was making me crazy to see this child being treated like an adult. He was working harder than anybody I knew, seven days a week, six to eight hours a day, and I was not about to let him miss the sunshine. So as soon as they'd take a break I'd say, 'I'm taking him out! This child needs air.' I refused to let this guy stay inside. Two, three times a day we would go for a walk. No matter what, I would make time. We'd walk and I'd talk to him and teach him about crossing the street. Every time that he would look at a tree, I'd say, 'That's a tree, Chris. Say tree.' We would walk and say the alphabet. We'd tumble in the grass. Physical exercise became a crucial part of his daily routine. That was a big thing with me.

I also tried getting him out in the world more. I'd take him for rides, bring him places and show him things. But whenever we tried anything new with Chris we had to set out very slowly. If we wanted to bring Chris into a new building he'd put up a fight. So we'd drive up to the building first for three days. 'Hey, great Chris!'

Each day we'd say, 'OK, let's go back!' He'd be so nervous in the car. Then maybe we'd stand in front of the building and then we'd go in the doorway. Next we'd go in the lobby. And it worked! We got him to visit new places. It was a very intense time. Very intense.

Another part of our program was participating in professional workshops. Rutgers workshops were regularly scheduled at our home so that we could learn how to progress. A team from Rutgers would come, but so would personnel from the IU. Sometimes there were twenty people gathered in a tiny room for these workshops. It was the most nerve-wracking time for me. I was so concerned that we make a good impression. After all, everyone was looking at us as the great example of in-home programming.

I went so far as to hire people to clean the house before a workshop because we didn't have time to do it ourselves. I'd get girls who were working maintenance at the complex. 'Want to make fifty dollars? Come at five o'clock and clean my house.' I was taking laundry and throwing it out. I didn't know what to do with it! There was catered food and people were actually making special requests as if these workshops were paid, catered events. It was crazy.

When Dr. Mary Jane Weiss, director of Rutgers Autism Center, came to observe she said this was the best in-home program she had ever seen. That complimented us, but it spurred us to go even further. Housework be damned! We had to get better.

6

Behavior Control

When we were doing the early stages of Discrete Trial with Chris he'd get mad every time we showed him something new. 'Chris, do this.'

'Ahhhh!' He would scream and throw a huge tantrum. Sometimes he'd attack you or run away. Matt Bowman's main philosophy with Discrete Trial was to ignore the bad behavior and try to work through it. So when Chris started to choke us, we just went on and did something else. Ignore the bad. Reward the good.

I understood that he needed special treatment, but there had to be another way to go. This was a very artificial reaction. The behavior merited more than just being ignored. I said to myself, 'What would I do if my daughter choked me?' Would I simply say, 'No choking, honey. Let's go on and play.' Of course not.

Issues were not being addressed. First, Chris was running wild. We couldn't yell at him because he didn't understand why we were yelling. We weren't supposed to stop him because then we'd be paying attention to bad behavior. We couldn't run to him every time because we were afraid, for example, that if he kept banging his head and we kept running over to him, he would start to bang his head just for the attention. There was no way to really know what he was thinking.

We had a daughter who was punished when she misbehaved. She knew there were consequences to her behavior and yet she had a brother who could get away with anything. She was beginning to resent him. Disabled or not, if he tore apart a room his behavior needed correction. We needed a little help.

We believe now that Chris' disruptive behaviors began to increase for a number of reasons. First, he was probably very frustrated with the program. Also, as he got older he was becoming aware that he was different. He began to see, 'All these kids play ball and talk to each other. I don't do that.' He was realizing that he was not communicating.

Naturally, as children with autism become more aware of the world they become more frustrated because they know they are different. I picture it like this: 'I want to tell my mom I love her and I love the park and want to go for a walk. Wait a minute. I can't do it! But I *know* what I want to do! Look at that little boy. He's talking to the other little boy and I can't do it!'

It must be very frustrating. And the more they know and the more they learn and see the world around them, the more it must get frustrating. I think this is a make it or break it time and it's very important to give them some tools, reassure them and be there for them.

Chris was learning by leaps and bounds. He had some excellent days with great receptive language. But there were also days when he wasn't tuned in at all and displayed more aggressive behaviors. We decided to hire a behavioral analyst. We paid her quite a bit of money to make twice-weekly visits, but we felt it was necessary to get the help.

The behaviorist had a few interesting ideas that we learned. She taught us to use time-outs and to have Chris take responsibility for his actions. For example, if he messed his bed, he had to clean it up. She also told us a few things that we knew were not going to work with Chris.

You really have to know your child. If you listen to everything that some analyst tells you, you're in a lot of trouble. There's nothing wrong with seeking help and there's nothing wrong with using some of the ideas, but all of them may not fit your child. You have to apply the knowledge you've learned with a great deal of love. Trust that you know what your child needs. What *he* needs. That's hard to do. And know also that you're going to make mistakes and you're going to yell and second-guess yourself all the time. I whip myself constantly. Did I do enough? Did I do too much?

What I'm really trying to say to parents is you have to go with what's in your heart, but you also have to realize that you need some skill. You might have to read a lot, listen a lot, attend seminars, or hire somebody. We gathered as much factual information as possible and then used it as instinctually as we could when dealing with special behaviors. We took a philosophy, used a small portion of it, and then went our own direction with it. Using our intuition along with our behavioral analyst's information, we started to manage Chris' behavior. But we always made sure to act as loving parents first and not as therapists.

We found time-outs helped control Chris' behavior and also showed Jessica that he too got punished. One time we put Jessica in the chair for a time-out and Chris started to laugh! It showed him, too, that they were both treated alike.

I also use a lot of love to help Chris control himself. If he is crunching his teeth and shaking his whole body in anger, my instinct as a father is to go over and hold him. 'Buddy, take it easy. Come here. Listen to me. Take it easy. Come on, let's take a walk.' I redirect him by helping him calm down and take the focus off what is bothering him.

The behavioral experts would say you can't do that, you're reinforcing the behavior. But what I'm saying is, 'Look, I'm his Dad and I'm going to act with love first.' What I'm trying to tell Chris is,

'This is OK. I understand it. You've got to calm down. I understand that you can't help this.'

I don't believe that's reinforcing the problem. I believe reinforcing the behavior is saying, 'All right. Take it easy. Here's a piece of candy.' In fact, I think to ignore his frustration is terrible. If I was a kid I'd be saying to myself, 'Why isn't my Dad doing something? Why doesn't he help me?'

Slowly but surely we began to let Chris know that he had to adjust his behaviors. Even though his neurons were telling him to act certain ways because it made him feel better, he was going to have to adjust. He had to adapt to the world around him. Even though his actions may not bother me, and I understand why he does them, they are not socially acceptable.

I can sit there all day and not care that people stare at my son. I will always be there to protect him, but that's not really my entire job. To fulfill my duty as his father I must give him ways to adapt to the world. I have to give him ways to shake his hand so it doesn't disturb other people. I have to be able to say to him when he screams in the restaurant that he must behave differently. 'Chris, in the restaurant people stare at you. So why don't you clap instead? Maybe in a few years you'll learn to tap lightly on the table and maybe you'll even learn to tap your leg instead.'

It used to be that when he lined up objects in the house, we had to step over them all. No one used to be allowed in the living room if he lined things there. If he lined something on the steps, you couldn't use the steps.

'I'd like to go to the bathroom.'

'I'm sorry. You can't go to the bathroom. Go outside if you have to go. My son has lined things up and that's it!'

But we started changing our attitude, 'Chris, if you want to line things up, it's got to be over here.'

He would get mad.

'Sorry.'

When I walked with Chris we always followed the same route, but I decided that I didn't want him to always follow the same pattern. So I said, 'Chris, today we're going a different way.' He got so upset, crying and screaming and pulling me. 'No, honey, I'm sorry. We're going this way.' I made him come, even though he was mad most of the time. He was still angry when we got home. The next day he didn't want to go out, but I still continued to walk with him every day. Three weeks later he happily walked everywhere.

We made a very conscious decision to work very hard, and I mean very hard, on introducing Chris slowly but surely to the world of things he didn't like or didn't want to face. Day and night we made him confront all his fears. Rather than say, 'OK, you'll never have to hear loud noises again. We'll protect you,' we said, 'You're going to hear loud noises and we're going to introduce them to you slowly so you can deal with them.'

Chris was wild and destroyed a lot in the house. It certainly would have been very easy to medicate. We medicate very quickly in this country. Parents and teachers don't want to deal with these kids. The behaviors can be very hard to live with and it gets very expensive to replace things, but too bad. We don't believe in medicating.

So what do you do if a child is running around throwing toys? I believe you use behavioral interventions to stop him. Chris threw everything. Chris will still today throw the garbage around and we tell him, 'Chris, pick up.' It took a long time for him to respond. Chris didn't want to pick up anything. He kicked and tantrummed, yelled and screamed. He didn't understand why he had to pick up. He ripped my daughter's paintings, threw things, urinated anywhere he wanted and bit things. That was Chris. He did whatever he wanted without understanding that he impacted on others. If you got in his way, he head-butted you.

So we said, 'Chris, no. You don't do that. Now you have a time-out. You sit there.'

'Turn the TV off because I told you not to rip that. Come here. Out of the room.'

And he would stomp his feet and flail his fists when we admonished him. We tried to work through it, but there were no quick fixes. Medication, group homes – these are quick fixes.

There's a very fine line between working through behaviors and giving in to them. If every time they tantrum you say, 'honey that's OK,' then you're giving in. Believe me, giving in is what I want to do most of the time. But they're smart so they learn and say, 'OK, I'll just bang my head and get out of this each time.'

What happens when your child screams and you say, 'OK, you don't have to do this now.' The child says, 'Hey, I scream and I get out of this.'

If the child screams and you yell, 'SIT DOWN!' you're not working through it either. To work through it you need to redirect. Go on to something else. Get some crayons and color. Switch what you're doing. Try not to make it a big issue so you can come back to the activity later without a problem. There are times you'll have to say no. There are times you'll have to say stop. You have to be smart. You have to think on your feet and be intuitive.

And you should have a little background. It's important to understand why children with autism display what appears to be disruptive behavior. 'I'm not gritting my teeth because I'm a bad boy. I'm not screaming because my mother didn't discipline me. Maybe I'm trying to block out all the noises around me. This is my reaction because my body tells me to do this.'

That's why I stress the importance of knowing what you or other people are doing when they work with your child. Here's a child who lives in his own world. Your job is to bring him out of it. He's basically saying, 'I'm very comfortable doing what I'm doing. I don't know anything about your world and I don't know what you're talking about. I don't want to know. It's offensive to me. It's rushing at me. I want to retreat back where I came. I don't want to concentrate on this stuff.'

So you must constantly engage him: 'Look at me. We're going to do this. Hear me. This is important.' That constant engagement, that constant paying attention and bringing him back into the mainstream of things is crucial. However you do it, getting a child with autism to connect is the most important thing you can do.

7

Communicating Without Words

'I can't communicate. I want to communicate, but I can't. I
don't want to look at you. I don't want to talk to you, but in a
way I do want to talk to you.'

Kids with autism must be very frustrated to live in a world where
they can't speak or understand language. It's difficult for them to
conceptualize. Say to them, 'Honey, are you happy?' What's happy
mean? You have to always show them. Using visuals is good. People
with autism think in pictures. Happy? Show a happy face.

You also have to break everything down. For example, show a
typical toddler a picture of a man on a boat in a rainstorm and ask
him what it is. The toddler will answer that it's a man in a raincoat, a
fisherman, a man in bad weather, or captain of a ship. Show the
same picture to a kid with autism and he'll say that's a button. They
key in on one thing. So that's what you're faced with when trying to
get a child with autism to understand and communicate.

Chris used to stand in the kitchen waving his hands and
screaming because he couldn't tell me what he wanted. I'd give him
a sandwich and he'd throw it at me. I'd give him a cookie and he'd
throw it at me. I'd give him a bottle and he'd throw it at me. Maybe
he wanted a sandwich with no jelly on it. It could take an hour and a

half to figure it out. We felt terrible! Here's this guy who knows what he wants, but he can't communicate it!

So my whole thing was to take away the frustration from my son. We decided to help Chris with a pointing program. Pointing would make life much easier for both him and us. How many times did I stand there at the refrigerator while Chris would collapse in utter frustration trying to tell me what he wanted? If Chris learned to point I could open the refrigerator or cupboard and say, 'Go ahead. Point to what you want.'

Pointing is also a great tool to help kids with autism participate more in life. Chris used to push my hand or arm toward the refrigerator like a tool. So I started to say, 'Chris, you can open the refrigerator. Let Daddy show you.' I put my hand on his. 'Now pull. Look, you're opening the refrigerator. Now what do you want?'

They don't like to get into life. It's kind of scary for them so when he'd push my hand I'd say, 'No. You get it, Chris. You want soda? Go ahead.' And you know what? He smiled proudly after he got it.

We actually used coloring as a method to teach Chris how to point. He always loved to color in books. But it was very hard for him to slowly control his crayon. When you're very hyperactive or compulsive it's hard to bear down. So we facilitated him and held his hand.

Chris got in the habit of picking out a crayon, giving it to us, and then pushing our hand down to the spot he wanted colored, and we'd color it. In other words, we did the coloring and he directed. It was good that he was directing and designing, but we didn't want him to just simply push us. It's very autistic behavior to use a person as a tool.

So what did we do? When he gave us a crayon we'd ask, 'What do you want us to do, Chris?'

He'd take my hand.

'No, no. Don't put my hand there. Give me your finger. Point to face.' He was pretty receptive and started pointing. In fact, he caught on so well that later we used pointing to help Chris with spoken language.

Another way we tried to help Chris communicate was with PECS. PECS is an acronym for Picture Exchange Communication System. It's a series of universal communication icons with Velcro that a child uses to form sentences on a board or book. The whole idea is to take the frustration out of communicating. The theory behind PECS is to enhance language and ensure interactive communication. For instance, if a child points without first getting a person's attention, the attempt to communicate may fail. But when using pictures in a hand-to-hand exchange, communication failures are usually prevented. In addition, the pictures are more easily understood than pointing or signing. Eighty per cent of parents whose children have autism report a decrease in tantrums after starting PECS.

You can buy a PECS book that will have all kinds of different pictures. Some include universal symbols for danger, going to the bathroom, or not feeling well. For the expression 'I want' it will show the words and a picture of a boy with his arms extended. It will even include sexual information.

Chris caught on to PECS in a snap. My wife, Jae, created her own book for him, but she didn't just cut out little pictures. She actually drew about fifteen hundred pictures of things that he likes. We also have a very expensive computer program called Boardmaker that she's used to make icons.

Using PECS, Chris was able to take the picture for 'I want' and put it on the sentence strip to connect with a picture of something else that he wanted. Maybe he would put it with a picture of a cookie. Jae drew a picture of his favorite cookie with M&Ms so he could specifically ask for that. He would put it on the sentence strip, hand it to us, and we would then know to give him the cookie.

Chris became a master of PECS. We used to laugh because he put together such complicated sentences.

One day he handed me 'I want sandwich.' The picture was a peanut butter and jelly sandwich cut in half. I handed him a sandwich and he threw it back at me. He gave the sentence strip to me again. 'Chris, this says sandwich. What do you want?' He looked through his book real fast and he put 'I want sandwich' and then a picture of a piece of white bread next to the sandwich. It took me a few minutes, but I figured out he wanted a whole sandwich; not one cut in half. So I gave it to him and, sure enough, to this day he eats his sandwiches whole.

He once wanted mum-like flowers that looked like pom-poms he played with, so he gave me the PECS 'I want pom-poms.' I went upstairs and got his pom-poms, but he threw them back at me. Then he pointed to the flowers and I understood what he was trying to say. The picture of the pom-poms was the closest thing he had describing the flowers.

Chris has even used PECS to show his frustration when trying to communicate with others. Once the therapists apparently didn't understand him so he put together a PECS that said, 'I want lizards with gas.' He gave it to them and just waved away and walked out.

Jae has also developed a system of putting up pictures in the car to represent places we go. Let's say we drive past the mall and Chris wants to go there. So he's thinking, 'Good. We're going to the mall.' Then if we pass it and don't stop he gets upset. Instead it might turn out that we're going to the doctor. So now we can put up a picture of the doctor and say, 'Chrissie, we're going to the doctor.' He might even respond by trying to take the picture down to voice displeasure. But in general, the system of car pictures is a great tool for us. They serve to assure Chris about where he's going and help him to prepare.

One other very important PECS book we have made is a social PECS. It is an excellent safety tool if Chris were ever in an emergency situation. By using this book Chris can communicate his name, where he lives, his phone number, the name of his Mom and Dad, the name of his sister, emergency numbers, the name of his cats and other significant personal information. I strongly urge any parent of a child with autism who can't speak effectively to have a social PECS so he can tell about himself if ever in need of help.

8

He Spoke!

I read a story one time where the father got mad at his son who had autism. 'You haven't spoken in fourteen years and I should just never speak to you for the rest of your life!' The kid suddenly talked, 'I realized that day that I thought my father meant he wouldn't talk to me for fourteen years so I decided to speak.' It was an amazing thing. So if your child with autism has no language today it doesn't mean he won't speak in the future.

I've heard countless stories of kids with autism who have surgical operations of which they know the date and then they wait a year to the day and start to speak. It's amazing what goes on in their heads: 'I had the surgery that day on January 14 so I had to wait three months.' When you speak to them years later, they'll explain, 'I didn't want to speak because of what a person said to me.' The mind just works differently. But these stories give hope for all parents praying their child will have full language one day.

Children with autism have two language disorders, called apraxia and aphasia. They can't process words coming in and they can't get them out. If you say to a typical child who doesn't have autism, 'Look at me. Pay attention. Do this,' that child will respond. A kid with autism has trouble even looking at you. What do you say when you want somebody to listen to you? You say 'Look at me,' and the eyes of a typical person go up and you know they're listening.

So I force Chris. 'Hi, Chris! Chris, come on, say hi.' I give him a direction with my hand and show him my eyes. Then I bring his eyes to mine. It's much easier for him not to follow my eyes and to stay in his own little world. It's very hard work for people with autism to focus. You do it naturally. They don't. Everyday we work on this with Chris, and still to this day it's a challenge. He recently went upstairs one morning and I said, 'Chris, see ya.'

He turned around and went, 'See ya.'

That means as he walked away he heard me and chose to pick up on it, but that was a result of constantly forcing his attention. 'See ya! Chris, I said see ya. What do you say?'

'See ya.'

Communication is very hard for these guys. They aren't born with that innate ability. You bond with your child because you say goo-goo ga-ga and that child looks up and repeats goo-goo ga-ga. 'Look at that!' you say, 'He's smiling at me.' You've found a way to communicate.

Not so with a kid who has autism. He doesn't have that ability. So you take my child and you say, 'Hi, Chris, I'm home!' And he turns away. He's simply not cueing in on certain things. This type of non-responsiveness causes a lot of parents of children with autism to give up.

The first thing doctors tell you is get a hearing test because symptoms of autism mimic symptoms of deafness. I have dropped a pile of metal plates right in back of Chris and he never turned around. I'd go right by his ear and yell, 'CHRIS!!!' and he wouldn't turn around. I remember what a marvelous feeling it was the first few times he finally looked at me after I called his name.

Once Matt Bowman got Chris to repeat a word, we did our best to encourage speaking. But even before that I always talked to my son like a human being who understood and communicated with me even though it seemed like he didn't. So talking to Chris was nothing new for me. I just didn't push him to respond. On a couple occasions when he was sick, Chris did say 'mama,' but otherwise his speech remained non-existent.

So I had one-sided conversations with him at bedtime saying, 'You know what buddy? If you don't speak, I can't understand you. It's hard. It'd be great for you if you talked because it would be easier, but you don't have to. I'm going to be with you no matter what.'

And no matter what we did I would constantly talk to him. When we took walks together I'd say things like, 'So Chris, do you like the trees?' I also did a lot of Discrete Trial to encourage his speech. 'Touch tree. Say tree.'

Then the amazing happened. One day Chris, my mother, Jessica and I were walking in the back with Chris. We were doing 'one, two, three' where you hold his hands and repeatedly lift him up on the three count. Jessica and I chanted, 'One.' Suddenly Chris replied, 'Two, tree.' Oh my God! He spoke! We started jumping up and down and actually fell on him. My mother was crying. I was rolling around. Jessica was pouncing on him. He never spoke at all and now suddenly he said two, three! We did it like eighteen thousand times after that and he repeated two, three each time. It gave us such hope. We knew that in there someplace was a lot of intelligence, memory and the ability to speak.

Then he got this thing where he would look at me and say a made-up word, 'holumbaday.' And I would look at him and repeat it. He would change the sounds and I would repeat the changes. Laughing, he'd trick me with a new sound pattern. I'd sit in that bed for hours while he verbalized all kinds of sounds for me to repeat. We did it back and forth, back and forth. It was a great oral exercise. But even more important, he saw that he could get power by making me repeat the words. I'm sure he was thinking, 'I can't say a lot of your words, but I can say these sounds.' I showed that not only do I make him do things, but he made me do things as well. I was listening to him and I was inviting him into the world. That's what you have to do.

The next step was to give Chris words that had power. Our cats were always all over him and he didn't like them so I decided to try and teach him the word 'go.' This would be his first word, one that he could use pragmatically. So he learned, 'Tow! Tow!'

And then I taught him 'stop.' Let's say I tickled him and he pulled away and made an uncomfortable sound. So I'd say, 'Do you want Daddy to stop? You say STOP!'

And I put my hand on him and he'd say, 'Dop.'

'OK. See ya.' Or when he wanted to be in his room by himself and I was bothering him. 'Do you want Daddy to go? Say GO to Daddy... Look at me... Go.'

'Tow.'

'OK. Bye.' And I'd walk out of the room. He started catching on.

Now we wondered what we could give Chris that would help him realize language is pragmatic; language means something. That's what they don't understand. So we taught him the word 'goodbye' to use with his therapists. Chris didn't like when they hung around after his sessions. They would talk, sign their time sheets, or do a little data work. I think he always felt they were intruding on his own time, or maybe they would take him back upstairs for more therapy. So he got mad and pushed them. Jae and I thought that maybe if we got him to say 'bye-bye' and the therapists left, it would be the perfect pragmatic, power word.

I told him, 'When you want your therapists to go, you can say 'bye-bye' and they're going to go.' Then we got all the therapists in a group and said, 'If he says bye-bye, get out of the house.'

And I'm telling you, the first time he used the word it was so funny. He looked up from his session and said, 'Bye-bye.'

The therapists said, 'Bye-bye, Chris,' and ran out.

He looked around, saw what he had done, and said to himself, 'Look at that, I say something and it means something.' That was the first time he really understood about pragmatic language.

When the therapists came in the next time he immediately said, 'Bye-bye. Bye-bye-bye. Bye-bye. BYE. BYE! BYE!BYE!' And he kept saying it. He learned the word and all of a sudden he thought, 'Whenever I say "bye-bye" they're going to leave.'

So we said, 'Chris, they have to go upstairs to school.' He got mad. It was so funny because then we had to explain that bye-bye does not always work. That was a lesson we never anticipated. But bye-bye was a big breakthrough for him. At the end of every session each day, he'd go downstairs, and say, 'Bye-bye.' And he said it sometimes with such glibness like, 'Hey, I can make you leave.'

That was a big key to me. This guy knew that bye-bye meant you go. He was keying in on the meaning of language and the meaning of life. He was participating, and we were giving him power.

Just taking a word like cookie didn't mean the same to him. He may understand that if he says cookie, he's going to get a cookie. But he doesn't understand what cookie means. He's really just parroting. 'OK, I said whatever you told me to say so can I have my cookie now, please?' That's how they think of it.

So you have to find words that empower them, like 'yes' and 'no.' 'Chris, do you want that? Yes?'

'Yes.'

'OK.' Now he's beginning to see that language has a reason.

We tried very hard to continue making Chris verbalize with everything he did. When we played ball I would say, 'Chris, come on. Let's play ball. What is this Chris? Say ball.'

'Bu.'

'Great! That's good.'

Very easily, we combined our pointing and PECS program with our language program. For instance, if he was coloring and gave us the crayon and pointed to the eyes, we'd say, 'Oh, you want eyes? Say "eyes".'

'Eyes.'

'Oh, you want blue eyes?'

'Blue eyes.'

'Great talking! I'll do blue eyes.'

He started to come over, tap me, and hand over paper and crayon. 'Honchers.'

'Oh, you want Honkers.'

'Din don.'

'And Dingers? OK, I'll draw them. Do you want the horns colored?'

'Yes.'

'Yes?' And I'll sign with the word yes. 'What color?'

He'll give it to me. 'Oh, yellow. You want yellow?'

'Yewo.'

'OK... Oh, look. Here's two crayons. How many crayons?'

'Two.'

'Good!'

So we used all our playtime to teach. 'Do you want to color the eyes now? No?'

'No.'

'OK. Good. What do you want to color?'

'Face.'

'Face! Good talking! I can color the face.'

Similarly, if he came over with his PECS to ask for something, I'd say, 'Oh, you want soda. Say I WANT SO DA.'

'A a sosa.'

What's peculiar about this disorder is one day he could say, 'I want soda' and then not speak again for months. You never knew. A lot of his words weren't clear, yet sometimes they were. So we hired Julie Fischel, a speech and language therapist. She helped tremendously!

Her whole basis of teaching was like ours. Give him power. You want more? Say it. You can get it. He started doing very well with her. 'More' was the first word she taught by giving him candy. 'Do you want more?' she'd ask after he had some.

'More.'

And then she started working on different ways to ask. 'I want candy.' 'I want M&M.' 'I want more.' 'More, please.' 'Yes.'

Yes and no were BIG things.

'Do you want more?'

'Yes.'

'OK. Very good. Here.'

We had to give him some sort of incentive. He doesn't like popcorn so we brought him some. 'You want popcorn?'

'No.'

'So you want candy?'

'Yes.'

He's come such a long way. Now he goes over to a therapist and requests, 'Roll, please. Sosa.' Sosa is soda.

'OK, honey. You're hungry? I'll get you a roll and soda right away. Thank you for telling me.'

So Chris says to himself, 'I want a roll and soda, and I can ask for it and this person will get it for me.'

Jessica, who is always the innovator, was the first one to teach him something called hand-over-hand. She showed us one day. 'Watch this… Chris, let's start! In a cabin in the woods…' She taught him to finger play to nursery songs!

'How'd you do that?'

'I took his hand and I showed him.' That's called hand-over-hand. And then she started teaching him songs because he hung around her. And being a little rock and roller she started saying, 'Chris, let's do NSync.' So she taught him songs and he loved it.

He liked to watch MTV and when we were walking in the street he came out with four verses of the Backstreet Boys, his favorite group. Unbelievable! We were in the car when he suddenly belted out songs. At first we thought it was the speakers, but there he was just singing along. It was pretty audible. If you knew the songs you could recognize them. We applauded wildly for our wonderful performer.

One of the things I didn't like about Discrete Trial was the way it taught language. If Chris said, 'I want play,' we would reply, 'Very good. Here's your chocolate.'

But he was thinking, 'I don't want a chocolate. I said I want play. So don't reward me with a chocolate. Reward me with play, and then I might catch on that language has a purpose.'

Or Chris would say, 'I want TV.'

Our response would be, 'We're not going to watch TV now, but that was good. Here. You get a candy.'

No. Let him watch TV. It's an immediate reward. Rewards for Discrete Trial should relate more to the action. If you say go, then I go. I don't give you chocolate when you say go. If I say, 'I want sandwich,' don't give me a token. Give me a sandwich.

'I want crayon.'

'Here's your crayon.' Now you're teaching him. I say crayon, I get crayon.

It's important to remember that people with autism think in visuals. So if you take a child with autism to a noisy auditorium, next time you say he's going to the auditorium his visual will be a noisy, chaotic room. And he will yell unhappily because that's what he's thinking.

People with autism will explain to you, 'It takes me a few minutes to reply to you. Take for example, when you say "I'm having a birthday party. Do you want to come?" I get a visual. That's the first thing I get. The visual may be a big red balloon. It's now taking over my entire psyche. All I see is this big red balloon. It's really overwhelming and I can't process anything else. So wait one minute. I have to get it out... OK, I'll come to your party. But the first thing I got was this overwhelming picture of a red balloon. It's hard for me to respond to you. So you have to understand how I think.'

So when a child with autism acts bizarrely, he probably is responding to his visual picture. Or if he takes an awkwardly long time to respond to you verbally, it's because he's first processing that visual picture.

People should also note that kids with autism have certain language commonalities. They may not be that expressive. Chris, for instance, is primarily monotone. It's hard for him to emote and learn expression. Sometimes he'll have a little force behind his words, but he's still experimenting with it. Pronouncing the letter d is also difficult. He says Daddy now, but it was so hard for him in the beginning. He called me Tooie, Tooie. Kids with autism leave off word endings too. It's hard for them to get that hard consonant sound at the end.

I also think they hear the last part of your sentence first. Let's say you yell, 'Come on, we have to go to dinner!' By the time they perk up to listen, they might hear '...ner.' So you really want to get their attention first and not use too many words. If you say, 'Come downstairs, wash your hands, set the table, and then we're going to eat dinner,' the kid's already said, 'Forget it. I've lost you.' First, work on two-step commands like 'Go get the towel in the bathroom,' or 'Go get the big towel.' Eventually he listens, understands, and follows through. It's wonderful to see!

And then there are the miracles of autism. I was there along with Jae and Michelle Warner, our therapist, when Chris suddenly stomped his feet and pronounced with great conviction, 'I don't want to be here any longer.' Everybody was dumbstruck. We all looked at each other. He was speaking in a typical little boy's voice, his real voice!

There have been a few of these rare occasions when we heard Chris' voice. He even sang with his little boy's voice once. It's really hard to describe, but you know it's his real voice. It absolutely makes you stand up. There's expression rather than that monotone. He seems almost to be breaking through to the outside world. There will be something he says and it's Chris' voice. You can tell that if he was a typical child this is how he would speak. We've told him, 'Great talking.' But what can I explain to him to get him to continue? It just seems maybe he's more lucid at the time. He just comes out of it.

It's eerie because I see that child in there. And it saddens me because I think, 'That's my little boy in there. There he is. I had him for a minute!' You want to reach out and grab him; just savor the moment. But it's gone. He's gone... But it's an uplifting moment too because I know he's in there, and maybe in a few more years he'll reappear for good.

I remember a story about a nonverbal boy with autism riding in the car with his father. Suddenly the boy turns to his father and says, 'I really like Count Basie.' The man almost crashed the car. His son never spoke before, and from that point on he spoke normally. The parents were afraid to ask him what made him speak because they were afraid he'd shut down. So years later they said to him, 'When you first spoke you said you like Count Basie. And we never played Count Basie. How did you know about him?'

'I don't know. It was just something that was in my head.'

I'm sure Chris has stored up six years of information in there someplace, and one day he's going to say, 'I hated that class you sent me to,' or 'You made me wear that ugly shirt one day.' We don't give these kids the credit they deserve. They have wonderful potential, but if we don't work with them the right way we'll lose them.

9

Potty Training

It was a quiet night and I was watching the kids while Jae was out shopping. Jessica and I were watching TV while three-year-old Chris was falling asleep upstairs in his crib. I started noticing an awful stench that began to permeate the house, so I ran to check on my son. Looking in his room I was startled to see nothing but feces! Feces everywhere. And nobody was in the crib! I looked down and found Chris with his legs completely spread out on the floor in the oddest position. Were his legs broken? I went in and touched him. He didn't act injured, but that didn't necessarily mean he wasn't hurt since part of his disorder was to defer pain. I picked up his feces-covered body, letting the dirt smear on me, and stood him up. Incredibly his legs were fine. Apparently there was so much dirt in his crib that he vaulted over the side and fell on the floor. And before he jumped he must have been playing in his stool and throwing it around the room. I spent the rest of the night bathing him, washing his clothes, cleaning his room and disinfecting the crib.

As our son's autism progressed, he evolved into a feces smearer. What a horrible time! I just felt so bad for him. After he had a bowel movement he didn't like the feeling of stool in his diaper, but he didn't know what to do. He didn't know to call for help or come down and show us. He would get up and simply remove the feces from his diaper and throw it.

Whatever remained he smeared on the crib, the mattress, the pillow, his face and his hair. He did this every time and all I could do was come up and say, 'OK, honey.' And he'd hug me. He always hugged me. It was like thank you, Dad. From there I would proceed to put him in the bath and scrub him. Literally two or three hours almost every night were spent cleaning; getting stuff off the ceiling, disinfecting the room, changing the sheets, scrubbing his nails, and washing his hair. But he was happy.

We worried because we thought maybe he was doing this because he got such pleasure from his baths. A behavioral management person once told us to handle it by telling him, 'No. I told you. You do not do that. Now you will clean it up. I will help you, but you're going to clean it up.' We could never do that, though. We just didn't think he understood what he was doing and would be troubled by our response.

Instead we chose to talk to him. 'Good trying. We know you're trying. Maybe next time you could tell us. Try not to throw it.'

And of course we tried to catch him having a movement, but it was so difficult. He didn't want to do it in front of anybody and seemed to wait till we weren't there. Since he usually went at night I tried sitting with him then to catch it.

He did stop throwing it around, and eventually he started coming downstairs to let us know when he had a movement. He came over to me, smiled and gave me a hug, and I cleaned him up! He'd even bring me a paper towel. I'm sure he will eventually be trained. It'll be late, but look how far he's come from smearing his feces on the walls and his face.

Our philosophy on toilet training for our kids was take it easy, they'll get it. It's not like there was a timeline we had to follow. Our daughter, Jessica, started early and then took a while to train, but it was all very natural and stress-free. Chris, however, was not responding normally to life at around age one-and-a-half, so it didn't seem like a good time to begin his training. Instead we just kind of sat back with him.

Once the Discrete Trial Instruction was running we decided that would be a good time to use part of the seven hours a day therapy for toilet training. It took a lot in the beginning to get Chris to even walk into the bathroom. Maybe he was afraid of the toilet or maybe he was just afraid of the room. Who knows?

So first we took him to the doorway. If at first he wouldn't go to the door we physically took him over. That's called a prompt in Discrete Trial. 'VERY GOOD! Here's a candy.' Once Chris went to the bathroom door by himself, he had to stand there for a certain amount of time. 'You did ten seconds! Very good! Here's a candy. Go sit down.' Then he moved on to walking into the bathroom where visual cues were set up to help him understand what he was doing. 'Pull down your pants. Very good! Pull them back up and let's go back and do it again.' In true Discrete Trial tradition the whole act was taught in small stages. 'Touch sink! Very good. Turn on the water.' This took months and months and months.

There were many fears we had to help Chris overcome concerning the bathroom – one of the biggest was sitting on the toilet seat. It was all part of a spatial fear he had of lowering himself backwards. So we placed a potty seat on top of the regular toilet seat, played music, and of course we gave him rewards.

We had to be very careful not to push him too hard, though. One time he actually shut down. The therapist was pushing him to sit longer and he responded by knocking the musical toy he played with and running out. He wouldn't go back to the bathroom entrance for two months after that!

Discrete Trial was great for teaching what to do when in the bathroom, but it didn't really teach him the internal signal. You've got to get in their head, 'I just don't do this for a reward. I do this when I actually have to pee.' It wasn't unusual for him to urinate in the toilet during therapy, but then he would wet his pants later. Obviously he was thinking, 'I did my whole bathroom routine. I went to the bathroom, pulled my pants down, flushed the toilet, washed my hands, pulled my pants back up, turned off the light, and got my reward.' But did he understand that he was supposed to do this whenever his bladder was full? Could he tune into that sensation?

Remember, with autism everything seems to be coming at them. When a typical person has to go to the bathroom, he's able to filter everything else out. 'I've got to go. I know I have to go.' But when this guy feels a twinge to pee, the lights are coming at him, the noise is coming at him, and he's playing with his fingers. Eventually he buries that pee sensation, urinates in his pants, and doesn't even know it.

So we constantly reminded Chris hoping that eventually he would feel the sensation. 'OK, let's go potty.' Every ten minutes, 'Come on, try potty. Try potty. Let's go. Try potty.' There was a lot of 'Good trying. Next time.' When he would touch himself we'd say, 'OK, come on! You have to go potty. Say "I want potty." Let's go.' He got annoyed. He got mad.

I also tried very hard to point out to him when he had an accident. 'Chris, your pants are wet. Let's get them off. You don't want to be in those pants. Come on, buddy! Let's go take them off. You don't like this.' In a way I taught him how and when to feel uncomfortable. Eventually he started to pay attention to the urination signals so he would not have an accident.

By no means was he accident-proof, though, until one day when we were in Ocean City. I decided that I was going to show him how I urinated in the urinal. 'Look, buddy. This is what you do.' And he came over and looked. He wanted to come with me a second time and I repeated the demonstration. That was it. He started peeing in the urinal. BANG! He was going. 'Guess what?' I came out proclaiming to Jae, 'Chris is peeing in the urinal!'

He's been dry ever since! Every once in a while when he's watching a movie he gets so involved that he pees a little bit, but then he realizes he's wet and he stops.

It's now come to the point where we have only to train Chris for bowel movements. Before we could seriously begin he had to overcome sitting on the toilet seat once again. When he learned to urinate, sitting on the potty seat helped him feel secure. But once he learned to stand and urinate, he no longer sat on a toilet. Now he's too big for the potty seat. So all of a sudden he's faced with pooping and he can't use the potty seat because it's too small for him. That means when he sits on the adult seat he feels a big open space – that same spatial fear he's always had. It's not a psychological fear. It's not like when kids say I'm going to fall in or worry where it goes. That's not it. It's leaning back. He can't lean back.

I got him to try again by sitting fully clothed on the toilet myself and having Chris sit in between my legs with his back against me. He felt more secure that way. Then I would back up, and back up again, and back up some more. Before long, I got up and put a pillow behind him so he was leaning against the pillow. The pillow was up against the back. Then I removed the pillow. He now holds on with his hands, but he definitely feels more comfortable. We practice as often as possible and I have him squeezing and pushing.

All we have to do now is catch when he's ready to have the movement. Unfortunately, there's one other problem to resolve. Chris' diet has caused him to develop a lot of constipation. Sometimes he'll go ten, twelve days without a movement. So we put him on Lactylose, a type of stool softener. We squirt a syringeful in his mouth and he takes it. Somehow he seems to know when medicine is important and always cooperates.

If we stop giving it to him every day, he becomes more and more irregular. So the doctor said to give it to him whether he needs it or not in order to keep him regulated. I've also been giving him more and more water. He won't ask for it, but I'll bring it up to his mouth and he'll drink. He still only has a movement every three or four days, though.

We don't attack potty training as much as we should, but it's so hard to find the time for such a time-consuming task. We just have to set aside a couple of hours every night before he goes to bed. 'OK, time for potty.' Luckily, he doesn't tend to have his movements outside of the home. He doesn't wear a diaper and he's become aware enough that he doesn't like it in his pants. However, we always carry a change of clothes and a bunch of paper towels just in case. It is one of those things that's going to take a lot of concentration, catching him at the right moments, and following up each time. I feel confident he will succeed.

10

Adventures In Eating

Chris' Menu

Bread and rolls – *Either potato or white bread. No rye, pumpernickel or French. They have to be soft, the real doughy kind. Not too hard. Never crisp.*

Doughnuts – *Powdered doughnuts. They can't be wet, have too much icing or sugar granules on them. No flavor inside. Must have a certain squishiness. Can't be hard.*

Peanut butter sandwiches – *Peanut butter must be on both sides of the bread and be thinly spread. Bread cannot be sliced.*

Candy – *All types. M&Ms, red licorice, caramels with the vanilla center. Must first be able to eat vanilla center by pushing caramel out with thumb.*

Chocolate – *M&Ms, peppermint cigarette sticks, Chicklets, caramels, candy necklaces and buttons. All chocolate must be cut into tiny pieces.*

Fruit – *Raisins, apples and pears. Apples and pears must be skinned, sliced and patted dry. Not soft or mushy. Put in freezer for a couple minutes before serving.*

Cereal – *Marshmallow Blasted Fruit Loops. Must be 'blasted.' Serve dry.*

Cookies – *Oreos. Must be able to separate and lick the cream first.*

Drinks – *Caffeine-free Pepsi, water. No Coke. Can serve with a straw. White milk on rare occasions.*

Chris was a voracious eater as a young toddler. I remember we were eating pizza when he didn't yet have teeth and he got mad because he wanted a slice. After he moved to table food he tried anything. He sat in a high chair using utensils to eat spaghetti, avocado, hamburger and even chili.

As the autism started to develop, not only did he stop sitting in the high chair, he almost completely stopped eating. Rather than use utensils to eat, he preferred to line them up. He lined up every spoon in the house. Suddenly he had a tremendous aversion to food and slowly but surely he started eating less and less until he was down only to cheese.

He'd come to the kitchen and scream so I'd ask, 'Do you want this?' And he'd push whatever I offered him away. 'How about this?' I'd spend an hour looking for things. We actually got him to lick an ice-cream one time while strolling him in the mall, but he refused to eat it again after that. Somehow he stumbled upon watermelon and made that his only food. For some reason he later stopped the watermelon. We thought maybe it was because the cold hurt his teeth.

Everything we ate made him sick. If he smelled or looked at our food he would gag and run away. The gagging was so terrible that he almost went limp. Our lives evolved so that there was no dinner time, no lunch time, no eating time.

For at least a year he was ingesting nothing but soy formula in his bottles. I tried putting different juices in the bottle, but to no avail. I tried squirting juice down his throat with a syringe, but all he did was gag. Horrible. He would only take medicine by suppository or injection.

This was about the same time Chris was beginning his in-home therapy program, and life for both Chris and us was overwhelming. The eating programs we looked into were very, very strict, and we were not willing to subject our son to that. Food was not one of the things we felt important enough to torture him with.

We stumbled upon one program, the dry spoon method, devised by Dr. Keith Williams at Hershey Medical. His claim to fame was that he never had a child who didn't start eating. His program was specifically created for kids with food aversion, especially autistic kids. The idea is to put the child in a chair and introduce whatever they like, chocolate for instance, into their mouth with a spoon and continue on from there. He was a wonderful man who came out to teach us, and even sent me his book before it was published, but I didn't want to strap my child to a chair and force-feed him.

So we decided to sacrifice diet for the sake of his learning. I've read about a lot of parents who simply said, 'I could care less if this guy sits down and eats. I'm happy if he'll eat anything, and I don't care where or when he eats it. We're doing eight hours a day of ABA Therapy and we're running all over and I don't give a damn.' And that's kind of how we felt. He was not malnourished and seemed to be growing.

Unfortunately, Discrete Trial was based on a system of rewards and it's usually done with candy in the beginning. You can't say to a kid who's just starting out and spinning around the room, 'OK, you're going to earn tokens and when you get five of them you can go away from the table.' They don't understand that. So you usually start out with a little bit of chocolate. Turns out that was one food Chris would eat. We were taking M&Ms and chopping them into little pieces and when he did something good we'd say, 'OK, good job. Here.' And he'd take a piece of chocolate and eat it.

Well, now his nourishment was candy and bottles. Chris' teeth were literally decaying out of his mouth and when the dentist said, 'Why don't you cut out some of this candy?' we couldn't. This was the key to his learning and his life, and he was beginning to thrive with the program.

Anytime Chris wanted the bottle he got it. Chris would give us the PECS symbol and pull us over to the refrigerator. I finally said, 'You know what? You can do this. Come on, let's do this!' And I taught him how to open the refrigerator. That was a big thing because he could get his own bottle. Only he couldn't open the bottle top, so he still needed us. Finally he pulled it open and was able from then on to get a bottle by himself. Little things like this were signs to me that my son wanted to do things; that he wanted to be an active participant in life. And I became increasingly happy thinking that he was a fighter with the ability to stabilize himself.

By getting his own bottles Chris was opening the refrigerator and being exposed to food. Somehow he began eating donuts. He went on the 'Dozen Donut A Day'· diet! We were ecstatic – he was eating solid food!

Sugar donuts were his love. I would get up every morning and run to the local market for them. They couldn't be wet, have icing on them, or have flavor in them. They had to have a certain texture – not hard, but somewhat squishy. Once I tried powdered donuts and he liked those too. Powdered sugar was good because if the doughnuts started to sweat he wouldn't eat them. So we dipped them in powdered sugar and kept them dry. And he was eating them! This was amazing to us. He was drinking formula and eating two dozen donuts a day, but we didn't care.

And then he found bagels. So his diet was formula, doughnuts and bagels. Next he added in peanut butter and jelly sandwiches. Somehow he decided against the jelly and insisted the sandwich not be cut in half.

We really started making a big push to get him off the bottles now, but he was so attached to them and they were his only source of nutrition. Luckily, the more he started to eat, the less the bottles came into play. We tried to get him to drink from a cup, but he refused to take his formula that way. In fact, he'd throw it at us. His mom drank a lot of Pepsi and she got him to taste that. He liked it and agreed to drink the Pepsi from a cup. This was a big event and we all, including the therapists, leaped around the room! In my house when things like that happen we celebrate.

We started introducing more and more food, and he began to lose some interest in the bottle. When Chris was about four-and-a-half, Jae decided to take the plunge and completely get rid of the bottles. She put them in a bag and hid them in a closet. She didn't throw them out because we didn't think it would work. So when he came for a bottle of formula we said, 'No, have water or have soda or have a roll or something.' And lo and behold, he didn't balk. He was reaching a point in his life where things were becoming easier.

We decided to set up an incidental eating program. By incidental I mean it's not something we sat him down specifically to do. I would just call him over while I was eating and say, 'Chris, taste.' Maybe I would take a piece of roast beef and put it right by his mouth and say, 'Take bite.' And he would try to get it down. I convinced him that he didn't have to eat it, just put it by his mouth, and then maybe taste it. In a way I was desensitizing his tactile problem. So now I can go over to Chris with a piece of pizza and say, 'I just want you to taste.' I'll put it to his mouth and he doesn't usually eat it, but he doesn't push it away or gag either.

My son has actually started to desensitize himself now. I've watched him go over to Chinese food, stand there and smell it. I saw him go over to a piece of rare steak, a pretty difficult feat because it's bloody and smells. But he touched it, sniffed it and walked away. The smells overwhelm him, yet he makes himself deal with them. He's saying to himself, 'OK, I want to eat this, but I can't. I'm going to make myself get over it.' That's why I think he's the greatest fighter I've ever seen. He fights all the time. I believe Chris knows what he's got, and he wants to overcome it.

Currently, cereal, peanut butter sandwiches, rolls, bread dough-nuts, cookies, a lot of different candies and fruit make up Chris' diet. The fruit has to be peeled and wiped dry with a towel and can't be mushy or wet. It has to be firm, but it can't be too hard. I'll take it, cut it, pat it down and put it in the freezer for a few seconds so it has a specific feel to it.

Chris is very texturally oriented and very tactile, which is probably why he has such a particular way of eating. He picks up doughnuts with the very tips of his fingers like they're contaminated and only eats the doughy part. Then he puts them down and picks them apart. Without holding them, he tears off pieces until all the inside dough is gone and all that's left is a shell. He does the same with sandwiches and pieces of bread.

For breakfast he'll eat Flavor Blasted Fruit Loops. He won't eat any other kind. We tried other kinds and that's the only one he liked. Lunchtime is peanut butter sandwich time. And maybe some candy. Oreos are the only cookies he eats now. He used to eat a big cookie with M&Ms in it and take out the M&Ms. He recently started eating pears, apples and raisins. When he comes home in the evening from school, he'll eat another peanut butter sandwich, rolls or doughnuts. I've seen him take seven slices of bread upstairs. He'll just go to a loaf, take slices of bread, and eat them. Children with autism often have a high acid content in their stomach so maybe he tries to settle his stomach with all the doughy bread. It's his own way of helping himself.

Unfortunately, there are no real meal times in our home. Life has just been too chaotic for us to plan and cook daily meals, not to mention everyone being home at the same time. We'd love to have him sit down and eat at a regular mealtime so that's something we'll have to work on. Chris does eat morning, noon and night, though.

We have tried a vitamin supplement with a syringe shot in the mouth, but he really gagged on that. When he was drinking his formula we weren't concerned because it had a lot of vitamins in it, but as he gets older he needs more vitamins and minerals. We're hoping with the peanut butter, fruit, raisins and fortified cereal that we're covering some of it.

Actually we're happy with Chris' diet. The foods he's added in are a big step when you consider he literally wasn't eating anything not long ago. If you think about it, it's not so terrible. It's kind of like a poor man's diet.

Hopefully in the next two years he'll add a couple more foods to his menu. Sometimes he'll take a bite of something new, and then another little bite. And then sometimes he's not in the mood. It depends on the day. But I believe in a few years he'll be eating a much more diverse diet.

11

Teeth

One day while Chris and I were playing I noticed a little something on his gum when he laughed. As I looked in his mouth I could feel the pit of my stomach collapse – there were abscesses all over! I felt sick at the thought of this poor little guy not able to tell me something was wrong. He never cried. He never even pointed. If I had only known, maybe some of this mess could have been prevented. But his front teeth looked fine and there was no outward sign of a problem. Now I had to quickly find a pediatric dentist who had a little experience with autism. It was almost an impossibility.

Chris was absolutely overwhelmed with fear when he went for his first dental visit. My wife sat on the chair holding him on her lap while I held his kicking legs. After giving him a quick exam the dentist reported, 'It's bad in there. We're going to have to put him under anesthesia at the hospital so I can perform the necessary oral surgery. There's no way I can even examine him when he's awake.'

He was scheduled for surgery at Brandywine Hospital, but there was still a big hurdle in front of us. I had to call the anesthesiologist and get permission to be with Chris while he was put under. What a fight! I had to explain that my three-year-old son with autism didn't understand what was going on and needed me there to keep him calm and under control. 'I don't care what your policy is. If I was a father of a woman having a baby you'd allow me in the room. Part of my son's disability is that he doesn't understand the world around him. He's young and he's terribly frightened.'

Permission granted. Now all I had to do was pay twenty-eight hundred dollars. The hospital stay was covered by the Access card, but the dentist wanted her payment up front.

The big day arrived and we left at five in the morning for Brandywine Hospital. I couldn't feed Chris because he was getting anesthesia, so naturally all he kept asking me for was a bottle. I kept pushing him up and down the corridor in a stroller and talking to him in an effort to distract his hunger. Finally, the anesthesiologist came and gave him some oral drops that made him a little woozy. Chris got goofy and started laughing while I scrubbed and suited up to take him into the operating room.

I laid him on my lap. 'Chrissie, your teeth hurt and we're going to make it better.' And he knew. He leaned back, closed his eyes, and I masked him. Once he was asleep, I put him down and watched them begin work. Then I joined Jae and Jessica in the waiting room.

We were just a wreck! Every four, five minutes a nurse came out and told us, 'Dr. Meliton found this problem in the back,' and 'Dr. Meliton found that.' Apparently his teeth pretty much collapsed when the doctor's surgical tool touched them. That's how bad they were. He was in surgery almost four hours. How could I not have noticed anything before?

We were devastated. Just devastated. Could we have prevented all this? I honestly don't know. I have heard bad teeth are a common problem for kids with autism, but that doesn't make me feel any better about it.

When he was an infant we cleaned his teeth with a washcloth. It was the best we could do since he wouldn't let us go near him with a toothbrush until he turned four. Drinking formula as his only source of nutrition didn't help either. We tried not to let him fall asleep with a bottle, but we were not very successful. Plus he drank twelve, fifteen bottles a day. We'd think, 'OK, the bottle's going to be gone soon.' But it kept going on and on.

To make matters worse, he had 'pica.' He ate anything! He'd pick up a piece of glass and put it in his mouth. He used to chew rocks and break off his teeth. The dentist said it looked as if someone had taken a hammer to his teeth. Well, I guess if you combine rock chewing with bottle sucking and a lack of nutrients, rotten teeth are not such a surprise.

After that first dental experience Chris' remaining teeth started to go. He went in two more times for oral surgery and basically ended up with a whole mouthful of metal.

One time Chris knew he had a loose tooth, but still didn't understand. So I was explaining to him what it was and he went over and got a scissor. He then gave it to me and pointed to his tooth. In his own very intelligent way he was telling me, 'Please, just get this out for me.' Of course, a typical child would know you don't take a scissor and cut out the tooth. But he reasoned to himself, 'Scissors – they cut things out, and I want this out. It doesn't feel right.'

His teeth are pretty good now. We brush them three times a day and have also taught Chris how to do it. He has learned to brush his teeth *and* his tongue. At first it was tough. His tactile sensitivity was a problem with the toothpaste. So we dipped a little toothpaste and then washed it off so there was just a little left. Hopefully any future disasters with his teeth have been conquered. We've also worked on going to the dentist and saying, 'Ahhhh.' At his last visit he sat in the chair and let the dentist examine him – a small feat for a typical child, but a huge breakthrough for Chris!

12

Gymnastics

One characteristic of children with autism is poor muscle conditioning. There was no way I was going to allow that to happen to Chris. I've always felt it was important for anyone's welfare to exercise and have good physical strength, and naturally I felt it was important for Chris; maybe even more so. As a person with autism he had lots of spatial fears, particularly a fear of leaning backwards, but he did, however, like jumping around. Maybe enrolling him in a gymnastics class would help.

So I enrolled Chris in a gym. We walked into our first class and there were people all over jumping and leaping and spinning and screaming. My son wouldn't do anything for two months, not even roll a ball. But I persisted and we kept coming back once a week and he kept crying once a week while we walked around the gym floor. Finally he pushed a ball. Then he lined up some objects. I playfully threw him in the air and lifted him to stand on my shoulders, and then I got him to run around.

Before he knew it, I had him running up to the long trampoline and I lifted him on. He looked a little puzzled like, 'Wait a minute, how'd you get me on this thing?' But then he started to bounce with me a bit. I knew he would love trampoline because he jumped all the time. He was very athletic and leaped and vaulted over chairs and on couches and loved jumping on the bed. Unfortunately, I bounced too hard and he twisted his ankle. So that was the end of the trampoline for a month. Once he got back on again, he'd either push other kids off if they came on during free play or run away.

Other children made him nervous. So, slowly, I introduced him to kids by bringing him to play on the floor fifteen minutes before his private class. A year went by and he started to really take to gym, but the instructor wasn't prepared to pick up the slack and work with him.

He didn't seem to know what to do with Chris and I ended up having to make suggestions: 'Let's try the bars because he loves that type of movement.' So I would put Chris on the parallel bars and he'd hold himself up, and I'd say, 'Support.' He loved it! Chris liked to control his body and move around. But the instructor just couldn't figure out how to teach him. He demonstrated to Chris how to do things, but that was just not enough. You can't put five movements together and say do them to a child with autism. Finally I got fed up paying this guy fifty dollars a week and we stopped the class.

I really wanted Chris to get some exercise, though, so I called up another gym, Prestige Gymnastics, and talked to Mike, the boys' coach. He turned out to be my daughter's old gymnastics teacher. The guy was very agreeable while I explained for an hour-and-a-half about Chris and what I wanted.

We went that night to Prestige Gymnastics and it was magic! First Mike, a soft-spoken guy, came up to greet us. 'Hi, Chris. Let's try to go out there and stand.'

I thought to myself, 'This isn't going to work.'

At first Chris didn't want to do anything, but each time he did a little more. Mike just kept working with him, and even when Chris was unhappy about the skill he was doing, Mike got him to go through with it anyway. Chris actually fell off the balance beam and got back up! My son was really conquering a lot of fears.

But it was probably I who needed to conquer my fears even more. I was always out on the floor crying, 'Don't yell at him! Don't touch him!' I was very protective. If I felt Chris was getting nervous I would tell the instructor to leave him alone. I was actually walking along with them. Even though Mike was an incredible instructor, I thought I was justified because this was a very overwhelming experience for Chris. I was also there, and still do stick around, in case something happened. Chris could have a seizure or throw a fit. It was unlikely that would happen, but it was good to be there in case Mike needed a little guidance.

I also asked Mike to work on specific problems that Chris had. For instance, backward mobility is a big fear for a lot of kids who are tactilely defensive. Chris' autism made it almost impossible for him to lean back from a sitting position. He loses all sense of what's going to happen. Lying down backwards, going through a tunnel, climbing on a ledge and putting his foot down were always scary for Chris. It's not unusual at all.

'I hate to see this guy when he's a big strapping sixteen year old male,' I said to myself, 'scared to death of these things when maybe I can help him.' So I read a lot of neurology and occupational therapy books, and went to Mike and said, 'Look. These are things that he can't do, but not because he's afraid. Neurologically he's unable. It's not psychological. Can you work on them?'

So he worked on the fears step by step just like he approached Chris with everything. First it was, 'Sit down.' Next it was, 'Chris, stand up... Sit down. Very good. Can you lean like this? Very good.' And then he may not have tackled that movement for another week or so. This gave Chris the knowledge that Mike was not going to force him to do anything.

Most people make the mistake of pushing. 'Chris, lay down. Come on! Let me help you.' And then they push him down. That's horrible to do to someone who is frightened to death! It should be done bit by bit. Mike taught him in the same manner as Discrete

Trial, breaking it down. He turned out to be a real professional, and Chris just loves him. All my son's spatial fears of going back with his head are gone. Chris will lie down, fall backwards on a mat, and lift his legs up when he's on his back. All these things used to horrify him!

I have finally faded out of the picture and I don't interfere with Mike at all. He's the coach, not me. If Chris falls off the balance beam Mike will say to him, 'Come on, Buddy, let's get up.' And I don't go right over anymore. Of course, I don't want my son to think I dropped out so every once in a while I'll run up and say, 'Chris, that was a great job! Give me five.' Then I get out of there.

My son is now doing more than most kids his age. Mike said to me recently that out of the five- and six-year-old kids that he teaches, Chris is in the seventy-five per cent range in skills and the top range for safety. Mike is not even concerned if he walks away and lets Chris do some things on his own. Chris, he says, always listens and is a pleasure to teach.

My son is now up to two hours a week of gymnastics and goes on every apparatus. He warms up, stretches, strength conditions, leaps off a trampoline into a pit, goes through a tunnel, goes down a slide and climbs up a ladder. These are all things he never would do before. He conquered all his fears and does all kinds of incredible stunts. They have him climbing a platform that even I wouldn't climb! Then he hangs ten feet in the air from the rings, swings, jumps and sticks his landing. He works on the vault, the trampoline, and does routines! He just goes from one apparatus to the other and he's strong and he's fit and he loves it.

I just marvel at my son. Somebody came up to me in the gym and said it's great that I have him here. But *he* goes out there for an hour and conquers everything, not me. Maybe I emphasized exercise and went out and found the instructor, but this kid is the one doing it! Look at him! All I did was help clear the path for him. That's what all parents should do. But I've never seen such perseverance and strength in a person. I just admire him. I do.

> We notice a lot of confidence and willingness to try new things since the gym classes started up. He used to hate to go backwards, but now he's OK about it. I know they really challenge him there. I've gone to gym class a few times and it's amazing what they do. He jumps off these big ramps into the pit! He really does stuff that as a little child, I'd be scared to do.
>
> He used to be very timid about all the sensory programs we did. For instance, one was sticking his feet in a bucket of corn and walking around in it. It sounds easy to us, but it was very hard for him. Now he's much more willing to try these activities and I credit a lot of this new confidence to his gymnastics.
>
> *Jenny Nielsen, therapist*

PART IV

Advocacy and Education

1

The Battle For Safety

A little boy with autism was found in front of a restaurant playing in his diapers. He traveled three miles through a ravine, a gully and across a main thoroughfare to get there from his home. The mother, a friend of mine, who happens to have two boys with autism, called the police when she found her son missing. She tried to explain that this child has autism and he took off when the screen door was accidentally left open, but the police really came down on her anyway.

A kid with autism once wandered into a record store in the mall. He couldn't stand the fact the CDs were not lined up according to color so he started rearranging them. He was very engrossed with his project and determined to complete it when the clerk yelled, 'Stop that!'
    The kid echoed, 'Stop that.'
    The clerk said, 'Hey, buddy.'
    'Hey buddy.'
    'That's it. I'm calling the police.'
    A policeman came and saw a kid frantically throwing CDs around. The clerk explained, 'This kid's nuts and he's a real wise guy. He's repeating everything I say.'

So the officer went over and tapped the kid on the shoulder, 'Hey, pal.'

The kid turned around and bit him! Angry, the officer knocked him down and handcuffed him. The boy screamed and cried.

'Where are you from?'

The kid couldn't answer them. Instead he was trying to crawl in the corner, and the more they pressed, the more he kept moving away.

One early hot summer evening we were sitting on the sofa watching TV with the front door left ajar to get a breeze. I answered the telephone when I turned and noticed Chris was no longer sitting with me. So I said to the person on the phone, 'Gee, my son's not on the sofa. Let me just look for him.'

Chris had taken off! My heart sank when I looked down the street and didn't see him. But then, I looked the other way and just caught him turning the corner. He was running on his toes wearing nothing but a diaper! Thank God, he turned left instead of right because right went toward the highway. He seemed to be going a route that we'd taken before. He was very route-oriented so I said to myself, 'Don't panic. He's going to follow our route.' I sprinted down the block, leaped over a parked car, and found him. There he was, just sitting there very happy. 'Hi, Chris.' No reaction. He just smiled as I took him back to the house.

I knew we had to do something fast to ensure Chris' safety. He wasn't even considered a significant runner, but we could not take the risk that he would dash out of the house again. A lot of these kids take off any chance they get. You open the door, BANG! They're gone. They see a space. They're gone. It doesn't matter if they're dressed. They just like to run. And they don't have any concept of danger. So you have an incidence of finding kids miles away playing in front of restaurants or sitting in a gully unable to communicate.

The first thing we did was install a screen door on Chris' bedroom. Perfect. We could see and hear him. And he could see out, but he couldn't get out. Maybe this seems odd, but we had to do it. Chris had no fear of danger, and if he wasn't being watched you never knew what he might do. He wasn't like other little boys who would walk out of their bedrooms and go jump on Daddy's bed. This child would go to the sink, turn on the hot water and burn himself.

Another immediate course of action we took to protect Chris was placing a little emergency ID tag around his neck with his name and phone number that said, 'I'm nonverbal autistic.' God forbid, if he ran or we lost track of him, this tag would help strangers identify and communicate with him. But he hated it. We tried it on his wrist, but in two seconds he'd tear it off. He just did not want anything on him. Like most autistics he could not tolerate materials touching him.

Then Jae came up with a brilliant idea. She just slipped the tag into the eye of Chris' shoe where the lace goes. We had him walk toward us and saw that it really stood out. If you were a policeman or a fireman, it was something you would see immediately. 'Wow, there's something on that guy's shoe! It's shiny and it's clunking around and I better take a look at it.' The best part about the tag was that it didn't bother Chris at all. So now we have peace of mind knowing that if a circumstance comes up when Chris is on his own and in trouble, he's wearing this tag that identifies him. I highly recommend a similar tag for anyone with autism or any other communication disorder. In fact, we are now offering instructions on our website at *www.autismhelp.net* for obtaining or making your own ID tag.

There's a saying that if you put a twelve-year-old child with autism in the mall with ten dollars, he'll starve to death. They simply don't have the ability to take care of themselves. So whether Chris has the ID tag or not, he still will cross the street without looking and still has the potential to wander away. The tag cannot lull us into a false sense of security. We have made it a lifetime safety project to diligently teach Chris how to cross the street, not to leave the house, to stay by us when we shop, how to talk to strangers and how to get help.

Part of our safety project was to also create community awareness of both autism and our son. We felt very strongly that an aware community was necessary for Chris' security. So we contacted our local newspaper and had articles printed on autism using our family as the focal point.

Another big step we took was to sponsor Awareness Days at our home. The idea was to get people in the neighborhood to know my son and learn about his disorder. I went all out for these functions. We had food, a band and politicians. 'Look, this is Chris. Say hello.' The Awareness Days were so successful that we've continued holding them a few times a year. People know Chris in our neighborhood, in the grocery store and at the mall. And believe me, it helps.

I always tell families with autistic children to get them introduced to the community! You don't have to hold Awareness Days, but at the very least, print up a flyer and pass it around the neighborhood. 'Hi. I live at 146 Elm. My son Christopher is six years old and has autism. Here are a few characteristics about the disorder. You might see him in the street doing this, or you might hear that. Don't be alarmed. Here's what to do. Please come to the house anytime and say hello to him. I want you to meet him.' If you want to take it a step further, hold a barbeque, invite your local state representatives and advertise it in the community newspaper's calendar. That's what we did.

Then I started thinking, what happens if someone encounters Chris who *doesn't* know him? What if they mistake him for being crazed, on drugs, belligerent, violent or aggressive? The police would certainly be called in to take him. That was a clear possibility, especially when he becomes a teenager. What if at age fourteen Chris is one hundred and ninety pounds of pure muscle and says to me, 'Dad, I want to go to the mall. But I want to go on my own.' What if at the mall he gets overwhelmed or somebody makes fun of him or he starts flapping, and somebody thinks he's crazy and the cops are called? The cop would see a strong kid who looks pretty normal and would undoubtedly conclude the teen is either nuts or on drugs. If Chris started having a seizure the cop would see some wild maniac and instinctively try to restrain him. Now all this poor guy probably wants is his dad, but he can't communicate that and continues to resist even more.

These thoughts scared me to death. So I impulsively called my local police, the East Hempfield Police Department. This was stupid because I had nothing written down and hadn't thought it through at all. 'I'd like to speak to the person in charge of training.' I got the lieutenant. 'Hi, I'm a father of a child with autism who lives in your district and I want to train your policemen.' He invited me down to explain my case to him and another lieutenant.

'What experience do you have?' they asked.

I told them I did a lot of work with autism and showed him news articles written about me. Then I said I was involved with the Pennsylvania Autism Society and that they could call Pat Houston, the president, for a reference. So they called. 'Yes. This guy is really good,' said Pat. 'As a matter of fact, I'll go with him.'

They invited me to do two lectures in a hall with fifty cops each time! I had never done anything like this before. I went up to the podium shaking with fear, tightly holding my little notes as everybody stared at me. I remember seeing one cop fall asleep while I spoke. So thinking everybody was bored, I sped through my presentation while Pat Houston taped me. 'Are there any questions?' I asked at the end. Yes! A lot of them! Turns out they were interested after all.

The lieutenant came up to me after the session and said in a big voice, 'You did a fine job. You're really a great dad.'

'That was just great,' Pat chimed in. 'I'm so glad you're doing this. We've been talking about doing this for years. And that you just did it is amazing. How did you come upon this?'

'I just felt it was the right thing to do. It was important.'

I walked away thinking hey, I could do this. And I called the East Hempfield Fire Department and the East Hempfield Ambulance Department. Then I started finding out that different departments all had different questions. The fire department wanted to know how you coax a child out of a fire. The ambulance department wanted to know if the children don't realize they're hurt how do they check them for injuries? How do you get a child in a car wreck to stay calm? They hit me with a million questions, and I was able to answer them!

I went on to call Lancaster City Police, the biggest force in the region, and spoke to Sergeant David Odenwalt, the training sergeant. This big, tough guy who trained with the Navy Seals says to me, 'Good shit you're doing! Come on down.'

'When?'

'Well, we train six in the morning every other Wednesday. You need three months to cover each group and I've got you booked.'

So there I went at six in the morning. It was hellish for me. I bartended at Scooters until three AM and then went off to Lancaster for a six AM training session. When I first walked into Sergeant Odenwalt's office I immediately thought I was in too deep. This was not going to work. Here was this big massive guy saying, 'You're a fucking good guy. I like you.' Then he took me into a room with about twelve cops and said, 'This is Bill Davis. He's gonna tell you some things and you guys listen.' And all these guys were sitting there, all big with crew cuts and it's six in the morning. But they listened and asked questions.

I was next asked by the Lancaster City Fire Department to do several sessions. One time the fire alarm sounded and they just took off in the middle of my talk. But these men were very interested and had tons of questions. Tons! Very interested. One time a District Judge came to listen. I was so nervous, but he followed me afterwards and also asked me a bunch of questions. People were interested!

Soon emergency personnel started calling me from all around. 'I'm from the Manheim Fire Department. I heard you do training and we want you.' The Lititz Ambulance Company called. I did just about every department in the surrounding counties and city including the State Troopers of Pennsylvania. Now I'm branching out to emergency workers in hospitals and am scheduled to speak to nurses, anesthesiologists and technicians.

I'm particularly excited about extending my training work across the country. The Kansas City chapter of the Autism Society of America is having me train their police department, and I hope to obtain corporate funding to sponsor a National Emergency Services Training Program for Autism. Along with conducting my own national training project I will be writing a manual that interested parties can use for training staff on their own. In the meantime I continue to write articles emphasizing the importance of training emergency workers about autism in national publications such as the Autism Society of America's *Advocate*.

The training sessions are very straightforward. Basically what I do is tell them about Chris, explain autism and its communication problems, how to handle a person with autism, and then answer questions. Most emergency service professionals I've trained know very little about autism, even the EMTs (Emergency Medical Technicians), unless they've already been exposed to the disability. Typical comments are usually, 'They're like the guy in the movie *Rain Man*. What's his special skill? They're all smart, right? So what does he do best?'

Dispelling these myths and stressing how difficult it is for people with autism to communicate is a very important part of these training sessions. I explain what PECS is so they understand when a person uses cards to communicate. I tell them a person with autism might use a computer to communicate. But mostly, I stress that in the majority of emergency situations the person will not readily communicate with them at all.

'Everything you know about communication you can pretty much throw out the window. You may have a child looking at spinning objects or throwing a ball from one end to the other. Very quietly get the child's attention and be prepared to repeat yourself over and over. "Are you OK? Are you OK?" Talking louder doesn't help. You don't want to touch their face, neck or back. And *never* sneak up on them. If you are faced with a child who has no language and is flapping and stimming, you must be very persistent, quietly gain the child's attention and go from there.'

I try very hard to get across that a person with autism should be made to feel as safe, secure and as unthreatened as possible. Don't get frustrated with somebody who appears to be paying absolutely no attention to you. They may be stressed and go to a favorite topic to make themselves feel better. For instance you say, 'What's your name?'

And they answer, 'The capital of New York State is Albany. The capital of…'

'I didn't ask you the capitals. What's your name?'

'The capital of Alabama is…' They go back to what's safe.

Try to redirect them. 'Hey, that's great talking. That's great. You know all the capitals. But can you tell me your name? Can you write your name?'

They may stand right up close to you because they can't differentiate between private space. They may be very loud because their volume is off. They may not look at you. They may walk away from you. They may attack you! You have to really dig down deep and think and be calm. It's going to take time. It's going to take a lot of time. It can be very frightening.

That's another reason ID tags are so important. If a person with autism is wearing something that identifies he has autism and who to call, it will save a lot of grief for everyone. Obviously, getting to the parents right away is best. They'll know what to do – ' Does he have that blue object with him?'

'No, I don't see it.'

'Well, that could be the problem. Find a blue teddy bear. He loves to hold it and that will calm him right down. In the meantime we'll be right over.'

If the police don't know a person has autism or how to deal with the disorder, the person with the disability ends up getting hurt. They get pushed around, put in jail, and admit to crimes they don't commit. Imagine sending your kid to the store and he gets put under arrest because he started waving his hands. The manager says, 'Hey! What are you doing over there?' The kid gets nervous and the manager calls the cops. The boy looks like he's refusing to pay attention so the cop grabs him. The kid bites and it escalates. Next they'll throw him in jail.

And a person with autism should *never* be thrown in jail. If he's violent or aggressive, yes, he may need to be restrained. I'm certainly not telling anyone to get hurt. Use caution, but never throw him in jail. Keep him in the holding room.

If a crime was committed chances are he has no idea what he did or may have even been persuaded to do it. People with autism are quite pure and generally don't lie or steal. Maybe he went in and took something he liked without understanding the whole buy/sell concept. I've seen my own son do that. He was in a store and saw his favorite toy. 'Oh, I like those lizards.' And he walked out with them. Are you going to arrest him for a concept he can't understand?

People with autism are also easy prey because they will do what they're told without thinking about it. There are instances now where street criminals are finding kids with autism to deliver drugs. 'Hey, take this package and deliver it here.'

'OK.'

So they are very easy prey. And later they cannot tell you what was wrong nor what was done to them.

Some people with autism are capable of functioning in society without anxiety and can be out on their own. But a good majority can't seem to make it in everyday life. They're too confused, too overwhelmed, too over-processed. They're easy prey and can be easily manipulated. The simplest thing becomes the hardest thing. A kid might be a musical genius, but somehow wanders off in the mall and doesn't know how to call his parents, can't buy food and he pees in his pants because he's so overwhelmed. So what do you do with somebody like that?

The most common concern for police is that not realizing he's disabled, they will overreact to a person with autism and mistakenly hurt him. They know that a mentally retarded person doesn't understand when their rights are read. But do they know a person with autism doesn't understand either? What happens when the police ask a question and don't get an answer? Surely they don't want to end up incarcerating somebody who doesn't deserve to be incarcerated.

That's why at these training sessions I try to fully explain the characteristics of autism and outline what a police officer might encounter. When called to a problem situation, they might find a child who appears belligerent. He could be violent, aggressive, appear deaf, or even spit at them. Imagine a cop's reaction if someone spit on him.

I emphasize that people with autism lack the ability to communicate, don't know what a facial expression means, and take things literally. If someone said, 'Keep your eye on the coat,' they might put their eye on the coat. An uninformed policeman would more than likely interpret that as wise-guy behavior.

The most common concern for firefighters is how to approach someone in a fire. There was one incident recently where twins burned. The biggest problem confronting firemen is that people with autism retreat. They see some scary looking guy coming at them with a fire mask and suit yelling, 'Quick!! The flames! Come here!!' and they cower and move further back. If the firefighter continues to yell, they might bite him or they might bite themselves.

The most important thing is to be calm, persistent, repetitive, low toned, keep low body language and not be overwhelming. Always speak with a very calming voice, 'Come here. Look at me. Come here.' Eventually they'll look and listen. You have to force the kid to pay attention. You're saying to him, 'I'm not letting you retreat. You're going to look at me. And when you look at me you're going to get some kind of reward – a high five, a smile, a pat on the head, a hug, a piece of chocolate.'

If you realize as an emergency service worker that you have no time left to slowly coax then you better grab him; but you better know how. Afterwards check really well for injuries because pain deferment among people with autism is common. 'Are you all right?'

'Yes,' the child might answer, but his leg is burned in the back. So check him.

'Most everyone realizes that if they had encountered someone with autism before my training sessions they would have made serious mistakes. Police, firemen, EMTs all know about alcoholics, diabetics and people with seizure disorders. They should also know about autism. Their mouths drop open at these trainings when they learn about the disorder. They're saying to themselves, 'I would have cuffed this guy. I would have knocked him out. This is shocking.'

A general consensus at my training sessions is, 'Thank God, you told us about this because we didn't know about it. We had no idea this disorder was so severe and encompassed so many behaviors. Now if we encounter somebody with autism we'll know what to look for and have the confidence to handle the situation.'

I was standing at the bank recently when a big guy with a crew cut came up to me and said, 'Hey, you trained us one day. And not long after, I was called to the mall and a kid was exhibiting exactly the characteristics you told me about. So the first thing I did was look for an ID tag. Turned out he had one around his neck that said he was autistic. I called his mom and dad and it really settled the situation. If it weren't for your training I would never have known what to do.'

All I wanted from these training sessions was to one day help someone. That guy made my year, never mind my day, because he cared enough to listen. And instead of confronting this kid or being confused about what was wrong with him, the officer cued in on the disability right away.

So I think it's very important that emergency personnel receive this training. It gives them cues to look for. And on a higher scale it opens their minds and reminds them that there are people in the community who don't fit their expectations. My son could be mistaken for a lot of things. I've seen the stares. But just because he's disabled doesn't mean he's stupid or a threat or should be locked away.

Parents must take active responsibility to ensure their child's safety. Get the community to know him. Register him with the police, fire and EMT departments. Teach your child about strangers and how to get help. When you're out in public teach him to stand on line with you and not to stray. Get an ID tag! If he won't wear it, use the type we devised for the shoe. Make an Emergency PECS kit. We did. If Chris has his PECS book and someone asks, 'What's your name?' he can answer through PECS with a picture of himself and the word 'Chris.' He is able to answer a whole series of social questions. 'Where do you live?' I live in this picture of a house that says 146 Elm. 'What's your phone number?' He shows a picture of a phone, 555–299–2960. If he ever gets in an emergency situation Chris will be able to answer. It's ridiculous to allow a nonverbal child to go without ID and communication tools.

Last, but equally important, get your police force and other emergency workers educated! It is said that people with disabilities are more likely to come in contact with the police than other citizens. And it is usually not for a crime. That means police are being called because people are frightened by unfamiliar behavior. Most police departments are very open to training sessions. So why not make it our responsibility to teach them what they need to know and prevent tragedies from occurring in emergency situations?

Tips for keeping your child with autism safe

Turn your home into a classroom

Ask your local police and firefighters to visit your home in uniform and talk to your child. Create a social story to prepare him or her for the visit.

Hold an 'Awareness Day'

Set up an information table, hand out flyers and invite your local state representative to your home. Advertise in your newspaper's community calendar.

Knock on your neighbor's doors

Introduce your child and describe some of the things they should be aware of like running and self-injurious behavior. Hand out autism pamphlets door-to-door along with your contact information.

Create an identification tag for your child

Include your child's name, phone number and important characteristics like nonverbal, runner or biter. Teach him or her to show it to someone if lost or hurt.

Contact your local paper

Demand an article on autism to raise awareness. Contact your local Autism Society of America chapter to help provide information to the reporter.

Register your child

Register and provide vital contact information with your local police, fire and EMT departments' computers.

Take your child with you

Take your child everywhere with you and let the neighbors, shopkeepers, emergency personnel and educators get to know him or her as an individual.

Place a special decal or sticker on the window

Put a decal on the window of your child's room indicating his or her disability in case of fire. The Emergency Alert Window Decal shown is available exclusively from the Autism Society of Illinois, 2200 S. Main St, Ste 317, Lombard, IL 60148, or www.autismillinois.org

A decal, produced by the Autism Society of Illinois

Teach your child about fire safety

Practice fire drills through repetition and a step-by-step approach. Continue to have periodic drills. Place smoke detectors where your child will hear them.

It was about a year and a half ago that Bill came to our police department and gave a wonderful demonstration for us on autism. Up until then, we only knew about the disorder from watching the movie Rain Man, but of course that's a movie and not real life. As police officers we work in a city environment of almost ninety thousand people dealing with all kinds of people. There are blind, deaf, mentally retarded, handicapped and autistic citizens in our community and it's important that we know how to handle each of their disabilities. We need to know how to communicate, how to help them and where to go if we don't know what to do.

There were a lot of things I didn't know before Bill's training session. I didn't know that if we put our hands on somebody who has autism, they may react a certain way by pulling back. Most police officers would initially take that behavior as resistance. Now I know what to expect and how to approach someone with autism. Until Bill's training session I was very unaware that loud noises or startling things can send people with autism into a panic. I also learned that a lot of autistic children are afraid of dogs. Being a canine cop, this was important for me to know.

Bill also explained that many people with autism don't speak. You look at somebody who may be ten or eleven years old and you would expect that child to speak and talk in sentences. A police officer may interpret someone not talking back to him as a sign of belligerence or attitude. So I would recommend parents have their child wear an ID tag like the one Bill has on his son's shoe. Anything that says, hey, this is what's going on here is invaluable. If an autistic child wandered away from mom at the store, mall or carnival, nothing could be more beneficial than an ident-a-tag that says my name is such and such and I have autism. It immediately helps an officer who might be wondering why the person isn't answering questions.

Our shift ran into a boy about ten years old with autism following Bill's training. It turned out that the information we received from the session was extremely helpful in dealing with him.

Police officers come into contact with everybody, including those with severe disabilities. We need to know what we're dealing with and how to resolve problems correctly. I had absolutely no idea how to work with people who have autism before I met Bill. And I'm sure that's true for most of the department. Knowledge is power when it's used in the right way. Thanks to Bill - he's given me the knowledge and the understanding of how to use it if I ever come across a person with autism.

Officer Chris DePatto, Canine Division,
Lancaster Bureau City Police

2

Fighting For A Public Preschool Program

Even though we were happy with our own in-home program Jae and I never stopped demanding the IU create a preschool class specifically for autistic children. We petitioned the Governor with a number of letters and phone calls. My call to the special education administrator was typical of the uninterested reception I was getting. 'Am I boring you?' I asked. 'Are you not listening to me? Are you doing your shopping list while I'm talking? Because I'm really getting angry. Trust me, I'm not going away.'

Eventually he directed me to a woman who was supposed to start a movement to improve the states' education of special needs children. I called her repeatedly to let her know that I was available, but surprise, surprise, she never called me back.

My state representative, Katie True, had been one of the few people who were very responsive to us. She even invited Jae to speak before a legislative committee on special education. It was kind of funny because Katie, a very conservative Republican, had never seen my wife in person. Katie's mouth dropped open when Jae walked in sporting a few tattoos and body piercings. 'Don't worry,' Jae reassured her, 'I can speak.'

Then Katie noticed that my daughter, Jessica, came along. 'Children aren't really allowed,' she said.

And Jesse answered, 'I'm representing my brother.'

So both Jesse and Jae went in to speak. Jae went before the committee and described the ordeal we went through to get Chris proper services and pointed out the need for autism education and awareness. Finally, the state of Pennsylvania in 1995 was recognizing the need to begin work with children of autism.

We continued protesting to anyone who would listen, and finally the government responded by starting to develop a special needs preschool class specifically for autism. I guess the pressure from us helped, but more likely they were afraid increasing numbers of parents would demand funding for in-home programs like ours. We were getting a lot of publicity, and the local government could no longer keep our program hushed.

The state decided to start a class modeled on Discrete Trial similar to ours. So now officials from the IU were not only coming to our home to check up on us, but also to learn from us because our program was so top-notch. I must admit my attitude was, 'Oh, wait a minute, you didn't want to pay for this. Now all of a sudden you're using it?'

When they found out I hired Rutgers University they were amazed. 'We've been after Rutgers and they simply won't come,' they moaned to me.

Here was my bargaining chip. 'I'll get Rutgers for you, but play fair with me. Don't interfere with my program.' I was very concerned they would cut our funding so I knew if I did this favor it would keep them under control.

I spoke to the people at Rutgers. 'Look, there's an opportunity here for you to start a program from the beginning. The local government wants to go with you and the people need you here.' Rutgers came and they still to this day run the Lancaster-Lebanon IU program.

Unfortunately, the IU slapped the class together very quickly. Rutgers did a couple of training sessions, but that was certainly not enough for people who were only aides, volunteers or special education teachers. Most of these people didn't know autism from cerebral palsy.

'You want to be an aide in our new autism class? We'll pay you six dollars an hour. All you have to do is attend a few sessions with an expert from Rutgers.' So they had people running a program for a very complicated disorder who only had a couple of seminars. I protested.

They asked if we wanted Chris to go there, and we said no.

'You've been clamoring for this classroom for two years,' they said to me. 'You went to the Governor. You wrote letters. You protested. Now you don't want to enroll your son?'

I said, 'No. You didn't do it correctly. I didn't ask for a badly run classroom. I asked for a professionally run classroom.' They hated me.

Before the class started, the IU held an open house. I'll never forget it. You could see the classroom and hear Rutgers speak about the concept. Naturally we were planning to attend and hear what they had to say when we got a call telling us we were not welcome. I said, 'What do you mean, I'm not invited?'

'Well, your child's not coming so we don't want you there.'

'Wait a minute. He's eligible. Maybe I'll change my mind and decide I want him to attend.'

'No. You're not invited.'

I called up the head of the Pennsylvania IU units and asked him what was going on. My theory was that Jae was now a known force in Discrete Trial and people came from all over to ask her help in setting up programs. With all her research and workshops she had become quite an expert. But the IU hired what we considered amateurs to run its program who were most likely unable to answer Jae's questions. And since it was no secret that I had a big mouth and would speak out about their inadequacies in front of all the other parents, they uninvited us.

Following my phone conversation the IU employees started treating me a little nicer, but basically I was persona non grata. Don't talk to that guy. Don't go near him. Yet, every other week there was a group from the IU still asking to come over and see our program because they were having trouble running theirs.

Once the IU preschool class for children with autism was in session, literature and notices were sent home to parents in their children's backpacks. Items like educational pamphlets or invitations to local conferences were distributed. Only we never got any information or word of any meetings. They were leaving us out.

Again I called the IU administrator, and said, 'Look, my son is part of the IU. I demand that I get every piece of literature that these kids get. It doesn't matter that Chris isn't attending the class. He's part of the IU. He has autism just like the others. If there's going to be a discussion on coping with stress at home given by someone from the psychology department, why aren't I invited? I want to be involved in anything you do because my son is eligible for this class and these services. You can't cut me out just because you don't want me there.'

Then I demanded the IU allow me to view the class. 'I'm sorry. My son is eligible and I want to see this class.' I actually did want to see it. It had been running several months and maybe it was a great class at this point. I didn't know.

So who's the guy assigned to take me to the class? The pompous idiot I threw out of my house a few months before. After a curt greeting he started throwing every term possible to show me he was the most knowledgeable guy in the world.

During the class a boy jumped up from the table and started flailing. A volunteer aide in her seventies ran over, pulled him by the shirt, and threw him in the chair. 'Oh,' I said to my guide, 'is that what we're doing now?'

'She's new.'

So I said, 'Oh. So if you're new you can manhandle the children. Is that your philosophy?'

'I think our session is over,' he replied.

In my opinion, they were very bad at what they did in the beginning, but fortunately they have increased their knowledge and are much better now. I've seen the class again, I've spoken to parents, and I see that they now have a little handle on what they're doing. I still wouldn't send Chris, however, if he was just starting out because I don't think the class is quite up to par yet. The program has expanded and they've taken the task seriously, but not until they can show me teachers with hands-on training who graduated with their doctorate or masters with an emphasis on autism would I send him.

The need for this preschool class that we so strongly argued for is tremendous. At my last count there were about forty kids in the Lancaster-Lebanon autism class. And some children haven't even been diagnosed and others have been purposely misdiagnosed. If a child is diagnosed with pervasive developmental disorder, PDD, then he gets a special ed teacher rather than specific autism instruction. Unfortunately, the teacher can't do much but babysit the child, and he doesn't progress like he should.

I believe as a special educator you are mandated to tell parents everything that's out there. Don't just tell parents about a general special ed class because it's easier and less expensive than outlining specific services available for each child's disorder.

Put it into perspective this way. If you had a child with a serious heart condition, would you send him to somebody who wasn't a heart specialist? No! 'I'm a pediatrician. I'll operate on your child because we don't have anybody else.' You would never allow that.

Instead you'd say, 'How dare you? I'll go to Boston. I'll go wherever I have to go to get the best help for my child.'

The same goes for providing therapy and education for a child with autism. A responsible parent doesn't want to hear, 'This woman is a special ed teacher who took a two day seminar with Rutgers University and now she's ready for your kid. She's never had any experience with children with autism, but she does nice little paintings.'

Your response would be, 'Really? What does she know about processing problems? What does she know about self-injurious behavior? Nothing? Well, I'm not sending my child.' That's the same response we had to the IU's new preschool program.

3

Helping Other Families

When Chris was first diagnosed we felt lost. There was not one family or organization to take the lead in guiding us through the maze of steps we needed to take. Finding the right therapy, school and knowledgeable doctors was an arduous task. There was so little information and fewer people willing to deal with us. I spent six months, eight hours a day on the phone calling lawyers, parents, educators, universities and doctors. I would read a name of somebody who wrote a book and call him. I had no idea where to get the information we needed.

I would have loved if someone took us in and led us along the right path. God, would that have been a help! Maybe that's why we've never refused to help anybody else. What a great feeling not to have a family go through what we went through! When a father asks me, 'When I go to this meeting what do I do?' it makes me feel so good to be able to answer him.

All I wanted was someone to direct me. 'OK. You call this number. Here are the three places in your area you can go to get a diagnosis, the books we recommend and the classrooms that are available. Let us look at your son and see if he learns visually and pinpoint the therapy he needs. Let's come to your home and help you a little bit. Let's tell you about the political movements in autism. Let's tell you about the cutting edge research in autism. Let's tell you about the future. Let's tell you about occupational therapy, support groups, doctors, immunization.' This is all necessary information that is not easily stumbled upon.

While working furiously to find expert help and schooling and running our own in-home program for Chris, our name started floating around. Other parents of children with autism started calling us for help and advice. We were painfully aware of the absence of a good local information source, and decided to form our own organization to help others. Jae called it FACT – Family Autism Challenge Team – and its purpose was to help with legal advice, fight for services, create awareness and teach what we knew about therapies.

We made great efforts to develop FACT into an informative support and advocacy group. I knew adult support groups could easily turn into coffee klatches because they often just sit around and complain. But support to me meant specific support for issues, and that's how I tried to gear the group.

I started calling area parents, inviting them to a meeting, especially those who were interested in the new autism class I fought so hard for the IU to create. I also invited the president of the Pennsylvania Autism Society.

At the meetings information pamphlets were distributed and guests spoke on a variety of topics including IEPs, vitamins and therapies. I especially tried to get the parents more involved in fighting for their children's services. 'Here's the Governor's number. Call and tell him we need funding for classrooms, trained teachers and awareness. Here are some forms to fill out. Mail them to your senators and congressmen.'

Most of them did nothing. I found that most parents came to us only when they had problems. 'Can I come to your house and talk about my IEP? Can I come and learn PECS? My son's not doing it right.' I didn't mind helping, but I minded the fact that they wouldn't fight for their kids' rights.

By now, the IU had set up the autism classroom, but the parents didn't want to hear about its inadequacies. Nobody was concerned. 'You have a classroom of children with very special needs and I am telling you they're not doing it right. Aren't you concerned?'

'At least he has something.'

One day we got a call from a woman whose son was enrolled in the new IU autism class. It was hard for this boy to sit still and he would bang, bite and kick under the desk so hard that he bruised his shins. So the staff devised this great scheme to wrap him in ace bandages. They had his arms, wrists and legs wrapped up. 'So go ahead, kick all you want. You're not going to bruise yourself now.'

The boy fell asleep after a Discrete Trial session and they just left him there. But he was wrapped so tight that his circulation stopped, his hands turned white and he became very cold. That's when they called the mother to come and get her son. She then called my wife for a ride and they took him to the doctor.

I was flabbergasted. 'Tell them you're suing,' I insisted. If my kid was wrapped up and lost circulation I absolutely would not sit back! The school clearly did not know how to deal with this boy's disability. They were definitely not professionals. My wife with all her studies and experience would have known how to deal with him. She knew how to move on, how to redirect and how to use a time-out. She certainly wouldn't wrap him up in bandages!

I was so frustrated with the people in our group. They just were not interested in fighting for their children's needs and rights. FACT fizzled out, but the people continued to call us because we had the knowledge. Essentially, I became the area consultant.

Our advocacy work for Chris now extended to advocacy work for other children with autism. Our number was out there. So if you needed advice or somebody to sit with you at an IEP, we were the ones called. Jae made in-home visits where she set up preliminary programs for the families.

The new IU classroom didn't want to set up PECS, the Picture Exchange Communication System. But a lot of parents knew about our system and asked the IU, 'Jae Davis has this beautiful PECS program and her son is communicating. Can we have one?'

They'd answer, 'Well, you have to wait on that.' If they set up PECS in the classroom they would need to set up a continuation at home. Only that would require a lot of time and work to send somebody to each house. So parents came to us instead and asked for help in setting up their own PECS program. How could we refuse?

It took Jae days to help each family. First she'd visit the house and learn what the child liked. If there was a special cookie he liked, she'd draw that particular cookie with the word spelled out on it. Then she'd teach the child how to use it and give it to his mother when he wanted a cookie. Pictures were needed for all kinds of circumstances including things like 'my stomach hurts' or 'I have diarrhea.' Anything you could possibly imagine, Jae would make for them.

It was very time-consuming. All the necessary pictures had to be found or drawn, mounted and laminated. In fact, we went out and bought a laminating machine. Jae easily worked six hours a day on those systems for other people. We've recently bought a computer program called Boardmaker that helps cut some of the work time down by letting her adjust and print pictures out on the computer.

Word of our work kept spreading and more and more phone calls came in. News articles were published about us and people would call. 'Hi. I read about you and called the newspaper for your number. Can you help?' One woman called because her son lived in Italy and there was no information there. Could we send her something? Even the IU referred people to us! There were a couple of employees who believed in us and they would give our number to parents who were unhappy about services. We got all kinds of calls and questions. 'How do I continue therapy at home?'

'How do we get speech?'

'We're only getting therapy for nineteen hours a week. Aren't we supposed to get forty?'

'I need a dentist.'

'I need a neurologist.'

So we were working with all these people setting up programs and working with their children in our home. When Chris finished his six hour day another child would go upstairs for two more hours. Jae was both setting up programs and running them. When the families needed therapists we lent them our own. This even led to problems with some of the girls branching out and cutting down on Chris' time.

Jae was exhausted. She was up at six in the morning and went to bed at three in the morning every day. I'd find her on the computer at one AM saying, 'I have to get this done before I go to bed. I promised them a program *and* I have to do Chris' program.'

We found that the families were becoming very reliant on Jae to run their programs and she just couldn't do it all. So she told them, 'Look, you have to hire professional consultants from someplace like Rutgers. I can't take you through a complicated step-by-step program all year. I'm not a PhD and I don't have the time, but a consultant can take you through complicated steps all year round. It's the only way you can keep progressing and teaching.' Sadly, most were complacent with keeping things as they were and did not build on their programs unless Jae did it for them.

I'll never forget one parent who came over and watched Chris on the monitor for four hours doing his program. I gave her every piece of information we had, and at the end of the day I thought she was going to say, 'Thank you so much! I'm ready to begin.'

Instead she complained, 'I was more hoping of a place I could send him.' I hate to be critical, but a lot of parents out there are looking for that quick fix. It's too much for them to work with their child on their own so they'd rather find a place to put him. They're looking for a magic bullet.

I find men, especially, are fixers. A lot of them will say, 'There's something wrong with my son. How do you fix this?'

'Well, you can't fix this.'

'My wife will take care of meetings and school, and then when he comes home he'll play with me, right?'

'No. He'll probably go in the corner. He won't play ball and he won't run outside with you. And you're going to have to go to the meetings and learn therapy if you want to communicate with him.'

'I can't do that. I have to work and earn the money.'

'It's not going to work then.'

Of course, I've met a lot of great fathers too. I lay out everything for these families – all the steps. This is where you go for diagnosis, this is the IU unit and these resources are available. I tell them about the law, how to go to an IEP, what the timelines are, what an MDE is, what the guidelines are, and how to develop programs for their child. We give them a preliminary program at home so that they can communicate with their kid.

We made a huge parent packet with laws and telephone numbers. The Autism Society's packets are basically an introduction with little pamphlets describing autism. We tried to make a more individual packet highlighting local services and answering specific questions.

There's not always an involved local chapter of the Autism Society, and I think that's a big gap. When you call up for help you want immediate answers, not a general pamphlet on autism. 'My child is screaming in the kitchen for something to eat. Please help me. Where do I go for services right away? Where do I go for a diagnosis? Who's the best neurologist? My kid's teeth hurt. Do you know what dentist can help him? Where do I go? He isn't eating. Is that normal?' These are the type of questions that need answers. 'All these laws they're throwing at me. Can you explain them to me? Where do I call? Do you have a good lawyer?'

One particularly sad case we helped involved an eight-year-old boy originally adopted by a Mennonite family in Lancaster. The Mennonite family didn't want him anymore because he couldn't work the farm so they threw him back into the system until someone else adopted him. He had terrible problems. His language deteriorated to nothing but a few words and he started biting himself. He'd pick his arm and bite or he'd bite you.

Jae set up a PECS program for him at his home and worked with him in ours. She just loved this boy and did everything for him. He loved clocks so Jae made a clock PECS so he could ask for his.

I was watching on the monitor one day when miraculously he spoke! 'Granpa broke clock.'

'Joey, Grandpa broke clock?'

'I want new clock.'

'OK, I'll talk to Grandpa.' This kid had never spoken and now was talking to her! It turned out that his grandfather was trying to fix the clock for him, but that wasn't really the important matter. He talked! Another day he turned, looked at the camera, and said, 'Good job, Joey!' Unbelievable how with a little quality work this boy started to progress!

The boy was in an autistic support class run by the IU in conjunction with a public school district. He was a runner, a very common trait of autism, and once when they took him out for recreation he wandered off the grounds. They never even missed him! A neighbor happened to see him walking in the street a couple of miles away and went up to him. 'Hi, Joey, what are you doing here?' The man brought him back to school, but the administrators never called the mother to inform her. That night the neighbor called and asked about Joey. Of course the mother knew nothing, so he told her the story.

I was later asked by the mother to go to Joey's IEP and request what her son needed. Before I went I decided to visit the classroom for a couple hours. I came with twenty-five questions. Originally I called the head of the class and said I had some questions for her, but she said to fax them to her. 'No. I want you to answer them now. Is it because you won't know the answers?' She hung up. So I went to the classroom teacher and asked her the questions.

'What's an SD Prompt?'

She didn't know. 'What's your background?'

'I took a two week seminar at Rutgers,' she sobbed.

At the IEP meeting I asked how they could ignore the boy's biting and language degeneration. Then the speech teacher came in. 'I observed you the other day singing a song about the weather with the seven children sitting around not paying attention, hitting their heads, and stimming,' I said to her. 'How is that helping Joey? He's not speaking anymore.' She couldn't give an answer. 'You're the speech and language teacher. You have no one-on-one, no therapy, nothing. You're singing a song. This boy needs an in-home program and intensive speech and language.'

Then this one woman said to me, 'Are you asking for the Cadillac of education?' She had some important title and couldn't answer basic technical questions like how to redirect behaviour.

'I'm sorry. By the way, are you going to build a fence? How dare you let this child run off?'

And the teacher jumped in, 'But it was only two times.' Now she revealed there was another time! The head of the district was sitting there in disbelief.

The woman with the Cadillac of education remark said to me, 'Well we have to find out whose budget this is. Is it ours or is it IU?'

I came so close to cursing at her. I said, 'You know what? I think I need to call some people about you. You disgust me.'

And another woman who's a psychiatrist stood up and applauded. 'Joey needs help and we aren't giving it to him. And I'm here to tell you that this gentleman is right!'

It was a very dramatic meeting.

After the meeting I went through the Governor's office and filed a notice of non-compliance. But the head of special ed offered Joey's family a full-time aide if they dropped the complaint, and they agreed. They even dropped the request for an in-home program. Following this agreement the family called me and said they no longer needed our help. I guess it was easier for them to keep in the system with an aide than to give the boy an in-home program. But it saddens me to think of this child who showed potential, now once again degenerating into oblivion.

Fortunately, we have advocated far more successfully for many others. We have helped twenty to thirty different families a year, and are still doing that. My referrals keep coming from more and more sources.

I became an area rep for the Pennsylvania Autism Society of America and anytime someone doesn't have a local chapter they call me. I'm also on the board of the Pennsylvania Autism Society. I'm a mentor for the Parent to Parent Network. The group had no one to represent autism before they asked me to volunteer. Now parents can call Parent to Parent and say, 'Hi. I live in the Lancaster area. My son has autism and I just want to talk to somebody,' and they'll give you my name. The Special Kids Network has my number. Even the Philadelphia Law Center has my number. Originally I went to them for free legal advice, but later they asked me to write an article giving my own advice to parents. The Center can only tell you the law, not other types of advice. So now when parents call to ask how to handle their IEP, the center gives out the article along with my phone number.

A lot of different people call me and I don't even know where they get my number. Some hear me on the radio talking about upcoming benefits for Chris. A nurse once came to a benefit and told me, 'I was driving my car and heard what you did on the radio station. I came to give you money.'

I've even given advice on the Internet. One woman needed help with setting up a trust. Later she emailed me, 'Thank you so much. We were just about to do everything wrong with our money. How come you're so knowledgeable about this?' It was really nice.

We once had a New York family call us a while back when they were coming to visit Dutch Wonderland, a Lancaster area theme park. They had a son with autism and wanted to know if Dutch Wonderland had wristbands to allow you to go to the front of the lines because their son was unable to wait. So I called Dutch Wonderland.

'Listen, my son has autism.'

'We don't know much about it. But sure, tell us about it,' the official said.

'I have a family visiting from New York. And you have to understand that children with autism can't stand on line because they don't have the patience.'

He said, 'Sure, we can give out wristbands for that.'

The next year when we went to Hershey Park I did the same thing. I brought the park authorities literature and explained the problems associated with the disorder. 'This is so wonderful. We knew nothing about autism,' said the Hershey management. Just like Dutch Wonderland, they now give out special bands for kids with autism and other disabilities. What a relief that was for us! Chris would be too nervous standing on long lines and it would have ruined the day for everybody. But thanks to these wristbands, kids like him can now have fun at an amusement park.

Most recently, a newly relocated family came over and watched Chris. My wife prepared a huge packet of everything from therapy to IEPs to law to a preliminary PECS program. We taught them how to install and use the PECS, went over their IEP, and discussed their son and his other sibling. We went over options, where to go, doctors, dentists, school. They sat for a half a day while we served them coffee and prepared them for their IEP. That to me was a day of support. It wasn't useless chatter.

A few days later I had a message on my answering machine. It was the father. 'I'd just like to say that we had a successful IEP, and if it wasn't for you we couldn't have done it. Anything I can do for you, let me know.' It was great.

Everything we do for these families is strictly volunteer. Preparing the packets, teaching, we've never ever taken money for anything. Lots of people offer us money, but it just doesn't seem right to take it. I always feel it's good karma to help someone without profiting. When we advocated for Joey, we spent a great deal of time and expense. I filed a lack of compliance motion with the Governor's office and Jae worked with the boy at our home and set up a whole therapy room in his house. She spent about five hundred dollars in materials, but only gave them a bill for two hundred. 'I just need a little money back,' she said, and wouldn't tell them what it really cost.

Jae worked very hard with another woman and her son for a good couple of years. She set up programs for her and even gave the woman a table, chair and toys. Once again, we never charged a cent.

Another call I got was from a woman who said, 'Mr. Davis, I read about you. I'm a stupid woman and I don't know how to do this. I need your help.' She was a Mennonite who had adopted four kids and had four kids of her own, one with autism. She came to our home and we went over everything. He was a tough case. I also went to two of her IEPs, and have answered many questions from time to time. This woman would always offer me money, but I wouldn't take it. It was just gratifying to help such an appreciative family.

Sometimes parents who have heard of us will say Jae and I are the ones who got it all started in our area. You can't believe what that does for me. We fought and fought and fought. And when they come to us and say, 'We just enrolled him in this program,' it is so rewarding to know that's the program we started. It really is. I cannot believe that we actually did all this.

Our lives became overextended in every way possible with all our advocacy work. Finances were a mess. The house was a mess. We had no time to even sleep. Chris' program was six to eight hours a day and required many more hours of preparation and paper-work. We had constant observers in the house, especially for workshops. And on top of it all, we had become extremely involved in community work. Huge amounts of time and money went to helping individuals, fighting the government for services, going to conferences, and working for various special needs organizations.

People have told us that we should start earning a living doing our advocacy work. Life is now at the point where we spend so much time and money helping others that I really may have no choice but to consider charging for services. I have no regrets for doing what I've done, though. I hope one day I'll be able to look at these kids and say all the work paid off. To know a child got help because of us when he was an infant and is now able to talk at age four, is very gratifying to me.

Promoting autism awareness to pretty much everyone he comes across is the most important thing Bill does outside of the home. He's just such a generous guy that he'll always take time to explain it. And he never makes you feel like your question is stupid.

One of my parent's friends has a three-year-old boy recently diagnosed with autism and Bill was so open to having them call him. Anyone who wants to know anything they invite into their home. They tell them to watch sessions with Chris and sit down for hours giving all the information that they have - which is a lot. They gladly put people in contact with help. The amount of people they have coming in and out of their home is enough to give me a headache! They're very open.

If you don't happen to come in contact with someone who has autism, where would you hear about it? Why would you know about it? I know with my parents' friends when they got the diagnosis it was, 'OK, now we have it on paper. We kind of know what it is from the little textbook definition, but where do we go from here?' It's a shock. What do you do? There are education, medical and social issues to worry about. Should we put him in a home? Should we put him in a school? There are so many questions. To have someone like Bill who's been through it and is so willing to share all the information is definitely a big asset for anyone touched by autism.

Jenny Nielsen, therapist

Bill's contribution to the community has been his autism awareness push. He's been on Channel 8 Live At Noon at least twice. He's done his own fund-raisers locally and for Kennedy Krieger. One was at the American Theater. Frankly, not all parents spend much time on public awareness. They rely on the organizations to do it through commercials. Bill really puts in a lot of time to solicit awareness when most parents are not willing or able to do that.

We always appreciate anything that helps the public understand autism. As a parent of a child with autism it can get real embarrassing and awkward when you're in public, especially if your child is an older teenager, and you have to treat him like a two- or three-year-old. If people aren't aware of the disorder your actions can be misunderstood. Some parents have actually had the police call them because someone thought they were abusing their kids. For instance, a parent might hold their kid's hand in public, but it looks a little awkward for me to hold a sixteen-year-old's hand to cross the street. Sometimes my teenage son who has autism will break down and cry and roll around the floor like a two-year-old. Some kids with autism run away and knock people down. So other parents in the grocery store look at you as if to say, 'Well, if you were any kind of a parent, you wouldn't let your kid do that.' Well, if he were a normal kid you're right, but he doesn't understand. He doesn't understand language. These kids' disabilities are communicative, behavioral and academic. It's very tough if you're a parent of a child with autism. So autism awareness is important. And Bill does a great job.

Pat Houston, President,
Autism Society of Pennsylvania

4

Telling the World

'Here's what I think of you. You're elitists. How dare you all sit here at this lavish buffet and tell each other what a great job you're doing while I don't have services I need! Maybe I won't eat and you can give that money to my son's classroom. What are you people doing? You have dinners and pat each other on the back, and here I sit trying to get speech therapy that you won't give me. You don't have the vaguest idea how to budget properly. You're very happy figuring out a long-range budget for ten years, but with autism the need is immediate, early intervention. I don't need you to help my son when he's eleven. I need you to help him now! When I say my four-year-old needs fifty thousand dollars, you look at me like I'm crazy and offer me ten thousand instead. No. Give me forty now. In three years I won't need forty because his needs will diminish if you give him proper early intervention. If you don't give it to me now you're sure to spend two hundred thousand a year on institutions later!'

Needless to say my tirade did not make me a big hit at this meeting of the LICC, Local Interagency Coordinating Council.

'According to you, Mr. Davis, we do nothing right! Is that it?!'

I smiled. 'You're close.'

The meeting's purpose was to get together all the agencies in our local area that deal with disabilities and develop ideas to send to the state council. Agencies like Schrieber, MHMR (Mental Health and Mental Retardation), IU 13 and S. June Smith Center were all represented. Not too many parents came to the meeting because they never heard about it. But somehow I was invited – an invitation I'm sure they regretted.

I was sitting there listening to each agency representative stand up, report on budget and brag about what they were doing with the money. 'We spent five million dollars on wheelchairs last year.' I got up and boy, did I go at them. They had nothing to brag about. Any parent of a child with autism could tell them how inadequate their services were. The guy from MHMR walked out after hearing me.

Unbelievably, after all this they asked me to run for LICC president. They needed a parent to co-chair with a professional. I declined their nomination, went to a couple more meetings and dropped out.

I decided I could be more effective other ways. I soon found my way into politics. When Congressman James Greenwood of Bucks County, Pennsylvania held a big press conference announcing his Advancement in Pediatric Autism Research Act it angered me. 'Oh, good,' I said. 'Here I am having so much trouble getting my son's needs met and this guy acts like a hero. He's talking about the need for awareness, and his own state has no services. Seems to me *he's* the one who needs awareness.'

I called his office in Washington and spoke to a woman who later turned out to be a good friend. 'Can I just tell you something? I'm here in Lancaster struggling to get services for my son. Screw Congressman Greenwood because he stands there and yells about awareness. What's he doing for me?'

'Mr. Davis, I understand. What can Congressman Greenwood do?'

'What can he do? Tell him to come and visit me and I will tell him everything I've been through.'

His visit to my home made front page news. Radio announcements were made. 'Congressman Greenwood to visit family and learn about autism.' I couldn't believe a congressman was actually coming to my home to visit! He was going to sit in on a Discrete Trial session so I had parents, a couple other kids, a therapist and Dr. Landa attend the meeting.

Congressman Greenwood turned out to be a really good guy who actually listened to us. First I spoke for about an hour telling him what we've been through. Then Dr. Landa, Kennedy Krieger's Center for Autism director, spoke very clinically about research. He next went upstairs and saw a session with Chris while Jae explained. Later the Congressman talked about the state of services, and explained his bill and how it would help. He gave us a copy of the bill, went back to Bucks County, and I decided to lend my support. Here was a man who actually cared enough to draft legislation that would appropriate more funds for autism research.

A group based in California called CAN, Cure Autism Now, was also a big supporter of Greenwood's bill. They got wind that I worked with him and called me up. 'We need cosponsors to support this bill. Would you be willing to lobby the people in Pennsylvania?'

So began my career as a lobbyist. I had a list of all the Pennsylvania representatives and started lobbying each one of them to cosponsor Greenwood's bill. If they tried to ignore me, I would not give up until they listened. I guess when they heard my passion and sincerity they gave me attention.

I ended up getting about ten representatives to support Greenwood's bill. Senator Rick Santorum was my biggest triumph because he was known as a very conservative tight-fisted Republican. When all these senators and congressmen started calling me to say they were cosponsoring the bill, I thought, wow, you can do anything. You really can! Next I would like the opportunity to speak before Congress myself. I think I deserve that.

My motivation was now high and we crazily decided to run a Christmas toy drive as our next project. We called it Toys for Special Tots. Here we were helping families, getting involved politically, and running Chris' in-home program and we decided to collect toys for kids with special needs! A unique aspect of the drive was the additional collection of incomplete toy and block sets for use in Discrete Trial programs. If somebody said, 'I have a game, but it's not complete,' we would say, 'That's fine. We'll take the chips and use them for color programs.' It was perfect!

We put drop boxes in about five places – Education Station Toy Store, a couple of restaurants, a bar and F&M College. There was one news article and no advertisements. Unbelievably, we got a call from the drop-off points every day! 'It's overloaded. Come pick it up.' We collected thousands of toys! Mothers walking in the toy store with their healthy kids were saying, 'You know what? Let's buy a little something for these kids who aren't as lucky as you.'

The box was spilling over everyday. My wife, an eternal perfectionist, wouldn't just take the toys as they were, though. She cleaned every one, made them look good, and divided them into groups. It took us twelve hours to deliver boxes piled high with toys. We borrowed a pick-up truck from a neighbor and went to S. June Smith, MHMR, Schrieber Pediatrics and the IU 13 and gave each agency about five huge boxes. I was exhausted.

'Next year we need some help,' Jae and I agreed. We were already planning next year's drive. The therapists helped us the following year and this time we gave a lot of toys to Kennedy Krieger.

We were too successful! The drives ended up being too much for us. I would have had to gather twenty-five more volunteers to continue so we had to stop any future Christmas toy drives.

By now I was gaining more and more notoriety. I did television appearances and was featured in numerous news articles. It didn't take long before I was asked to serve on the board of the Pennsylvania Autism Society by the president, Pat Houston, who appeared on a TV news show with me. He invited me to a meeting and announced when I arrived, 'I'd like to introduce you to the newest member of the board.' That was the first I had heard of it too, but I happily accepted the position. All the board members already knew who I was through my advocacy work and fights with the IU to get an autism class. It was very gratifying to learn that they all knew and appreciated my work! Before long I became a rep-at-large for the Society. Now anyone who didn't have a local chapter would call me for information or help.

Speaking my mind and fighting for autism services made me lots of friends, but it also made me enemies. When we first started our program I was desperate to find replacements for my F&M therapists who left for summer vacation. So I started calling different agencies for direction. They were all so indifferent about helping. When I called Schrieber I was told, 'Do you think we're an employment agency?'

That was it! Every time I called this place they brushed me aside. 'You know, I called you a couple years ago when my son was diagnosed with autism and you told me you didn't know where I should go for help. Then you gave me some worthless telephone numbers to call. What you really did was give me the runaround then and that's what you're doing now! Thanks very much.' I hung up the phone.

What really angered me was that they couldn't be bothered to even try and help. If you're in the human services business you don't say 'I don't know.' You say, 'Look, I don't know, but let me make some calls and get back to you. I have a whole network of people who might be able to help.' Nobody would do that for me.

Not being satisfied, I called the organization's administrative office. 'I'd like to speak to the man in charge.' It so happened that it was Bill Jefferson's first day as president. He got on the phone and I told him the story. Shocked, he asked, 'May I use this story? I'm having my first meeting today.' Finally, a person with sense!

Following my conversation with Bill Jefferson, he nominated me for a program at Temple University's Center for Disabilities. Every year they pick twelve parents of children with disabilities in Pennsylvania to take their Parents in Partnership course. It took place in Harrisburg two or three times a month for eight, nine hours a day and was meant for the participants to bring back knowledge and information to the special needs community. The course covered the history of disabilities, how to go to a board meeting, how to advocate, and institutions. Experts, advocates and people with disabilities all guest-lectured.

I found it pretty interesting even though I was already doing a lot of what they taught. After a while, however, the two instructors really began to dislike me. Their philosophy to make friends with agency administrators was in exact contradiction to mine.

My whole philosophy is that this is my child, I know what's right for him, and I'm not playing games with you. I don't want to learn how to go to a board meeting and be a nice guy and I don't want to make friends with the advocate. I am there only to get the services my child deserves.

Needless to say they didn't appreciate my philosophy. They were there to teach these people how to interact and I kept interrupting to disagree. 'Excuse me, but why do you say that's what I must do? This is my child and I'm fighting for his rights. Why do I have to compromise?'

'Well, you have to learn to get along.'

'No I don't.' They really were annoyed with me.

I may not have agreed with everything they taught at the Temple University course, but I did follow through with my commitment to bring awareness to the community and advocate for children with special needs. I began conducting training sessions for ambulance, fire and police personnel and speaking to chapters of the Autism Society, HACC (Harrisburg Area Community College), Franklin and Marshall College, and Penn State.

My college audience is mainly students of psychology, special ed and medicine, but anyone can attend. The talks cover Chris' history, our in-home program, characteristics of autism, communication difficulties, and what you can do when you encounter a child with autism. The students are always a great audience. They just jump with questions. Most of them don't get a lot of information on autism so when they get somebody to speak it's very exciting to them. If they're really interested I let them come over to the house and watch a session.

All kinds of groups have asked me to speak about autism. They often get my name after reading news articles about me. A church group that had one autistic child in their after school day care even asked me to speak to the teachers.

I was once invited to a conference on autism put together by the IU and CISC, the Central Instructional Support Center of Pennsylvania, normally in charge of disseminating information on autism and teaching IU teachers. This particular day kept me going for a long time. During the conference, parents would get up and voice complaints like, 'My son's not speaking and he's not getting any services.' But then they would come up to me during lunch and say, 'Are you Bill Davis? Thank you. We heard about you. My son's in a class because of you.' It was wonderful to know that at least *I* was doing something to help others, even if the agencies weren't.

But I wasn't the only activist in the family trying to bring autism awareness to the community. Jessica felt it was important too. She's written papers about autism and has me talk to the students at her school each year. When she began listening to rock and roll radio and heard the morning show with all the banter she suggested, 'Dad, they should talk about Chris.'

'Let's go down and meet them,' I said. So we went down to the radio station one morning and we brought a flower. 'Hi! Bill Davis. I'm here with my daughter. She wants to say hello to Lauren, the DJ, and give her this flower.'

When Lauren came down during the break to say hello I introduced ourselves. 'I'm going to be very honest with you. My daughter would like to let the world know about autism and her brother and what we're doing. Here's some information for you.'

The woman said she'd read it over the weekend and get back to us, but she never did. I tried calling her a couple times, but she never answered my calls. I was really annoyed that she fluffed off my daughter like that. Then Jesse started listening to Pat Kain, the evening DJ. Still annoyed, I decided to call him. 'Listen, let me tell you a story about what your studio did to me,' and I started telling him.

'Gee, that's horrible. Would you like to send me material and come on the show?'

'OK.'

'When do you want to come on?'

'I don't know.'

'What about next Monday at eight o'clock?'

'OK. Can I bring my daughter?'

'Absolutely.' Now this was a big deal! Pat Kain! All the girls loved him.

Jesse and I walked into the studio that Monday night with all kinds of t-shirts and things. Pat introduced himself and said, 'To me you sound like an intelligent guy. I read everything you sent me. Let's get on the air and talk.' So they put headphones on me and we talked for an hour. He didn't play any music! This was a rock station, yet people were listening to me talk! Pat became a good family friend after that, and has helped me greatly with my advocacy work.

Funny, but my money woes have also played a big part in my quest to promote community awareness of autism. Providing a child with autism with all the help he needs is extremely expensive and was a huge financial burden for us. We were literally starving. Whatever I made at work that night was exactly what we had. We were fighting all the time for money. I was dying. I just didn't know which way to turn. Then my bar customers got together and decided to sponsor a day for collecting funds for Chris. It was very small and consisted basically of me behind a bar and a big jar. They actually collected about five, six hundred dollars and said to me afterwards, 'If we had planned this right we could have made a lot of money. How about you do it again?' Thus, my career as a benefit organizer began.

I began by working on an auction and asked all the beer and liquor salesmen for merchandise. They gave me mirrors, neons, shirts and glasses. Then I called teams like the Philadelphia Eagles and Flyers who sent me footballs and signed baseballs. A local hairdresser said she'd shave some guy's head so I could collect two hundred dollars.

Pat Kain put me on the radio to announce the benefit. 'Come to our home. We'll be out back. We have free food and some t-shirts to give you. The police will be there. Katie True, our state rep will be there. Senator Arlen Specter's office is represented. Come by for a lovely summer afternoon and learn about autism.'

It was held at our home and Chris was outside jumping on a trampoline while we barbecued. We gave out pamphlets from CAN, Rutgers, the Autism Society of America and Kennedy Krieger. Fact sheets were passed out and people came by to ask us questions. That benefit grew into many more successful benefits. In fact, we started doing two, three a year turning them into combination Benefit/Awareness Days. They were huge.

By the time we ran our third benefit at Hall's Café, the newspaper ran an article and we put out some flyers. Pat Kain now had a tradition of putting me on the radio to talk about the benefits and then afterwards he would blast it with community events announcements. All day long you would hear, 'Autism event with Pat Kane on Saturday. Come rally round.' It was such a big event that you couldn't get in the place! We had about five hundred people. News people were even there.

Businesses donated items for us to sell, but we really tried not to bang everybody out for money. There was no entrance fee and food was free. Money from the open bar went to the restaurant. Each event earned anywhere from a couple hundred to three, four thousand dollars. And that was wonderful! Every penny went right to Chris' therapy and education.

But the main idea of the day was awareness. Last year we had two grandparents come, 'We heard this on the radio and came because we think our grandchild has autism.' One parent came with her little boy who had autism and he played with Jesse all day long. The events are really nice with a very local flavor. We have representatives from the police and fire departments, local folksingers, entertainers, radio personalities and artists. We've even had the mayor of Lancaster. These events, unfortunately, have become a full-time job to organize, and I'm uncomfortable about accepting money like that. So we're probably going to stop them. They definitely served their purpose, though.

That doesn't mean my career running other benefits has stopped. I've already done a few for Achievements at Kennedy Krieger. They include the toy drive, a benefit at the American Music Theater in Lancaster and a beautiful silent auction at Burkhart's Furniture, a fine furniture store in Lancaster.

I was recently approached by a guy sitting at the bar having a martini with his wife and child while waiting for a table. 'Aren't you the guy I read about in the paper? How's your son? We read that you do benefits and I'd love to do something with you. How about a polo match? I play polo and my club's raised good money doing benefits. Can we do we one for you?'

'Sure! Let's do it for Kennedy Krieger.' So he is now planning this benefit. I hope to do that and another American Music Theater benefit for Kennedy in the near future.

Funny how bartending turned out to be such a huge help over the years! Not only has it allowed me to get quick cash and work at night, it's helped me network. I've met people from every walk of life who have helped us out in one way or another. Customers have attended our Autism Benefits and Awareness Days. When college girls from F&M came in I'd ask them their major. If it was special ed or psychology I'd tell them about our internship program and send them to meet with my wife if they were interested. And of course, bartending has allowed me the flexibility to take days off so I could devote myself to advocacy work. If you're the head of IBM you can't take days off, but if you're a bartender you can say. 'Lisa's taking my shift. I'm going to Baltimore for a few days.'

I have one other important bit of advocacy work I'm now involved in. A Baltimore group called Pathfinders For Autism just incorporated with the purpose of dedicating itself to issues with autism. It's a small group of very influential people including BJ Surhoff from the Orioles, marketing executives, bankers and lawyers. Most of them are also parents of children with autism. Dr. Landa is also on the board and I'm sure she's responsible for their invitation to have me join.

Pathfinders' ultimate goal is to build a cutting edge center for autism. It would incorporate clinical services, genetic research, a school and safe harbors for older people with autism. Obviously that's not going to happen overnight, so first its goal is to get known and seek funding. I have a lot of faith in the group's future.

Everything takes time and everything takes work. But I've learned that even the smallest action can lead to positive results. I will never regret one day of advocacy work I've done, either in politics or for private families. I will never regret pushing for the special autism class run by the IU or running autism training sessions for emergency workers. I know that I have made a difference in the lives of many children and hope to continue making even more of a difference in the future.

Bringing autism awareness to the world has become my life's direction. It is how I nourish myself. If I could train educators, pediatricians and emergency personnel, speak at seminars and spend time helping families and kids disabled by autism, I would be the happiest guy in the whole world. I'd like to turn around twenty years from now and say, 'I've trained nine million policemen and spoken to countless groups.' That would be my life's work. That would make me happy.

Driving in the car one day, Jessica said to me out of the blue, 'If Chris is cured tomorrow, don't stop fighting for these kids.' Every time I feel tired I think of Jessica's comment and it spurs me on. I've never really considered stopping advocacy work, but sometimes people get me so frustrated and I think that maybe I should just focus on my own son. But then I help a family who soaks up everything we tell them, and I think of all the hurdles they would have jumped without us. What a great feeling! And occasionally I get that person who says, 'You're the guy who started the program that my son's in now. Thank you so much!' That really does it for me. It's all the reward I'll ever need.

The first time I met Bill was the first time he came in for an interview almost three-and-a-half years ago. My impression was somebody very dedicated to educating people about autism. But more importantly, he was dedicated to taking care of his child. His family is the most important thing to him. He seems to spend every waking hour working for them, supporting them, and trying to better their lives. It was evident after meeting him for the first time that his family is first, and then the cause of autism is his next biggest priority.

I don't do a lot of interviews on my show. It's mostly music and funny stuff. I expect people to change the station if they hear a lot of chat. So it was a big surprise when I interviewed Bill about autism that people were actually listening and paying attention. Unless I say something about Backstreet Boys, I don't get a lot of phone calls about much. So to get the number that I did about Bill really surprised me.

After the interview people called asking whatever happened to that guy? How's his kid doing? What's going on with them? So we've followed up every six months to a year because there are people genuinely concerned about how he's doing and interested in how Christopher's doing.

What Bill does and how he does it is great. He has a knack for getting air-time and press about autism. Being on the radio, being on television, doing the benefits, all are making a difference, especially in this area of Pennsylvania.

Just about the only thing I knew about autism was from the movie, Rain Man, but Bill has done a fabulous job educating me and others about the disorder. I think he's really the only person doing it. I've never heard of anyone else in the area championing autism and it never crossed my mind to actually get involved with it until he called the radio station. We have lots of representatives for multiple sclerosis, cerebral palsy, and Toys for Tots. So you hear plenty about all of those. If he wasn't speaking out about autism, I think there'd be a big void.

Pat Kain, WLAN-FM DJ Lancaster, Pennsylvania

Bill's wonderful at bringing about public awareness of autism. It's good that he does because I think a lot of people don't know about it. They think that people with autism are freaks and scary and should be institutionalized. Bill going out there and talking lets people know that these are human beings with feelings too. They have needs, wants, desires, likes and dislikes. They're just like everybody else except that they have a learning disability. By bringing awareness to the community the average person will meet somebody with autism and not be taken aback and frightened by it.

Melissa Bennett, therapist

5

The Mainstreaming Myth

Our in-home program for Chris was working out wonderfully. His development was miraculous. But we felt he was missing out socially and decided we would try to find an outside kindergarten class for him to attend in addition to what we were doing at home.

When we began looking my philosophy was that mainstreaming was the way to go. My son was a US citizen born in Lancaster and he deserved to go to the same school his sister and all the other neighborhood children attended. That was my belief and I was not going to lie down without a fight. I fought for a preschool class dedicated to children with autism and got it. And I would fight for a kindergarten class with appropriate education as well.

Everywhere I went people applauded my efforts. I was invited to conferences, covered in the media and contacted by other parents. Inclusion was a word I believed in until, that is, I learned too much.

When Chris turned five he was eligible for the public school system's kindergarten, but disabled children are allowed to wait one more year and that's what we chose to do. We didn't feel he was quite ready and we wanted time to research the program thoroughly. That same year officials from our school district approached me and said, 'Can we sit in on your IEP with the IU because we want to be prepared when your son comes to school?' I had the reputation of being the one who would sue you in a minute and yell at you, and they had obviously read a little bit about us and were frightened. Letters I wrote to the paper almost everyday had big headlines – 'Pennsylvania doesn't meet the needs of autistic children' or 'School fails at special needs education.'

In order to make a responsible decision about whether or not to send my son to the public school's autism-support kindergarten class, I naturally wanted to visit it. To my dismay I found out that the program was run by my nemesis, the IU!

The public school system, because it knew nothing about autism, farmed out a contract with the IU. My school district was not under the auspices of the IU, but in actuality it was saying, 'The IU has experience. We don't. They'll run it.'

So I went to visit these kindergarten classes and I was shocked. They were horrible! There were kids with all forms of the disorder. That scared me because children with autism are very imitative, and you can have a child who's normally not self-injurious come home and start hitting himself in the head because he learned from another child in his class.

The class was unbelievable. The teachers essentially babysat these children, hoping to God they could get through the day. They had these kids with terrible speech and language problems, all types of motor skills that are lacking, and who do they get to come in to teach language? A singsong voice teacher who says, 'Now we're going to sing a song about the day... Clouds are forming everyday...' And the kids were just sitting there shaking their heads and self-stimming.

I went up to her. 'This is how you teach language? You're like a folk singer. What are you doing? When did you ever teach kids with autism?'

'Well, Sir, I...' And she was all defensive. 'I've been doing it this way for thirty years and I will continue to do it this way.'

'Have they spoken?'

'No.'

So that's what I was confronted with. The kids were just sitting there and not learning anything.

But I really wanted to do this right, so I invited the woman who was going to be Chris' kindergarten teacher to come to my home and meet with him and see my program. She was a very nice lady, but really had no expertise in autism. I asked her a few basic questions. 'If he does this, how would you respond? Would you redirect with a prompt?'

She started crying! Why? Because she couldn't answer me. And she said, 'I really try.'

'I believe you try and I believe you're a nice woman and I think you have a good heart, but I don't want you teaching my kid.'

I was really in a fighting mode after observing that special ed kindergarten class for autism, and met numerous times with the district's special ed coordinator. But all I got were lies and frustration. It was an unending fight. All the specifics I felt were necessary for a successful autism kindergarten program were being ignored.

I fought for therapists. They said they only hire aides. 'I don't want aides,' I responded. 'An aide? You're talking about a five dollar an hour worker or volunteer with no knowledge! I want skilled therapists to be with my son during the day to help him. It's the only way he'll survive.' Then they argued with me that they would train them. But the word aide to me meant somebody who sits with you and helps you go to the bathroom. My son needed a therapist, somebody skilled in the world of autism and able to communicate with him.

I got tired of fighting and came to the conclusion that the public education system was not ready. Why was I fighting? Fighting for what – more programming, getting kids with autism into public schools, changing the public education system's attitude? Wonderful goals, but I clearly was not going to win my fight anytime soon.

'What am I really doing?' I thought. 'Taking a child who has no language, very little communication with strangers, sticking him in a classroom with twenty-six kids with all kinds of things going on, and asking him to survive. Why?'

Summer rolled around and we put Chris in the Kennedy Krieger Achievements summer program. It was really wonderful. So now we had a choice. We could enroll Chris at Kennedy Krieger's kindergarten and pay thirteen thousand dollars or send him to our local public school program and stick to my belief in inclusion.

I decided to give it one more stab at my summer IEP and fight for my son's right for free appropriate public education. I even retained a lawyer. But it was to no avail. We just kept battling back and forth. They were arguing budget and policy and nobody was interested in what was good for Chris and how he learned.

I found myself standing up and pronouncing, 'OK. Bye-bye.' They all looked at me. 'That's it. I give up. This is not an argument about therapy or theory or policy. This is you sitting there not understanding a word I'm saying. You have no idea what my son needs, and I'm tired of arguing with you.'

'In lieu of FAPE, Free Appropriate Public Education, I'm sending my son to the Kennedy Krieger Institute Center for Autism and Related Disorders and I will pay for it out of my pocket. From your own conclusion you agree that my son still needs an in-home program as well as school. So I am asking for continued funding of my in-home program, which will now be less since he'll be going to Kennedy Krieger, and I will continue his speech and language that is already covered under insurance. I don't want anything more from you. Goodbye. All of you go out and have a drink. You're rid of me.' And they all were dumbstruck. 'Goodbye.'

Parents who sit back once their special needs child is attending public school are making a mistake. You cannot rely on a substandard public education system to provide a beautiful education for your child who needs a lot more than a 'normal' student. Parents must be one hundred per cent involved or it's not going to work. The onus is on them to get the proper education for their children. I have had so many meetings with my daughter's teachers and I know what homework she has and I know what's going on. At least I could do that for my son.

I used to walk Jessica to school and there would always be a group of special needs kids lined up outside waiting to walk to their class. It was a life skills class. Life skills teaches kids activities like going to the bathroom themselves and combing their hair. The children had all kinds of disorders, including seizure disorders, but they were all just thrown in together. I would always talk to the kids in this class and somehow I met one particular little boy. The little guy began to wait for me to walk him in, and it really saddened me to think that this had become the biggest part of his day.

One morning I watched a teacher pull this boy, throw him up against the wall, and say, 'If you don't walk on line, you're not going outside, do you hear me?' I immediately reported her, but the reality was that she was representative of the typical attitude. 'This child is an animal. He serves no purpose. He's a burden to me.' Why did she get in the field? The system stinks.

We're supposed to take care of these guys. This is what a neighborhood is for, parents are for, what a school system is supposed to be all about. All these special disability rights and laws were originally put into place to protect children's rights. And parents must make sure they're being enforced.

You don't know what they're doing in school during the day unless you're there. That's always been a pet peeve of mine. Don't drop your disabled kid off and hope for the best. Visit three times a week. Get reports every week. Have conferences every week. You can't allow these children to fend for themselves.

I've seen horrible things in classrooms; kids being pushed around and disciplined heavily. 'SIT DOWN! No, Sit down. Now you sit there!' So if your kid is in the corner spinning and he's not listening, instead of trying to work it out and get his attention or redirect him, the instructor has this stern attitude. It's as if your child doesn't matter, isn't human. I've reported a lot of teachers and done compliance reports with the governor's office. It's a shame. It's the scariest thing to think how your child could be mistreated.

A news article I recently read said that three autistic children in New York got on the bus to school. They were ages three-and-a-half, four and five. The only others on the bus were an aide and a new bus driver. The driver couldn't find the way to school, and the school radioed him to stop and tell them where he was so they could come and get him. But he refused and drove these kids from eight-thirty in the morning till four-thirty in the afternoon. The school never called the parents and never went after the bus driver. So they had three kids missing for almost ten hours!

These kids had no language to communicate that they were hungry or needed a bathroom. They were soiled, wet and hungry. So when the bus driver dropped them back home at four-thirty they couldn't tell their parents what happened. They couldn't tell the bus driver I peed in my pants. They couldn't say we're hungry. Can you imagine? 'I'm wet. I know I'm wet. But there's no way I can tell anybody. I don't even know what to do.' What a horrible thing! That's what can happen when you throw your kid in the system.

When I sent Chris to the IU's preschool class I didn't see a lot of signing work with the deaf children. I didn't see a lot of anything for any of the kids. And I believe that was typical of a lot of special education.

A lawyer once told me that special education can be very easy for teachers because they simply go in and spend the time. They have an excuse. 'There's not much I can teach these guys, anyway.' I witnessed the attitude in Chris' class. 'We're going to make Santa Clauses today. It's Christmas. Here. Take this cotton. Put it over here. Take the glue. Here. You made a Santa Claus. I'm sending it home.' Or it was, 'We're all going to sit and sing.' And the kids were not brought in to participate and were looking all over the place.

The real work, the meat and potatoes, especially with autism, is hard. It is laborious. It is intense. And it is a lot of hours. The system is not prepared to do that.

Children with autism can learn if you teach them the right way. They just have to be introduced to things slowly. Their conceptualization is different than the norm. Our system is very willing to set up special reading classes for kids who are slow, but it doesn't recognize the fact that kids with autism are slow too. They're different in how they learn, but they can be reached if time, effort, and training are invested.

Most special needs kids are screwed. If parents don't have the money or the backing, they can't get the proper programs for their kids. A lot of it is money. I've even had parents of children with other disabilities angry about the money we spend. They see that kids with autism get a lot of money when the programs are done right and feel it is unfair. 'How come? How come you have an in-home program and it cost twenty-five grand a year and my kid is going to this little classroom?'

The argument from the education bureaucrats often is that they only have one or two autistic children in their district. So I say to them, 'If you had one kid in a wheelchair, would you not build a ramp for him? Would you say, "We only have one so let him crawl through a window?" Or if you only have one deaf child, you don't teach him how to sign? You have to remember that just because my son is the only one with autism it doesn't mean he doesn't deserve an appropriate education.'

There are a lot of people out there who say, 'My son will not be segregated. He will be included. I want him mainstreamed; I believe in inclusion.' But if you put your child in a class with twenty-five kids and he sits in the corner, what have you accomplished? Who's it for, him or you?

I have come full circle on this. I believe public education is not ready to successfully take on this job of inclusion. I don't know if they'll ever be ready. So why should I expose my son to a classroom where he'll be lost, possibly ridiculed, and will learn nothing? If he needs a special classroom or a special school to come alive, that's fine.

At one point we thought we would move from Pennsylvania and I called Dr. William Penn, head of special education in the state. 'I want an exit interview. Your state has failed me and I want to tell you about it.' So we drove up to Harrisburg and I told him all we had been through.

He responded, 'There are countless numbers of IU units in Pennsylvania and we recently started a unit for autism. How fast would you like me to get things developed? We're doing the best we can.'

'You're so full of it. Tell that to my son. Tell him you don't have the time. Tell him when he's fifteen and he can't speak and he can't have a job that you're doing the best you can!'

The reaction from the overall public is that special ed kids aren't going anywhere. What are you doing putting so much effort into them? You're wasting our time and our money. Let's pour it into the kids who are going to learn and become productive.

The philosophy in this country for treating people with physical and mental disabilities has always been out of sight, out of mind. That's why institutions grow. 'We don't want to teach them. We don't want to take the extra time or the extra money. You can't really do anything with them so get them out of here. You'll forget about them in a few years. They're better off.'

So unfortunately, you're never going to get a phone call at home from the head of the special ed department saying, 'Guess what? We just read an article on autism and we're putting in this new therapy! This is really good!'

You have to do it yourself. That means constant education and always updating yourself on what's out there. Talk to doctors and PhDs, read books. Find out what fits with your child, and somehow get it. Maybe you'll have to raise the money or borrow the money. Maybe you'll have to put together the program yourself. That's what we've done for Chris in the past. And if we can't find or afford a suitable program for him after kindergarten, that's what we'll do in the future.

I first met Bill about three years ago when we did a TV program on Channel 8. I always love meeting other parents of autistic kids. Everybody always has a unique story to tell and Bill's is certainly unique. He prefers the home program and raising the money himself. That's very unique. Most parents usually use the public system. People are pretty much consigned to it. Before that, twelve, fifteen years ago all they pretty much had was a residential system for severely disabled kids.

Mildly disabled kids sometimes get ignored in the classroom. Some of them get by and technically graduate, but it's similar to a lot of kids in city schools who get pushed through even though they don't know the material. It happens to a number of kids with autism. If the parents are really intent on sending their kids with mild autism to public school, there is often a tendency for the schools to ignore certain things and allow the kids to get pushed through the system so they graduate with their peers. That's been a big issue the last six, seven years. The school districts don't like to separate the students and push them back.

There are pros and cons on both sides. It's tough to draw the line. Some kids don't do well socializing and don't want to socialize. So why push them? It's one thing to encourage them to do a little more. It's another thing to plop them in and force them. Sometimes you do more harm than good. It depends on the parent's wishes, the ability of the child, and the level of severity.

Pat Houston, President,
Autism Society of Pennsylvania

6

Kindergarten

When the Kennedy Krieger Institute Center for Autism and Related Disorders developed its Achievements kindergarten program, they invited us to their open house. We were very anxious to see what they had done because we weren't happy with the school program in our public system and wanted to find something else for Chris. The Kennedy program was very impressive and we decided to send Chris to their summer class.

We worked for weeks beforehand to get him adapted to the idea of going to this strange place for school. Over and over again we used visual stories with words, called 'social stories.' They're a great way to show children who don't understand concepts what will be happening. 'When you come to school Amy will be here. See Amy, Chris.' And then you build: 'Amy will then go to the sandbox.' If you just read to them, 'You will go to school today and will have fun,' what does fun mean? 'You will be happy.' What does happy mean? They don't understand that. So you might have to show them a room full of balloons or a picture of a person smiling when you say, 'At the end of the day you will be happy.' But you couldn't just write 'happy' and tell him, 'Chris, you will be happy.' He wouldn't know what your were talking about.

We did other things to help him too. For instance, Jae drove him to the school everyday. 'This is where you will be going to school. Let's walk in the lobby… OK, now we're going home.' It was all to get him used to the routine and understand what to expect.

I will never forget the first day of summer session at Achievements. We were nervous wrecks and packed everything in the world for the day, extra clothing in case he got wet, extra peanut butter sandwiches, soda, special candies, books, little pictures – everything we could think of that would remind him of home. They lined the boys up at the door and Chris marched right into the classroom. Jae and I watched from the viewing room. There was a little crying, a little first day jitters, and a little confusion just like any kindergarten. But Chris and the other children took to it. He even started to play!

Before long this guy adapted beautifully. It all fit, probably because we had good timing. He was now able to understand things and was more comfortable with his own ways and the ways of the world.

The summer program was perfect. But would we send him here for kindergarten? The public school was not meeting our needs, but going to Kennedy meant a lot of money and a major time commitment. Since it was out of state for us we could not get any funding and we would have to travel five days a week, an hour-and-a-half each way. But it was such a good program we decided to give it a shot.

Such a professional staff! All have college degrees and backgrounds in speech and language, and all have trained with respected autism programs like Kennedy Krieger or TEACCH in South Carolina. They really know how to work with autism. If a child is stimming, the teacher might say, 'Quiet hands. Let's listen.' What a pleasant change from all the people who just grab these kids and sit them down. Even singing songs is expertly done to communicate with the children. Amy, Chris' teacher, dissects the songs with sign language and pictures so that the words have meaning. If the kids fail to learn a song then she knows how to handle it and they eventually do get it. She knows each child's individual quirks. What more could you ask?

We don't believe you can use only one philosophy when working with autism. A child is not a philosophy that fits neatly into one strict way of thinking. Different methods work at different times. So you have to think on your feet, and that's what I see them do at Achievements. All the different methods for working with autism are incorporated the same way Jae and I have been doing for years, only we didn't know all the formal names to them. The program uses TEACCH, Discrete Trial, Lovaas, and Greenspan. They use just a little bit of everything; whatever is good for the child.

The program is set up with a lot of visual cues and a schedule board for each child. On the boards are picture schedules. The teacher points and tells them, 'Look here.' It may say circle time so they move the picture of kids sitting around the table. There are pictures for the art center, playing outside, gym, singing, potty and lunch.

Learning to communicate is a major part of the day's focus, and using different communication methods is a rule of thumb. They even change the room around to help the kids. One activity is centered around a calendar. 'What day is today? It is Monday. Put Monday up on the calendar... What's the weather outside? Let's look. Oh, look, see it's cold. Put the cold on... What day is it?' Chris now goes to the calendar and will count the days that are blocked off until he gets to the current day. 'Twenty-two. Yes! What is it like outside? Let's see... Oh, it's cold.' Then he dresses a figure for the weather. He's doing just what a kid would do in typical kindergarten. But most importantly, he's learning how to communicate.

And the communication lessons never stop. The children and teachers eat lunch together and the teachers make them request their food. 'Sandwich please.' 'Sosa please.' And then they give it to them. If a kid reaches out they say, 'No. What do you want?' She might sign and he might give her a PECS or verbalize, 'Sanwich.' The kids play together. They sing. The other day they sang BINGO, B-I-N-G-O with all the accompanying claps.

The best part about Kennedy Krieger Achievements is how well they know the kids and how very closely they work with the parents. It's quite normal for Chris' teacher to have something like the following conversation with me: 'I saw Chris was a little afraid to go on the ladder today. Do you know anything about it?'

'Yes. Here's the story.'

'OK. Why don't you work with him in gym and I'll work it out here and tell the OT.' All of a sudden, everybody's on the same wavelength. They always want to know what we're doing at home. They'll ask, 'I saw Chris doing this when I said hello. Does he do that at home?'

'Well, lately he's been doing…'

'Does he sing a bye-bye song?'

'Yes…'

'He was singing it to me.' *That's* really knowing your child. It's perfect for these kids.

The school is wonderful. The only curriculum change I would like to see is a little more classic education. In other words, they're not learning science, history, or how to count. In that respect it lacks a bit.

Chris became a regular guy at Kennedy. He goes to school. He plays with his friends, eats lunch, does artwork. I don't have to be there anymore. I just think of him as going to school like any other kid. It's a wonderful feeling. We made the right choice sending him. He never would have gotten that exposure to listening, sitting, and working with other kids if we continued working with him at home on our own. These things probably would have come much later and that would have been a shame. Achievements really catapulted him. I'm sure it's a combination of things we've done, but this school certainly has played a big role. Chris is much more social. He takes directions and joins in a structured program.

It's a beautiful school. If it progressed into the elementary years it would be perfect. Unfortunately, it's not set up like that and he will graduate from the program this summer. There's no continuation. There should be, but politics and money play into everything. Ideally there should be continuity so the teachers can pass information about each child from one year to the next. Hopkins does have an elementary school program called LEAP, but it just doesn't fit what we want for Chris.

In the meantime we are searching for a primary school program comparable to Achievements' curriculum. We've looked at every program in Baltimore and they were mainly for very severe, self-injurious, or constant care children. Any good program we might consider is way too expensive for us to pay on our own. Most charge about forty-eight thousand a year and I can't afford that kind of money. So guys like Chris are in the same boat. They're smart, not self-injurious, teachable, but have very little language or sociability. They can't make it on their own in a mainstreamed class, but it's hard to find an affordable non-restrictive autism program.

When I look at a program for Chris, I look for trained people and their methodology background. Are they able to fall back on Discrete Trial, TEACCH, Lovaas, or Greenspan? They should be skilled at using methods that reach children who think in pictures, children with processing and language problems. Can they help Chris communicate using language, sign and PECS? That means if Chris makes PECS for a sandwich and they know he can say it, they ask him to verbalize. 'Tell me. Tell me.'

'Sandwich.'

'Good!'

I also expect to see patience in a good program. You need a cartload of patience to be a teacher for the day with a child who has autism. You get bitten and scratched; they run and move constantly. After a while, it's very hard. For instance, it took me fifteen minutes today to take Chris to the bathroom when we got to school. He wanted his shirt a certain way, and his pants weren't tied right. He didn't want to go. Then he wanted to flush all the toilets and see the water. Then he wanted me to go. Then he wanted to play, and then he started to stim. To me this is typical, but a lot of other people would be yelling, 'Come on! We have to go to school! Go to the bathroom!!' You can't do that, though, because they don't understand they're being difficult. It's horrible to yell at a person who doesn't know why he's being yelled at. So I look for patience.

The other two things I look for are education and continuity. I would like to see classic American subjects taught like spelling, history, arithmetic and science. And a good program should also continue though all the grades.

Ideally, we would like our own school district to form a class for children with autism ages six and up. I recently started negotiating with the Assistant Elementary Education Superintendent for my school district. He asked me, 'What would you want for your son if we were to resume our talks?'

And I answered, 'It's much simpler than you think. I want personnel who have graduated and done their Masters and Doctorates in autism, not a special education teacher who's taken a seminar. These should be people skilled with years of practice with autistic children. And I want a full, thought out program that follows the children through the years, not a program that abruptly stops after a year or so. That's all I want.'

'Well, what do you suggest I do?'

'I suggest you come down to Kennedy Krieger Achievements and observe my son's program. See how he's flourished, has friends, reads, follows a schedule and plays. Take note of the quiet environment and how they work with him. Talk to Dr. Landa, head of the program, and if you like the program and really want to do something concrete, hire her. Have her institute a similar program in our district and then use her as a consultant until you stand on your own two feet.'

What I am saying to them is if they really want to do this right, they have to attack this disorder as a separate entity. I'm not saying I want to segregate my child. I am saying that my child needs some special things and I don't think you can give them to him without a specialized program. I'm not ashamed of him going to a specialized program. And I am not going to force inclusion so that he is lost and twenty-six other kids are held up because you have to deal with him on an individual basis.

Right now we'll continue working with the school district, continue our search for a good private program and hope for the best. What's the worst? I refuse to send him anywhere and we simply run our own program just like we've done in the past.

7

Future Schooling

'Do what's good for the child' – *Lynn Medley, Assistant Director, Kennedy Krieger Institute Center for Autism*

When Lynn Medley first imparted her wisdom to me I was in the throes of struggling with therapies and deciding what education was right for Chris. She helped confirm for me that my own instincts about my child were what I should follow, not some public bureaucrat's opinion or some new philosophy. By following those instincts I feel Chris received the best education possible over the years. But now I am once again at a difficult crossroads determining where Chris will continue his schooling. The Achievements program ends for him this summer and we have to choose which direction he will now travel.

By law I can demand that my school district provides appropriate education for my son next year, and the officials very cooperatively agreed to visit Achievements so that they might possibly put a similar program together for Chris. However, once they made their observations they changed their tune. 'Look, there's a good program in a nearby school district,' they told me. 'It really makes no sense for us to create a program when a good one close to here already exists. Why don't you take a look at it?'

I agree with them, but why wasn't I told about this other program six months ago, a year ago, or two years ago? I also just found out about one more program in another nearby district that's supposedly good. Why didn't they too tell me about that one as long as we were going other places to look?

The first of these schools I observed is a regular, neighborhood elementary school with a whole wing devoted to disabled children. It has two autistic classrooms, a physically handicapped classroom, a mixed disabilities classroom, a life skills classroom and then an older life skills classroom. There is a speech teacher who does one-on-one, visits the classroom, and does group work. The school tries to mainstream wherever the opportunity presents itself. Let's say my child was very good at reading, they'd put him in a standard first grade reading class. That's one of the advantages for a child with a lot of intelligence who's able to function. He can then attend regular gym class or maybe regular science class. Assembly and lunch are held with everybody together, and the kids all have buddies.

It's a beautiful concept and a beautiful school. They even go so far as to have kids who are bed-ridden with breathing apparatus. The autism support classes are divided by age, one for younger kids and one for older kids. The classes are set up perfectly – visual cues, little cubbies, eight kids, one teacher and four aides, and maybe one-on-one for a child who needs it.

Here's what I didn't like. First, it's a long day from nine to three-thirty. Second, they don't allow parent visitation. You can schedule a visit every now and then, but they really don't welcome you. I'm not saying they're beating the children behind closed doors, but I want to see what my son can't tell me. I want to see what's going on. Also, in the younger classroom where Chris would be, I didn't find the instructors to be experienced or professional enough. They seemed to deal mainly with the more verbal kids, and

Chris would get lost. He's a sensitive guy. I just can't imagine him sitting there all day being pulled and pushed around.

The older class I found to be extremely demanding. I realize they want the kids to fit into the mainstream of life, but some kids can get destroyed in the process. And is it that important to me that he learns mathematics this year because the teacher says so, even if he's terribly unhappy and pushed and over-processed? Or can he learn it later? Or maybe he'll never learn it. I don't really care.

I was once at a symposium led by four adults with autism. They were fairly recovered, if recovered is the right word. As children they were all placed in school and they all said they contemplated thoughts of suicide being stuck in the class all day. It was overwhelming and they just couldn't take it all.

That's the thing I don't think school officials understand. Maybe they have aides, maybe they work one-on-one, but if my son overloads where do they give him a safe spot? How do they know that he's having a tough time? How do they communicate with him? How do they recognize signals that he needs some special attention? And how do they separate the young man from the autistic young man? Will they think he's misbehaving if he's overloaded? They're not experts. They're all either aides or volunteers or special ed teachers who have taken some courses in autism. The people at Achievements went for their degrees in autism or with an emphasis on autism. They did all their training in classes with autism so they understand every movement, every nuance.

In a public school classroom like the one I observed I'm sure there are some kids who fend for themselves, are very verbal and take part in the activities. There are such varying degrees of autism. You're going to have kids who hop on the bus and are very verbal. You're going to have kids who are able to get what they want. But my child's just not like that.

Chris, all alone in a strange situation where they're not paying attention to him, is going to go off in a corner by himself and start to finger play because there's no stimulation. If he's uncomfortable and has to go to the bathroom he's not going to ask. If he starts to walk over to the bathroom and they say, 'No, sit down,' he's not going to say, 'But I have to go to the bathroom.'

I'm afraid he won't be able to handle himself in one of these classrooms and that the teachers will not be alert enough to work with him. My son really doesn't have a lot of common life skills. The littlest thing can set him off terribly, and yet, a robber can come in and he won't be phased by it. I'm not saying he's going to remain like this, but he has very weak self-help and self-preservation skills. If I said we're going to go to school now he would walk out the door half-dressed. He just doesn't know he has to put the rest of his clothes on. I have to recognize all my son's strengths, but I also have to be aware of his shortcomings so he doesn't get hurt. I really feel an intense public classroom could cause him to regress or shut down. He just isn't ready right now for that type of experience.

It's not a case of me letting go. Let go how? Dump him in the classroom? It's not like I'm taking this very verbal self-sufficient child and protecting him. He needs a lot of love and care. This is a little guy who couldn't manage to call for help, or know what a fire is, or know when he's being physically abused or pushed around.

We're in negotiations with the school district now and they're trying very hard. I will listen, but my gut feeling tells me he wouldn't be happy there. They'll probably look at me and say, 'You know what? We give up with you. Now you don't like this. Now you don't like that.'

I don't fault them for being exasperated with me, but I can't just let myself stick my son anywhere. I know I'm overprotective, but this little guy has had such a sweet life. He's come so far. I don't want to ruin all he's accomplished. What's best for Chris at this point may just be a continuation of our own home school program. It's important we make the right decision. If we choose the program that's best for him, I know we can look forward to my son's continued development and participation in the world around him.

PART V

Learning To Cope

1

Socialization

Chris was standing on line with four boys waiting to begin their first day at Achievements kindergarten class. He looked around, saw each one stimming, then he looked up and smiled at me! My wife turned and said, 'He knows they're like him.'

I often wondered what my son thinks sets him apart from other kids he sees, or why the kids at school are like him. His reaction that first day sure told me he realizes something. He seemed to know immediately that the kids in his class were alike and he felt very secure.

It was wonderful to see him happily be a part of a social group. I've always made it my mission to help Chris learn to participate in the world. From the very beginning I always felt it was very important for me to acknowledge even the smallest of accomplishments. I'd just go crazy over them. If he drew circles with different colors he'd hear me exclaim, 'OH, is that beautiful! Look at that! MOMMY! Look what Chris did!' And he'd get a smile on his face. Building his self-esteem was the first step. Learning to share his joy of an activity was next.

It was important to let him know that doing things his own way was fine and that he didn't only have to do things our way. Of course, it's still necessary that he learn the ways of the rest of the world because he lives in a society that will measure him and we want him to get along as best he can. But that doesn't mean he can't be applauded for doing things his way.

We've had to be careful not to take away his innocence and spontaneity while teaching him to function socially within the outside world. For instance, he likes to take off his clothes in the bedroom and dance while he looks at himself in the mirror. I'll say, 'You are a beautiful boy!' And he smiles and preens and waltzes around. Who cares? But he also has to know he can't take his clothes off in a restaurant. Not for my sake – believe me, I could sit in a restaurant with him naked and tell everybody to turn away. I could care less. It's for his sake. 'You're going to go to a restaurant and you can't take off your clothes because you're going to get in trouble.'

I've read stories where fifteen-year-old boys with autism mastur-bate in the middle of dinner. And they look at you as if to say, 'Why not? I want to do this now. That's my feeling right now.' So they push everything else away and they don't realize it's not acceptable. It's the parents' job to teach them concepts and how to be social.

Unfortunately you also have to teach them about strangers. And there's the irony. 'I want you to be social and pay attention to everybody; something you don't do naturally. That means you must talk to everybody and react. Wait a minute! There's a catch here. Now we have to teach you about strangers, people you shouldn't talk to or look at.' That's very difficult stuff. Kids with autism can't conceptualize ideas like these. It's very hard.

Sending Chris to kindergarten at Achievements had a wonderful impact on his social skills. Before kindergarten, Chris didn't have any friends. None at all. We always had a birthday party and there was nobody to invite so we'd have his party when Jesse had one. That way there would be people for him too.

But once at Kennedy he started looking at the other kids and playing with them. He'd put hats on them and accept things from them. He would watch them climb so he'd climb. They held hands and all responded to each other.

He's even made a close friend named Jimmy. We keep up the relationship by visiting Jimmy's family and going places together. One of the most poignant times I remember was when Jimmy cried and Chris reached over and put his arm around him. Seeing Jimmy's tears, my son wiped them away. That was really special. The teacher just stopped in shock because kids with autism aren't supposed to make friends or have feelings.

Christopher plays a little with my daughter's friends too. She teaches them how to respond and they'll tickle him or play ball. Sometimes he even tries to kiss them.

My son also has favorite places he likes to visit where he knows people. The other day we went to Damon's Restaurant. He sits in the booth, turns on the music, switches the TV channels and even goes up to the bar to get the kids' cups. He looks at the bartender who says, 'All right, Chris. Get your cup.' And Chris gets the cup and gives it to him.

'Sosa.' And the bartender gives him soda – no ice, half full. Everybody knows him. So it's wonderful!

But then he does things like go and watch TV at a table where a man was already eating. It never occurred to him that you don't sit with another person. I happened to know the guy and asked, 'Do you mind if my son sits here?' He said it was fine, but Chris has yet to learn about social boundaries and other social rules.

Autism and stares from strangers often go hand in hand. Parents with autistic children always encounter the attitude that we're bad parents because we have very typical looking children who appear to have big behavioral problems. 'Why aren't they stopping him from these odd noises? Look what he's doing with the silverware. He's not even eating. And he's screaming, he's loud, and he's moving back and forth and rocking! Why don't they do something?'

When Chris and I went out in public, especially when he was younger, he ran around throwing things and flapping his hands. People would give me dirty looks as if to say, 'Why don't you tell this kid to stop?' There was no question they thought I was a bad father. Talk about lack of support! Parents of children with autism are made to feel like social pariahs.

But I gave the stares from strangers very little thought. One time, however, I let a woman have it for staring at us. I remember Chris was walking in a store with his bottle when he was about four years old. A saleswoman tapped a coworker and pointed with this incredulous look as if to say, 'How can they allow him to use that bottle?'

I went up to her and said, 'Hi. Are you concerned about my son drinking a bottle?' And she stammered. I continued, 'Well, let me tell you. Number one, that's the only form of nutrition he has right now, if you don't mind. He has autism and he's not eating a thing. So if it doesn't bother you that much, I'm sure you won't mind him drinking his formula this way so he won't shrivel up. Is that OK with you?' And she just kind of melted away.

When I confronted people in the beginning it was because I felt they just shouldn't be staring at him without understanding. Chris was not a bad boy. He was not a boy with psychological problems. But he did have his own set of issues to deal with, and I felt how dare they look at him like that. So it was more of a quick education. I felt I owed it to them, and I owed it to my son.

I learned later on that my role was not to change the world to suit Chris. Instead it was to help him fit into the world. So now if somebody is looking I will try and educate them in a more subdued manner. I'll especially key into the people who are looking with sensitivity. They have that kind look on their face that says, 'Gee, I wonder what's going on.'

And I'll say, 'Hey, Chrissie, say hi... By the way, Chris has autism.' If somebody's really, really rude and gives him a dirty look because he's near them flapping his hands then I'll say something. But overall I've become less protective.

That doesn't mean I won't lay down my life in a minute for my son. It does mean, however, that I realize I cannot change the world for him and he's got to fit in to a certain extent. It's a harsh reality, but not every mall is going to have somebody who knows Chris. Not every diner is going to have a woman that moves from the fan. I realized I was doing him more harm than good by jumping in to clear the way every time. Maybe in the beginning it was good. Maybe he needed to be protected and people needed to be shoved out of the way. But now I want him to understand that people stare. He's got to be able to cope, and he has started to do that somewhat. The stares have lessened, and Chris is learning to be more and more of a social person.

I think of Chris as a very triumphant human being who has a different set of problems than most. He has to be helped to fit into society only because it helps his life, not because *I* want it for him. We simply know that it's better if you can communicate and have human touch and human relationships. So we continue to help him socialize, and are rewarded with the most incredible hugs from a boy who's learned to give love.

I noticed a tremendous increase in Chris' interaction recently, especially with spontaneous verbal requests. I think it's probably a combination of things. When I first met him, I noticed there was not a lot of eye contact. The only way that I saw him spontaneously communicate was with his PECS. He would bring me the PECS and I would say, 'OK, what do you want?' Very rarely would he even verbalize it. He would just show me the PECS card, whereas now he'll just say, 'ball, soda, soda please,' without even needing to look at the pictures. That's a huge difference.

He's very playful too. He will definitely pull you by the arm and make you do whatever he wants to do - play with his little Honker dolls or tickling. I'll tickle him for a while and he'll laugh and laugh and laugh. And he looks you right in the eye. He likes pressure on his head. I guess it feels good to squeeze his head. So he'll grab your hands and make you squeeze.

Bill is always grabbing him, hugging him and teasing him. But at the same time if Chris doesn't want to do something Bill will just say, 'Chris, tell Daddy no. Tell Daddy go away.' They're constantly interacting. I think the program's great, but education can only do so much. A lot of his progress is who's around him and how they're treating him.

Bill is incredible. He's an incredible father. Great man. I've never seen him without a smile on his face. And it's got to be tough. Just being a father in general is tough, let alone dealing with anything like a child with autism, financial pressures and public involvement.

He's just the best father I can possibly imagine. Always playing, always laughing with Chris. You hear him say, 'OK, we'll go for a ten minute walk,' or 'I'll take him for a car ride and go to Damons for dinner.' He spends every free second interacting with Chris. And if Bill walks in the room, that's it. Chris immediately wants to go play and tickle. It's like this 'dad smile' comes on Chris' face that you don't see with anybody else. I can't say enough good things about his relationship with Chris.

Jenny Nielsen, therapist

2

Laughing And Feeling Joy

Kids with autism aren't supposed to have a sense of humor. Well then, make jokes and *teach* them to enjoy humor. Life is funny. It's your job to give love and teach this child to be a kid. Hug and play and laugh with him. Tell him he's funny. Roll on the grass and run. Every time something silly happens I point it out to Chris. 'That's funny! Look at that. That is funny.' And he knows what's funny now and laughs all the time.

As an infant, Chris was always quiet and a loner, but he was very affectionate and laughed a lot. He seemed to have a core sense of humor right from the start, but his humor along with so many other qualities started to slip away as the autism progressed. If I was to fight for my child, I knew that teaching him educational skills could not be my only job. I had to teach him to be a kid and laugh again.

A normal child will come to you and say, 'Come on, let's roll the wagon,' or they'll bring their friends to play Ring Around the Rosy. But if you don't teach a child with autism how to initiate play, then why would he? He certainly doesn't want to play with others. The whole disorder says, I am unable to be social. I don't want to be around you. I don't even want to be in your world. Why should I initiate play? So you have to present scenarios to these kids that encourage social qualities.

My theory is if the ability exists to add or spell, then it also exists to feel joy. So much time and effort is taken to break things down to teach these kids educational skills. How about breaking humor down so they can learn that too?

I was determined to teach Chris laughter and joy, and took every opportunity I could. Sometimes we'd walk and playfully fall down. 'That's funny!' I'd say. 'Isn't that funny? Ha ha ha!' Maybe he didn't get that it was funny at first, but he didn't get that yellow was yellow until we repeated it a hundred times either. Eventually it clicked and he said, oh, these are the colors. Ask my son what's blue, what's yellow, he can do it in a second. But even more wonderful, he now realizes what funny is! He has a spontaneous laugh just like everybody else.

I went about teaching Chris humor without a great plan. I was very careful at first because I didn't know how he'd react. Today I will do a funny dance or make a face or throw him around, but I wouldn't dare do that a year ago. Little actions could upset him easily. One time I coughed and he was frightened to tears thinking I was hurt.

So I had to work very gradually. If he had the slightest smile I would encourage him. We did a lot of tickling and other silly stuff at first. I started out by light tickling on the arm, but was careful never to touch the neck or face because only appendages were safe to him. I think he loved the tickling because it was removed; he didn't have to look at me. Other forms of physical enjoyment would have been more imposing. Hugging is too full of emotion and playing games like patty-cake requires close attention. Tickling, on the other hand, was something that allowed him to just laugh and lose himself in abandonment without focusing on the other person.

I worked very hard at making routine activities pleasurable. I paid attention to every nuance, noting the smallest of moments when Chris was enjoying play. One time he lined little Teletubbies on the bathtub, took them up in the air, and went, 'Bye bye, Poke,' as he dropped each one. That was real innovative play and I encouraged him. 'Chris, that is so funny. Do La-La now. Goodbye, La-La.'

Not only was I letting him know that creating ways to have fun was great, I was letting him know that I understood his actions and was willing to step into his world a little. Whether or not I really found his actions that funny wasn't the point.

It was important that he found activities funny to *him*, not me. For instance, he loved saying sounds for me to repeat. Did he have to say the Gettysburg Address? I was letting him know that his way was good too. 'I can learn from you. And I can step into your shoes, and if you want me to repeat these things, fine.' When he sings a song the words are not discernible, does it matter? No. Instead I tell him, 'That is such great singing. I love that bird song. That is great the way you sing it.'

I think it's painfully obvious to a child what you think of him. When dad comes home and doesn't play and roll around with him, he knows he's being excluded somehow. He's probably thinking, 'I see other kids playing ball, but I'm not. All right, maybe I don't want to play ball. Maybe I don't even understand what ball is or the concept of why I run from here to there, but why isn't anybody playing with me? Why isn't anybody attempting to do this with me?' The dad might not get the same response as he does with other children, but that should not stop him from playing with his child. Not doing these activities further damages the child's self-image by reinforcing the attitude that he is strange or different.

How can you expect your child to learn to enjoy play if you don't give him the opportunity? For example, Jesse and I taught Chris to bat a ball. We stood behind him, did hand over hand, and he hit the ball! 'Yay!' He jumped up and down just like any other little guy. I play with him as physically and game-oriented as I can because I think it sends the message that he deserves to play just like every other kid. And every time you play physically, have fun and laugh, neurons are working and cells are moving. It's great therapy.

They say kids with autism have inappropriate laughter. Well, even when Chris had that so-called 'inappropriate' laughter, I just laughed along with him. I think it's good. I guess I have inappropriate humor myself. If he splashed in the bathtub and started to giggle, what's wrong with that? Maybe it was the water or maybe he just thought it was outrageous that he was sitting in the bath, I don't know. But he was laughing. What's wrong with laughing? So I would go and laugh hysterically with him. 'You are so funny. I can't stop laughing.'

I'm sure it resulted in Chris saying to himself, 'This is nice. I'm laughing. He's laughing. This is something good.'

We should always empower our children in every way, and knowledge is not the only way to empower. Joy and humor are highly powerful weapons. Let your children know that they are entitled to the same joys that others have. I feel very strongly that it is a parent's job to teach their child with autism to experience joy. You already know it's your job to teach life skills. If your child speaks, you reward him by saying, 'Good job. Good talking.' But if your child plays a little joke or has a little laugh, it's equally important to reward that. Tell him, 'Great! You are funny! Isn't that funny? You are so good when you laugh. Go ahead. Smile again.'

Now he knows, 'Hey wait a minute. Not only do I get a reward for matching colors or brushing my teeth, I also get rewarded when I laugh, hug, or smile.'

I think we're too busy rewarding structured learning activities. 'You got the right crayon. Good boy!' OK, but what about when he picks his own crayon and creates a line? Tell him, 'That is beautiful. What a great color.' That way he draws more because he is rewarded for the pure joy of creating on his own. Reward him for being a kid. We need to help these children learn how to understand emotion. Reward them for being funny.

I tried doing that with Chris right from the start. And it only took a few months before we started to see some changes. He was now coming to sit by me while I put my arm around him! He was even lying in my arms. This was the same child who wouldn't look at me a few months before! I can't begin to describe the joy I felt from this.

Families forget that their job doesn't end after school or therapy or doing a data sheet. Nor does it end after fighting for new laws or marching on Washington. I hear parents say, 'I teach my son Discrete Trial and he's learned to match every item.' So what happens after that? 'Well he goes downstairs and he sits in the corner.'

That's the worst part to me. Why are you letting him sit in the corner? If you can teach him to match every animal, why not teach him that he's to stay around the family and laugh?

We do that all the time. 'Chris, don't go upstairs. Stay with us. Come on, we're all going to sit here and play. Isn't this fun? Chrissie's with Jesse!' We are really teaching what it's like to be in a family and what it's like to be a loving child. And over the years that's what he's become. Now he'll come down and stay with us or he'll pull one of us down to wrestle. The other day I fell asleep and he was jumping on me and laughing. He knew I was asleep, but Jae said he was playing with my nose and trying to wake me up. He was experiencing the joy of being a child.

The other night he made a joke! Now for a guy like this to make a joke, it's amazing. Jae had asked him, 'Do you want to see some movies before you go to bed?' And he mockingly replied, 'No. HAHAHAHA!' Of course he wanted to watch a movie! He looks forward to it everyday. The fact that he could find sarcastic humor and then present it is miraculous to me. Here's this almost nonverbal child making a joke.

He's always trying to do funny things now. He's a very sweet, funny guy. Sometimes he laughs so hard that he actually falls down. He also has a fake laugh, a fake cry and a sympathy look where he buries his head down. He's beginning to truly show emotion and uses it to be part of the family. If a child with autism reacts to humor or emotion, you must not only recognize it, but really reinforce it. This is a crucial job for a parent or your child may never experience joy.

I think parents get too caught up in this world of special needs with the law, inclusion and concepts. Of course these are all important, but my experience is that you better start centering on your child. People argue with me, 'Well, we never would have any rights…' Of course there's got to be legislation and movements. I'm the first to go out and protest. But that's only a very small part of your responsibility. If your child is languishing in the corner, playing with his fingers while you're out at a rally you're not doing your job. There's nothing more important than helping your child learn to laugh, play, and feel joy.

Christopher looks so normal. When you look at him he has beautiful blond hair and blue eyes. You would never think that there was anything wrong with him. He's very affectionate for an autistic little boy, just wonderful.

I think Jae and Bill realized that all the academic stuff is important, but the most important thing is to teach him affection and to teach him that they're always going to be there, and to get him into a routine for him to depend on them. I think that's really important and I think they've done that really well. They've given him every opportunity they possibly could. Gym class, for instance. They don't have a lot of money, but they struggle just so they can send him. I've never seen anything like it.

I think they're really the best parents I've ever seen. Honestly.

Kim Egger, therapist

Chris has a really loving, fun personality. He enjoys things and laughs a lot.

Melissa Bennett, therapist

My first impression after meeting Chris was, 'I can't believe this child has autism.' You might expect a child who has a disability to be different in some way; maybe doing his own thing, separate. And that's not Chris. Chris is very social. He is a smart, energetic, good-looking child and if you put him in a line-up and say, 'OK, pick out the child who has autism,' I wouldn't be able to do it. He is energetic, involved and interested in things. Not what I expected. I guess my stereotype is Dustin Hoffman in Rain Man, just kind of sitting quietly in the corner with his head down humming to himself, and that's not Chris.

Pat Kain, WLAN-FM DJ, Lancaster, Pennsylvania

The one thing that sticks in my mind about Chris is he's such a happy little boy. A lot of things are definitely challenging for Chris, but he meets the challenge and is always laughing and joyous. He has his moments like any child. But I think what they've done to accommodate him has really helped him be such a happy kid all the time.

Jenny Nielsen, therapist

3

Music

Music is sometimes described as an expression of the soul. In Chris' case it has been an expression of his soul as well as a means to soothing it. My son has always responded to music, even when he was little. I remember music always being around while Chris moved and danced. I think it always affected him.

Music is a big enjoyment for him. We sing a lot together and have fun making up our own songs. I'll take a song that he sings and put his name in it. Or sometimes he'll just walk around the house humming and singing to himself, and I'll always tell him how nice that is.

During Chris' early autism days we tried using music to calm him down, especially in the car when he was in an agitated state. Mozart worked to a certain extent. We also started turning MTV on in the house a lot. When he was confused or not focused he'd often walk around not knowing what to do with himself, stimming and touching objects. So offering him music was our way of tying to get him to center. I'd say, 'Come on, let's listen to music.' And we'd sit down, watch MTV, and it calmed him a little bit. MTV became a big thing with us because he liked both the music and the visuals.

We found as time went on that Chris began to choose his music and it became a natural therapy. He'd sit down, turn to MTV and listen to music. He'd lean over in the car and point to the CD player or he'd take his tape and put it right in the tape deck by himself. 'Oh, you want to hear the Honkers. All right, I'll turn off the radio.'

I think it's a good idea that all parents use music with their children. It certainly can't hurt. It's soothing. Some kids with autism may have problems with volume where they can't stand certain pitches and loud noises or they pick up low noises. Sometimes the telephone rings and they could go berserk. You may turn on music and they pick out a high pitch that makes them uncomfortable. So you have to see. Kids with autism are all different. You really have to bear down and say, 'What's good for my child?' Luckily, my son's never had problems with sound. Music was always good for him.

I once took a seminar with Dr. Porges, a big proponent of auditory training. He says that children with autism lack use of the nerves and muscles around their eyes and ears that normally perk up when someone says hello to you. They don't pick out language like we do and don't work those muscles, so we have to teach them to listen.

We have Chris use headphones for auditory training. A lot of the tapes try to eliminate background noises, especially disturbing bass sounds. Originally he wasn't cueing in to anything, but now he can literally identify hundreds of environmental sounds. Play thunder and he'll point to a picture of a storm. Play the flush of a toilet and he'll point to a toilet. He's gotten very good at listening. Some of the sounds an average adult probably couldn't identify.

Celtic music was one of the first pleasing tapes we played, but quickly we moved on to other types of music. I found he loved the rhythms of Van Morrison. He just falls right into sync with his songs. There's one song by Morrison called 'Caravan' with a part that goes, 'la la, lala, lala la.' It's a very lyrical song and Chris loved to hear it in the car. One day at home he poked me. This was before he had advanced that much. 'Lalalala,' he sang.

Chris listening to a tape, photograph by Carol Nielsen

'What?'

'Lalala.' He wanted to hear the song! I immediately responded. So music has even helped him to learn that when he asks for something he gets it. He loves to choose his songs. He can read every cassette and CD. He will go and put one in the cassette player and if he can't quite get it to work he'll pull you over and show you to fix it.

When artists are played on the radio, he recognizes them. He loves girl singers and right now is infatuated with TLC. He likes certain rock music, some rap, classical and, of course, Sesame Street music. His sister Jessica taught him all the popular teen music. He knows every MTV song and belts them out whiles he dances right to the beat. The boy's got great rhythm! I turn on music just to watch him dance. Backstreet Boys and NSync are among his all-time favorite groups.

I'll never forget how my son used to sing Backstreet Boys in the middle of the sidewalk. People were hysterical as he'd sing with abandonment. He loves to perform! My daughter has a poster of NSync above her bed that Chris looks at. He then gets in front of the mirror and starts singing like he's one of the group. He'll go back to the poster, touch it, and dance with them. Then he goes back to the mirror and sings some more. Not all the words are clear, but enough of them are to know what he's singing.

I think Chris has a particular fondness for NSync because of their song, 'Bye Bye Bye.' Remember, his first command word that he really learned to use was bye-bye. He would say it to the therapists when he didn't want to work with them. So whenever he hears 'Bye Bye Bye' from NSync, a big smile comes across his face.

When Chris feels a lot of stress he always sings 'I Want It That Way' by Backstreet Boys. My wife has even made a PECS icon in his communication book for the song. In fact, Lynn Medley from Kennedy mentioned at a conference how he uses the song with his PECS for expression.

Children's songs are also in my son's repertoire. He loves a certain bunny song that he can only sing a word or two of properly, but I know what it is. So I'll say, 'Oh, you're doing the bunny song,' and he laughs. He takes great delight knowing I recognize what he's doing.

He especially likes to act out and sing little scenes that represent a part of his life. Particular characters draw him in because he identifies with them. All day long he once watched a video scene where a turkey comes up to a window and gobbles to the lead character, a dog. The dog says, 'I didn't understand you.' And a chicken then clucks to interpret the rooster's request. 'Oh, you want to hear John Denver,' answers the dog. John Denver proceeds to sing 'Inch by inch, row by row...' Chris loved watching this over and over again.

Here was a character who could only express himself with indistinguishable noises, but he still was able to get the other animal to figure out what he wanted. Fascinating that my son picked this out! Later he came to me and made a motion like the turkey. Luckily, I pay attention to how he keeps busy, and recognized what he was doing. I gobbled, clucked, and ended up doing the whole scene, even the song. Chris squealed with laughter and quickly made 'Inch By Inch' one of our favorite routines.

Chris is a survivor and doesn't let adversity stop him from enjoying his world. Music is a means of expressing that joy for him. The following story is one more example of that.

It was a cold winter night and Chris and I were leaving the mall to go home. It was freezing outside as we walked to the car. I put my son in the car, gave him a roll, put on his seat belt and locked his door. I went around to my door, put the key in the lock, and it broke off! There I was standing like a jerk saying to myself, 'OK don't panic. Try and get the door open. Call somebody.' And Chris was sitting there looking at me like, when are you getting in the car? I didn't know what to do. I couldn't leave him alone in the cold car smack in the middle of a parking lot!

A friend of mine had gone into Damon's Restaurant so I signaled to a woman. 'My son is locked in the car. Could you run into Damon's? There's a big guy named Jim Christian sitting at the bar. Just tell him to come out and help me.' She was very nice and said OK.

Here comes Jim. I said, 'Jim, can you call my wife? I think she'll be home by now.'

Well, there was no answer so he left a message. 'Your son's locked in the car. We need the key. You've got to come here right away.'

I knew a lot of the kids that worked at Damon's and they all started coming out to us. 'Call my wife!!' I shouted. So she got a million messages saying, 'Your son's locked in the car. We need the key.'

Jim then suggested he call mall security. I never even thought of that. So he went and got security because I wouldn't leave the car.

Security came and the guy said to me, 'Fill out this form, Sir.'

Being very upset I responded, 'Listen to me. Do you see the kid in the car? OPEN THE DOOR!'

He opened the door and started talking to Chris. 'Hey! You cold, buddy? You OK?'

Agitated, I said, 'My son has autism. STOP! Let me get him out.' I signed the form, thanked the man and we went into Damons.

We were listening to music after this harrowing event while we waited for Jae, but there was no sign of her. Suddenly Chris started to dance to a song on the jukebox. You've never seen anything like it. He was moving to the beat and four girls turned around from the bar and good-naturedly started playing with him. 'You are so sexy!' they told him and each gave him a peck on the cheek. Jae walked in frantically worried about her son locked in the cold car only to find him doing Mambo #5.

Locked in the car? He didn't care. It was time to sing and dance and enjoy the rhythms of life.

4

Honkers

Chris has always gravitated toward characters and stories that seem to express similar circumstances as his own. Like all children, he loves Sesame Street. But his favorite characters are the monsters.

He loves the monsters, and if you notice, the monsters are all different from everyone else. The monsters, known as Honkers and Dingers, don't speak and may look funny or scary, but they're still regular guys. They laugh and they cry just like everyone else. Because they can only speak by honking their noses, Chris probably feels he is much like them because they communicate through sound and gesture. Just like the monsters, he behaves differently and can't speak like others, but he's a normal guy inside too.

There's one song he loves about the monster Frazzle that describes how he expresses himself when he's happy or sad. I think that's what strikes my son. Here's this blue furry thing that's ugly and completely outside of society, but he eats dinner and takes a walk and sings just like everyone else. Chris loves it.

It's not that he doesn't like the other characters too. He actually likes all of them. He likes Elmo and does a computer program called 'Elmo's Color Workshop.' He listens to Sesame Street cassettes on the way to Baltimore and knows all the songs by heart. He watches a Big Bird movie in which Big Bird is kidnapped. It's sad in parts and Chris seems to feel the emotions so much that he starts to cry. But he especially loves the monsters. Last night I bought him Baby Natasha, a little monster. I think he truly feels for these monsters and understands what they're experiencing.

Since Chris loves Sesame Street so much, I thought it would be perfect to have some of their merchandise displayed at a recent benefit. I spoke to the head of public relations who agreed to send me materials. While talking, he started asking me some very technical questions about our therapy program for Chris. It turns out he worked in Applied Behavioral Analysis. We ended up having a whole discussion on Rutgers and Discrete Trial.

I also decided to see if I could get representation on Sesame Street for autism. It started out merely to get a child representative for the disorder on the show, not to use Chris. They've had children with Down Syndrome, children in wheelchairs, deaf children and, I think, blind children. 'Here's a population that's over half a million and growing,' I said to a woman on the production staff. 'It's the third largest children's disorder. What's the possibility of getting some representation?'

I explained to her about Chris' love of the characters, how he watches Sesame Street movies all the time, how he freeze-frames the movies and tries to color them, how he has Sesame dolls, Sesame cassette tapes and how he memorizes and sings the songs. I told her how he particularly loves and relates to the Honkers who communicate by honking their nose. I even told her how an article was published about us going to Sesame Street Live and being brought backstage to meet the Honker characters. 'I'd really like you to talk to the producer,' she said. 'I don't see any reason why we couldn't put your son as one of the background kids. Here's the producer's name, Michael Loman. Write to him. Here's his address. Include some of the articles and explain to him why you want to do this.' So I did that just last week and now I'm waiting to hear from him.

What a wonderful way to bring awareness to the world about autism! And what a wonderful opportunity for my son to be surrounded by all the characters he so dearly loves. Thrilling!

5

Making Ends Meet

Financial problems are a fact of life for an average family with a special needs child. Thousands of dollars face me all the time just for Chris' care. I just had a legal bill come in for a thousand dollars. I owe Chris' private school, we bought books on autism and we just redid his home classroom. I'm constantly juggling from here and pulling from there, hoping to pay all my bills. We're in terrible debt. Car payments I'm always two months behind. Rent I pay on the last day possible. Our phone bills are always huge because we call all over for information. It's very stressful. Whatever money we get, whether it's earned, borrowed, a contribution or a tax return, it goes right out! It weighs on me terribly.

Living like this used to make me nervous. It's a horrible feeling to think everything is slipping right out from under you. Here I am, a man in my forties living from paycheck to paycheck. Very scary. And there's absolutely nothing I can do about it. If I made a hundred thousand a year, I don't think it would help at this point because we'd just spend the extra income on better therapy for Chris.

I had a lot of dreams for the future when my family was young. We had a few pennies put away, we had a budget, and I was earning a decent living. We spoiled our kids, but we certainly weren't buying jewels or yachts. Then when Chris' autism set in, the money just started to fly out the window.

Our lives were completely engulfed in finding the best help for Chris. There was not enough time in the day to accomplish all we needed. Everything else in my life took a back seat, including my job.

Originally when Chris was a baby I was very involved in the food, beverage and hotel business and had planned on becoming a hotel general manager. But I found as the disorder started getting more and more noticeable, I just didn't have time to devote to a career. So bartending became my job of choice.

I started working three, four bartending jobs at a time. Carrying uniforms in my car, I'd bartend morning, noon and night. I was in a constant state of exhaustion and was becoming the meanest person in the world because I was so overtired. To make matters worse, I barely had time to squeeze in for Chris. I was torn apart between trying to earn money for my son and finding time to spend with him.

The more money we spent, the less it seemed important. My biggest priority was researching and obtaining the best therapy for Chris and spending time working with him. So as I started reducing my work, more and more bills started piling up. The interest on the payments kept building and our finances went out of control.

We went through fifteen thousand dollars just to set up Chris' in-home therapy program. My mother helped us a lot and the state reimbursed some. I presented them with every pay stub I had. But I'm not much of a businessman and originally didn't keep very good records, so we were reimbursed by the state for about half of what we spent out of pocket. When they learned I was paying our therapists twenty-five dollars an hour they fell down laughing. I had no idea how high over the going rate we were paying these girls! They wanted to pay seven dollars, but I got them to agree to nine. We also got three hundred dollars a year from the state for equipment and one Rutgers workshop. It probably costs them twenty thousand dollars a year to fund our program.

Believe it or not, that still hasn't been enough. With overtime and using two therapists at once for certain therapies I probably spend three, four hundred dollars extra out of my pocket every two weeks.

Money is spent in countless ways. There were times we had to hire expert consultants like Ruth Donlin for several hundred a pop to straighten out the program when we ran into trouble. We had to buy tons of materials and other incidentals for the various programs we ran. My wife, being the perfectionist she is, would not compromise and if she saw a piece of equipment that would help Chris she would buy it whether there was money in the bank or not. I'd say, 'How did you buy that?'

'I wrote a check.'

'Well, the check's no good.'

'Too bad. He needs it and we'll find a way to pay for it.'

We never fought about it. It made me a little nervous, but I was amazed at her bravado. She would stop at nothing to help our son. We just bought an item that runs around three hundred dollars. Everything's always hundreds of dollars. But if my son needs something I will get it no matter what.

Conferences are another big expense. Jae is going to a conference in New York, for example. It's a very important conference. But with hotel, food, travel and the books she'll probably buy it'll cost me a thousand dollars. I don't have it, but I'll get it somewhere. It's worth it because I know she'll bring back invaluable information and then create a program to facilitate it. The end result, however, is that we run over our state funding allotment all the time. But that's OK because we're making great strides with Chris.

One thing we won't do is take money from the state to pay for our own salaries. Jae has her name listed as an employee only because she wants to show the state we're giving Chris therapy and we're not lax, but she writes underneath it 'not to be paid.' Even when we're short of therapists because of illness or vacation we do not take money for administering the therapy program. We don't ever want to be accused of taking money inappropriately.

An average person caring for someone with autism has to change his mind about money. You can refocus on material goals years down the line when you get your feet back on the ground and can begin again. A lot of the mothers I know with autistic children have the same attitude. 'You know what? I don't have anything,' they will say. 'We were going to buy a house, but too bad. It doesn't matter anymore.'

Now that doesn't mean you should be careless about your finances. It is crucial that you plan for your child's financial future. You must have good knowledge of the law concerning inheritance, money, social security and guardianship. Spell things out in case of unforeseen events. You never know. God forbid, the two of you get killed in the car tonight, what happens to this little guy? You should certainly write your will and name people. I've named my cousin and my daughter as trustees.

Another thing to have that is not actually a legally binding document is a description of what your child's day is like. This would be read in court. In other words, if I explain how Chris is comfortable at home, wakes up in bed and then watches TV, a judge would see firsthand what my son's life is like on a daily basis and would be more persuaded to put him with a family member rather than in an institution.

I'm also adamant about trust funds and estate planning. Know what can happen to your money. It's very important to know that if you leave fifty thousand dollars to your son and it's not in a trust fund, the government can use it and say he can't get social security. Instead they'll dole his fifty thousand dollar inheritance out to him on a monthly basis. That money will go in a minute!

Chris has a trust fund specifically for the enhancement of his adult life. That money can be spent on therapy, a vocation, dentistry, special shoes, whatever is not considered a basic need. Money intended for life enhancement can't be touched by the government.

Here's what can happen without a trust fund. Let's say a father leaves a hundred thousand dollars to his two sons, fifty to each. One of them is disabled and is in a state institution. The institution finds out that this kid has fifty thousand dollars and says they're not paying anymore because he has his own money. So who's going to pay? The brother at home says he's unable to pay for his sibling's institutionalization, and takes him out of the institution to live with him. In about two years, everybody's money is gone including the other brother's. The kid goes back to the institution and the state now pays for it.

A lot of the money issue is not spoken about. I guess when you have somebody with a disability you expect people to bend a little bit with your monetary obligations. People who run these special needs programs need to sit back and examine why they got into the field. If you're really in this profession to help people, then I think you should set up some funding scholarships. I know there are some out there, but talk to the average parent and you'll hear, 'I can't afford to send him to that private school or therapy at home. I can't go for the extra speech. There's just not enough money to do it.' And that's sad.

Is it fair that a wealthy person's child may be speaking and yours is not only because you didn't have the money to pay for the best therapy? That's the harsh reality in the world of special needs. The wealthy man doesn't know what it's like not to find the money for his child's therapy. Most kids are screwed if they don't have the money or the backing to get the proper programs.

There are hundreds of thousands of adults out there who cry every night because they cannot pay for the therapy that their child needs. I have. Where am I going to get that next hundred dollars from? How many checks have I written and hoped would clear? How many times have I worked extra and we've done without? People don't realize that. I get up every morning and say, 'Jae, here's ten dollars for gas. When you come home I'll have a little more money from work and we'll buy food.'

But then I remind myself, what's the worst that can happen? If we can't find a program or we don't have money, I'll go out and get it or we'll do something at home. We'll make do, but my son will always get what he needs. Maybe we won't move to Miami where there's a brand new school for autism. I would love it for him, but maybe we can't afford that. But I will always see that my son gets the absolute best we can afford. I will not let him waste away because we don't have enough money.

Would I love more money? Absolutely. Would I love a big house? Sure. Anybody who says no is lying. Would I like a new car? Yeah, I would like a new car. Who wouldn't like a new car? But these are all expendable. It's those times when Chris laughs or puts on a hat and performs for us that are irreplaceable. Those are the moments I treasure. They're what hold the true value in life.

6

Total Involvement

'Jae, let me take you to dinner and the therapist will stay with Chris. Jessica's here to watch also.' This was the first opportunity we'd had in over a year to go out and have someone reliable babysit Chris. We got to the car, looked at each other, and went back in the house.

'We can't leave. Everybody get up and let's go together,' I said. We took the therapist and the two kids and we went to dinner. We just couldn't leave him, not because we were so scared to do it, we just felt that we wanted to be with him.

My life changed in many, many different ways when Chris was first diagnosed with autism. Our focus went entirely on Chris. Everything. Everything was dropped; my other children, marriage, work, money. There were no hot cooked meals, cleaning, or romance – nothing. Who cared? Everything was dropped until we became a little more centered, until we got a grip on what we were doing with Chris.

Initially I felt an immediate need to do and learn everything I could for this child as quickly as possible. I almost felt like I could conquer the disorder once I understood it. This world of special needs opened up and we became part of it.

There were times we didn't sleep because there was so much to learn and other times we couldn't sleep because of the disturbing nature of what we did learn. A couple people told us about institutionalization and seizures to look forward to in our son's future. One of the fathers I called told me, 'He'll probably become self-injurious and aggressive. It's lots of money and lots of disappointment. We put him in an institution and see him every weekend.'

I responded, 'I didn't call you to hear about an institution. I called you for some help. I'm looking for someone to tell me what's out there for my child, not how to get rid of him.'

The more involved we got, the more there was to tackle. There were so many different issues. How do I get medical care? What's the new therapy? How do I get services? Money, wills, trusts, estates. Tackling the world of autism became a whole lifestyle.

There was and still is a big drive to be as involved as I humanly can to help Chris. This is not because of guilt. It's because I feel that it's necessary. I think if anybody can help a child it's the parents. I can send my child to any school and follow any philosophy, but *I* must be keyed in to him for these things to work. It's a twenty-four hour a day commitment. It really is. Unless your child has a higher functioning form of autism, you're going to lose him if you don't constantly key in to what he's doing.

I'm sure I never would have gone to this extreme in caring for Chris if he did not have his disability, even though I think I was already a very good father before he was born. I always paid attention to the little things with Jessica; we read, went over homework, took walks and talked, and I tried teaching her different things all the time. People made fun of us because we were so involved. 'You're always with her. You're at every school function. You're like Mr. and Mrs. Perfect parents.' I always felt it was the parents' job to get their children prepared for life.

Unfortunately, a lot of times this disorder is so intense and the child so severe that you can be the most dedicated parent in the world and still might not get very far or end up picking the wrong program. On the other hand if you pick the wrong program, but you're totally involved, you will recognize the mistake. We've picked many wrong programs and taken many wrong turns. We've shut down our program, begun again, and changed it. We've rearranged his room. It is such a fragile disorder with so many intricacies that it is very easy to do something wrong. But if you are in tune, you'll catch it.

For instance, I noticed when we started Chris' language program he stopped speaking and he would hit himself in the head. Well, that's something you should notice! Time to stop the language program. Let's do it a different way or let's approach it differently. Here's a child who can't communicate and if all of a sudden he screams when he enters the room, you know there's something wrong. Unfortunately, it's not always that obvious. Sometimes whatever's wrong could be the most minute thing.

You need to be completely involved in order to catch the little things. Chris used to perform in front of the mirror with a hat or bowl cocked to the side of his head and then made it fall. I happened to know there was a Sesame Street scene where Fozzie Bear is a policeman who gets roughed up and his hat falls off. Thank goodness I knew what he was trying to do and was able to say, 'You're Fozzie, aren't you?' He'd laugh with delight and perform the scene again for me.

Can you imagine if you're showing off for your parents and you think you're doing beautifully and nobody recognizes what you're doing? How horrible. What a blow to your self-esteem! So even if you don't know it's Fozzie, at least say, 'You are so funny. What a great job! Look at you. Do it again!' Make your child feel good about himself. I think people are too quick to walk away, and so are educators.

Instructors for kids with autism need to learn more than the average teacher and give more personal attention. It's a fact, not a decision. If the teachers and therapists aren't alert all the time they miss things. That's why Chris' class is kept down to five kids.

But even in Chris' wonderfully run class, things can be missed. I happened to observe one day when a little boy was acting very aggravated and wouldn't sit still. The teachers kept telling him, 'No. Sit and eat lunch. No, sit. Stop. No, you cannot go there.'

Do you know what was disturbing him? One of the posters on the wall wasn't straight. All he wanted to do was fix it. Kids with autism can't stand seeing something askew. They need order. But he couldn't say, 'Could you just move the poster, please?' Finally his mom and I figured out what was wrong, knocked on the observation window, and pointed to the crooked poster. The teacher let him go over and fix it, and after that he sat down calmly.

It's very easy to mess up, even for professionals. The idea is to recover. We as parents are not experts and can certainly do the wrong things. It's important to catch the mistakes, though. If you catch them, you're on the road to recovery. You might try a million things and be frustrated and sit there crying while your kid keeps screaming. But don't give up and eventually you'll hit upon the solution.

If you keep trying you'll get it. You may not know who to call, but if you keep calling you'll find somebody. You may not know where to get money. You may not know what politician to hit, but I'm telling you, if you make a hundred calls, one of those calls you'll get the right person.

On the pessimistic side, this is a devastating disorder and it is very possible that your child may have such severe problems that you still may be unable to help him. Autism is a devastating life-long disorder, and there may not be anything wrong with you as a parent if your child is not progressing. You've got to look into yourself and know that you gave it one hundred per cent.

Maybe we're lucky with Chris' improvement. But it wasn't just the programming and the work we did. You've got to really love the child. I'm one of these guys who believes love conquers all eventually, and you've got to pour every bit of love you have into him.

Helping your child also means sacrifice. I'm not being dramatic. You are really going to lose everything. Your other children will suffer. Your marriage will suffer. Everything you know about life will change. I want to state it very factually. We yell at each other. We get tired. We give up half the time. We cry.

Unless you're fantastically wealthy you'll have no money. You'll have no social life. It takes a lot of believing in yourself. I think you have to say to yourself, 'You know what? I can do this. I'm going to fail a couple times, make stupid mistakes, look stupid, but I'm going to keep going.'

My wife always says she sees what he sees and I feel what he feels. If Chris is frustrated with something, she'll look at it and be able to fix it. If he's unhappy, I'll go up to him and say, 'Come on. Let's go wrestle,' or 'I know you feel bad. Let's take a hot bath together.' We just work at it all the time. Twenty-four hours a day we work in some way with our son.

I know it sounds very easy for me to sit here and say you need time and money. A lot of people aren't willing or can't do it. Some fear they don't have the ability. My first reaction is, bullshit. Too bad. You're going to *have* to do it. You have to make that commitment with children who have autism. If you don't, your child's going to be put in the system. Sure, some people do manage to flourish in the system, but that's not the norm.

People say to me, 'You're doing such a good job. It's amazing how you drive such a long distance everyday for school, manage to pay so much money, and spend so much time with Chris.' But I don't think of us as extraordinary parents. I really don't. I'm not trying to be humble. I don't understand how anybody would do less.

We said that we would always, always be there for him. This was the pact we made in the beginning. I will never give in to sadness, or difficulty, or lack of funds. NEVER would I give up my child or send him away because life gets too hard for us. He's not going anywhere, no matter what.

There's a story I read about the power of parents. Two tribes of Indians live by a mountain. One lives at the bottom and the other lives at the top. The mountain is horribly icy and craggy and difficult to climb. The tribe from the top comes down one day on a raid, steals a baby and scrambles back up. All the braves from the bottom tribe attempt to go after them to retrieve the baby, but they keep falling and slipping. They're winded, bleeding, and cold. Failed, they sit at the bottom of the mountain breathing hard and tending to their wounds. Suddenly they look up and here comes the baby's mother carrying her infant down the mountain. They turn and say to her, 'We're the bravest of the brave, the warriors of the tribe. *We* couldn't get up the mountain. How did you do it?'

'You're not the mother,' she replied.

I always remember this story because its message is true for all parents, especially ones of disabled children. All those doctors, therapists and fundraisers who care may be important, but they're not the parents. It is the parents who make the ultimate difference. You can have no knowledge at all, but if you act like a parent and are there for your child no matter what the circumstance, your child will reach his potential and be happy. Total involvement is the key.

I could write a book about all that Bill has done. I think he is very humble and very giving. He doesn't expect praise for what he is doing. He just considers it as a normal part of life. It's absolutely amazing. I know that parents want to do their best for their children, but Bill and Jae have gone to extremes in trying to help their child. I think they're exceptional. And the wonderful thing is that they think it's just the average work that everyone does. Their whole lives surround their family. They just put three hundred per cent into their children and they love it. You can see that they're stressed out and tired at times, but they just keep on going and going and never complain or wish that Chris didn't have autism. The most wonderful thing is they love Chris for who he is. They don't also wish he was a normal child. That's Chris. That's their son, and they do what they have to do for him.

Melissa Bennett, therapist

The Stress Of Daily Life

TO DO LIST

Take out garbage
Clean kitty litter
Feed cats
Let Chris watch movie
Take Jessica to school
Work out twenty minutes at gym
Pick up dry-cleaning
Pick up liquor for bar
Food shop – buy Chris' rolls; must be baked fresh daily
Get gas
Pick up check for Benefit
Go to bank
Let Chris color
Make calls for Benefit
Have Chris try new computer program
Make calls for advocacy work
- Don't forget to return call to family in need of help
- Check with Autism Society
- Call state representative

Give interview to reporter
Take Chris to gymnastics
Drive Chris one-and-a-half hours to school in Baltimore
Meeting with Dr. Landa

Drive Chris home
Stop at mall – get Chris to walk around
Go to work
Jae – Set up therapy room
Jae – Touch base with therapists
ABA Therapy for Chris
Jae – Staff meeting
Bathe Chris
Put Chris to bed
Prepare for next day
- Pack food, clothes, car, back-up bag, school bag
- Prepare data for therapy
- Prepare apraxic and aphasic speech cards

People don't realize that you put a hundred per cent of your time, energy and money into a child with a serious disability. I wake up in the morning and don't even have time to make coffee. I grab the leftover from the night before and I gulp it down with two aspirin. That's how I start every day. I only get a few hours sleep, and run all day long.

You go through the day and you think what *didn't* I do today? I didn't have him drink a lot of water. I didn't have him exercise. He wasn't on the computer. He didn't read. He's watching too many movies. He's by himself too much.

Last night I came home from work and Chris was in the bath. I hadn't played with him yet that day, so I got him out of the bath, we played and then lay down together. It's constant. I always think I'm not doing enough because what I'd ultimately like to do is spend twenty hours communicating and setting up little programs to help Chris.

But then I also must remember to allow him time to be a kid. If he wants to watch TV and sit on the couch it's not fair to take that away from him. After all, he goes to school six, seven hours a day, has speech and does gymnastics. Yesterday morning I had the speech teacher come over privately for the first time in our house and Chris was mad because he usually lounges around in the morning. He worked a little bit with her, but then he cried. He wanted to watch TV. He kept pushing her out of the room because he wanted time to himself.

Scheduling gets me stressed out more than anything. I find I have absolutely NO time to sit down. Before I know it, the day is over and it's one o'clock the next morning. All I long for is time to read a book, take a walk or watch a TV program. Occasionally it happens, but that's not the norm. Every minute of my life is scheduled.

And then there are all the things that are unexpectedly thrown at you. Last night, for instance, we started to wind down and I gave Chris a bath. I ran downstairs to get him a soda and when I returned I saw that Chris had had a bowel movement in the bath. This is not unusual for him so he just pushed everything to the side. There he was calmly sitting in the corner not dealing with it.

As I cleaned and dried my son I told him, 'You know, you're doing a good job. One day you're going to go to the potty and I know you're trying and we just love you.' And he hugged me so hard and smiled as if he just needed that little encouragement. Then I went and cleaned out the tub, disinfected it, put Draino down the drain, and put him to bed. I ended up falling asleep with him. When I woke up it was seven o'clock in the morning, and I immediately got on the phone for two hours about projects, benefits and school.

Later I drove Chris down to Baltimore for kindergarten. As we were driving he spilled a little soda. He can't tolerate the wet against him so I had to pull over on the highway and change his shirt so he would calm down. There's no normalcy to our lives whatsoever.

Chris probably doesn't go to bed sometimes until one o'clock in the morning. It's very hard to get him to bed earlier. He doesn't fall asleep until he wears himself down. You would think during the day with running around, long drives to and from Baltimore, school, therapy, gym, walks, swimming, wrestling with me and a bath that he'd fall asleep. No. He's up and jumping and we've done everything we can. Sometimes when he's tired he'll put his head next to me, squeeze hard and start flailing. It's like he's getting all the stress out of him. We start at nine, ten o'clock putting him to bed and he usually doesn't fall asleep till one in the morning.

Everyday life with autism generates a million stories. For instance, Chris had a deathly fear of dogs and one day he and Jae were outside sitting on a bench when a dog came quietly over. Suddenly I heard Jae yelling for me while I was taking a walk with Jessica. We ran back and found Chris passed out. He had gone into seizure when the dog came up to them. The dog hadn't done anything, but Chris went off anyway. Just another day for the Davis family! We've learned to laugh these things off or we'd go crazy.

Communicating with Chris is often another source of frustration for both him and us that we deal with on a daily basis. He may want a movie that he can't find so I'll usually say to him, 'Go to your PECS.' But he flips through sometimes and can't find the picture of what he wants. Then I search through the movies with him. Sometimes it takes two hours until we find what he wants.

I remember one time he was looking around the house so angrily. He kept looking in bags and looking around. I didn't know what he wanted. When I left for work I noticed four rubber lizards lying by the car. He likes to group them and I figured out they were what he wanted. Obviously they were dropped the day before when leaving the car. I came back inside and said, 'Look what I found!' He got all excited and started flapping his hands. I knew immediately they were what he was looking for. But if I wasn't in tune to him all the time I wouldn't have known that.

Chris' needs pretty much take center stage, and things like household chores are done in whatever spare time we have. Every once in a while Jessica will do the whole house to help everybody. Otherwise we all try and help with the vacuuming. Jae's the laundry person. And there's no such thing as ironing anymore. In fact, I had to wear blue shirts at my last job and when I couldn't find my new one I asked Jae what happened to it. She said, 'You had to iron it. I got rid of it.' She just threw it away or something because she refuses to iron. I don't think we even know where the iron is. So if you want something ironed you either go to the dry-cleaner or use your rear end to press it.

Recently the clothes piled up so high that it looked like we were taking in people's laundry. Our dryer had broken so we were lugging the wash down the block to our complex's laundry room. I decided to help out by taking all the laundry and have it done professionally. It cost me ninety dollars. Now people would say I'm out of my mind. But you know what? I brought home a carload of folded laundry and my wife didn't have to do it for a couple of weeks. It was a big treat, and I don't think anyone realizes how important that is. Jae was so thankful.

Little indulgences become important to us. The fact that I can walk across the street from Chris' school and take ten minutes for myself to buy a sandwich is a luxury. As much as I want to devote my life to my son and others, it would be very nice to say to my wife that today we're going to dinner. What a luxury it would be to get out a little bit!

But luxuries are not a part of our lives. There are a number of things that we could use. We're so cluttered and crowded in our home that more space would be a blessing. A bedroom for my wife and I would be nice since we made ours into Chris' therapy room. An office would be great too. There are tons of files and computer work we need to store.

I see so many things go by the wayside in exchange for working with Chris. Our health is neglected. We're just pushing too hard all the time and almost physically break down. Our lives are tiring and demanding, but we don't consider it a burden. In fact, I long for *more* time with Chris.

People constantly ask me for help and advice, but sometimes I have to refuse. I've learned that sometimes I simply have to say no to people. I can't be at every meeting and every rally. I can't write every article. It's very stressful for me. Sometimes saying no can be more stressful than taking on the job, however. But then I catch myself and say, 'We're going to stop for a bit. Let's watch TV. We're not going tonight. Cut his therapy session and we'll go to the mall.' Breaks like these help ease us a bit.

I wish there was time to find outlets for my stress. I can get pretty hard to live with at times. I bark at people, get very jittery and can't concentrate. There's no way for me to blow off steam. I'm lucky to find twenty minutes to work out in the gym. I'd like to take a self-defense class but I can't afford the time or expense. So my biggest daily relaxation is feeding the little squirrels outside our home every morning.

Socializing would be a great way to relax, but there's no time for that either. My best de-stressors are Jae and Jessica. They both know how to say things that soothe me.

But Jae gets pretty cranked up too. It's very hard for her because the burden of therapy is mostly on her. She's created so many therapies and so many innovations and then has to carry them out as instructions. Chris' whole program constantly changes and she must monitor it very closely. That means scheduling, changing the room, changing paperwork, changing data sheets, creating programs on the computer, facilitating them, teaching the students how to carry it through, watching how they do and correcting them. She's under a lot of stress with it all and I think she has less time than I do. She'll always say, 'I don't know how you do what you do,' and I'll always say, 'I don't know how you do what you do.' I personally think she is incredible.

I really don't mean to sound like I'm complaining about our lives. You hear about people in difficult predicaments all the time who manage. 'My daughter went to the hospital and I spent my life savings getting her the best surgeons.' What sort of parent wouldn't do that? Are we to forget therapy for Chris so we can buy a boat next year? Am I going to send my wife to work so we have more money? These are not even questions for me. THERE ARE NO ISSUES HERE! 'Honey, I have to work so we can get the house.' No you don't. Live in a smaller house. There's not an issue here.

And even with typical kids there shouldn't be this problem. What's more important, your lifestyle or your children? 'Honey, you've got to get back to work and we'll put the baby in daycare because we need the money from that second job.' Are you crazy?

My wife is a smart independent woman. She got along very well without me before we were married, but she chose to stay home with her kids. We had kids late in life for that reason. We were ready. Does she like to get away? Absolutely. Is she boring or incapable because she doesn't have a paying job? No. She likes being with her kids. Who's she going to leave them with? No one else could possibly love or care for them as much as she could. What could she possibly do that's more important than raise our children? But parents do that all the time with typical kids, and I think it's wrong. I can't even fathom doing it to a disabled child.

Taking a second job for more money should not be an issue here. Skimping on expensive services your child needs should not be an issue. Pay for what your children need and live a little less luxuriously. Grow up and realize that it's not the material things that bring happiness.

Yes, we carry some great burdens, but we are still happy. It's the love and strength of our family that keeps us that way. With each new challenge our love gets even stronger. And it's the strengthening of our love that makes the stress of daily living easier to, get through. People come up to me all the time and say, 'I could not do what you do.'

And I say, 'Yes, you could. If it was your child, you would do it too.'

8

Secretin, A Potential New Weapon

The word was out. Thanks to an evening news show the world learned of a drug miraculously curing autism! Its name was secretin, an animal hormone originally given to people with pancreatic problems. When a child with autism was given secretin for pancreas and stomach problems rapid changes suddenly came over him. For no apparent reason this child began to elucidate and speak. The only change in his life was secretin.

Once this episode aired every parent in the entire world who had a child with autism wanted secretin. It was a chance. Who wouldn't grab at the opportunity for a cure?

I immediately went to Chris' pediatrician to start my son on this possible miracle drug. We spent two days together discussing how we thought the hormone should be given. Infusion was the method of choice by most, but I refused to put my son through that. To infuse you first had to test if the recipient was allergic to it. So after a short infusion you waited fifteen minutes for a reaction. If there was no sign of allergy, a long infusion was given. The kids had to be strapped down. It was a horrible ordeal. I felt there was not enough evidence of a cure for me to put Chris through that so we decided to give him secretin by injection. The problem with injections, however, was that we had to play with the amounts in order to find the right dosage.

Giving and getting secretin took us into a whole underworld of drugs. Since it was not meant to be given for autism we went to the pediatrician's home secretly for the first injection. A few days after Chris' first dose we began to notice a different child. Not a miracle, but we noticed some changes. He had more receptive language, less aggression, better bowel movements and was more artistic. Naturally we wanted to continue it, but now we couldn't get a hold of more hormone.

Ferring, the pharmaceutical company that produced secretin, was quickly overrun. Doctors were prescribing it off-label for autism and everybody was trying to get a hold of it. The company didn't even have enough for people with pancreatic problems. It was nuts. People were calling the government. The pharmaceutical company was out of it and it was not going to make anymore. I called everybody – neighborhood doctors, pharmaceutical companies. I would do anything to get my hands on secretin.

The situation quickly got out of hand. We heard of neurologists who were charging six thousand dollars for an infusion! One day our phone rang and it was a woman whose family I helped when their child was diagnosed with autism. 'Bill,' she said, 'you helped us. I'll help you. I have secretin.' She had gotten a hold of some in South Carolina. So we paid her and went in on it together.

Luckily, we were able to continue giving Chris the secretin. But now we had to play with how many cc's of the hormone and how many injections he needed for it to work. We noticed him fading after a couple of weeks as the secretin wore off. He was acting a little more confused, like 'Hey, wait a minute. I was seeing clearly and now I'm losing it.' So every month we had to play with how much and how often to dose him. We eventually administered the hormone every twenty days.

Obtaining secretin, however, continued to be a problem. Our supply from South Carolina ran out and we again had to find another source. This time we found a woman whose kid wasn't being helped by the hormone so we bought it from her. Now I think we only have two vials left. We've been doing this for about a year and a half.

The doctor only charges us fifty dollars, but each vial costs anywhere from two hundred and fifty to three hundred and fifty. Once you open the vial it has to be used right away or be discarded. And unfortunately, a whole vial is too much, so you either get another kid to go in with you or you throw it out. There's no use saving it. It's not going to do anything.

Keeping the unopened vial fresh is difficult too. You have to freeze it, and when we take it to the doctor we bring it in a cooler packed in ice. He always asks us questions about how Chris is doing, whether there have been any reactions and then he gives the secretin; two shots, one in each buttock cheek. Chris doesn't like being there, but he marches in, gets his injections, rubs his rear and moves on.

We've now learned that secretin has been sold to a drug company called Repligen which is trying to make a synthetic version of the hormone. I don't know how long that's going to take, but hopefully the synthetic version will be more readily available and safer.

We haven't seen any side effects from the drug, but you never know. I called a doctor who's doing work with it in Minnesota and she said you have to realize that as pure as they say an animal hormone is, it's never one hundred per cent pure. There's always the chance of a virus being spread.

In the meantime, secretin continues to be studied. We wanted Chris to join a study at Johns Hopkins, but because he was already taking the hormone he couldn't participate. So far I am not aware of any studies that have come up with concrete conclusions.

From our own experience, though, we believe secretin has helped Chris improve. I wouldn't say it's a miracle. But he seems more attentive, better able to understand commands and language, speaks a little more, and is less aggressive. Over all he appears more lucid. When we stop secretin we see him become a little more aggressive, a little more confused and have more episodes of flailing. So we definitely link the changes to the secretin. Admittedly, we are doing a million other things to help Chris along with the disorder. But the rise and fall of symptoms along with amount of secretin he gets tells me that I can't discount it.

I'm not aware of that many cases where parents claim their kids were cured of autism by secretin. However, most feel it has worked to a certain extent. At the very least it does help the stomach problems that afflict so many with this disorder. The bottom line is you might see great improvement, you might see a little improvement, or you might see no improvement. But parents who saw this one show and said, 'My God, my child will speak! It's a miracle!' were terribly disappointed.

Dr. Bernard Rimland, one of the founders of the Autism Society of America, has always said there's a link to hormones and diet, but nobody would listen to him. Now researchers are listening, and they'll probably discover a whole combination of hormones and enzymes that will help people with autism. As seen with secretin, though, autism is a vastly complicated disorder. One child could get secretin and nothing happens while another gets it and huge changes take place. Studying secretin, however, is at least a start to finding what I hope will be a cure.

9

Steps To Take

People always come over to me and ask, 'How did you set up such a wonderful program for your son? How have you made such strides with him?' My answer is that we didn't wake up with all this. It was a lot of hard work – day after day, trials and tribulations. You don't suddenly have programs and good schools in front of you. There are a number of steps you have to take.

Knowledge

The first step we took was to get information coming into the house. Our name was placed on every association, catalog, book and conference mailing list we could find. Then we searched the web for every autism site, got on every list, posting, and link there was. Of course, you've got to exercise caution when using the Internet. One site I clicked onto said, 'Kids with autism in Arizona have been cured by eating adobe bricks. Send us money and we'll give you an adobe brick that will cure your child too.' In all probability kids with autism probably had pica, just like my son had, and they were eating the commonly found brick for minerals. Perhaps a few months later some of them began to talk, and someone made the assumption that adobe was behind it. Most likely, though, speech was brought on by something like therapy. Anyway, adobe bricks don't cure autism, and Internet sources should always be checked.

Don't let a few questionable sources stop your information quest, however. You need to empower yourself with knowledge. Read. Travel. I called everybody on the phone. 'Hi, I read your name in a book. I live in Lancaster and have a kid three years old with autism. Can you tell me a little bit about what you do?' They talked to me. If they didn't talk to me they'd give me another number and that person might have given me another number or a book to read.

I remember when I started studying educational law I read a law journal article describing IEPs by Marty Kotler. I found him at the University of Delaware and telephoned him. We exchanged ideas and then I asked if he would be my lawyer. He wasn't licensed in Pennsylvania, but referred me to his friend, Dennis McAndrews. Dennis McAndrews is my lawyer to this day. If I hadn't been aggressive enough to make that call, I never would have found such a wonderful lawyer. So you do what you have to do.

As you empower yourself, shape that knowledge into what is good for your child. In other words, don't just read Lovaas and say, 'I know Lovaas now.' Read Lovaas and pick out bits and pieces of what works for you. Don't be afraid to say, 'My child doesn't learn language like that so I'll find a language teacher who can help us with a different approach.'

Eventually you may hit roadblocks when trying to find the best help for your child. Don't let that stop you. Fight with all that knowledge you've gained. That knowledge is your power. Fight for your child's rights. Decide for yourself which therapy and education is good for him rather than what other people offer or tell you, and then go get it. Never veer from it. Remember, you don't have to be brilliant, or have connections, or have money. You just have to persevere.

Introduce

I think one of the best things you can do as a parent of a disabled child is gravitate toward a small community so people get to know your kid and he has a network. This is not because you want to hide him away or you need him to be accepted. Having everybody know your child is good. Much of our community knows my son, and I bet if he ever got lost people would know him. Even now he's learned to go up to the store counter and pay, and the guy at the counter knows him and tells him, 'Good job, Chris.' If he's by himself when he's older and goes up to the counter stimming, people will know why. I'd prefer that over no one knowing him or understanding him. And you'll find most people are supportive. So if he starts acting in an odd way, chances are someone will know him, be able to identify him, explain he has autism, and call us.

Peaceful place

Another step we took for Chris was to create a safe home environment. This world has so much noise and so many pictures, and it's so fast! They have to learn this, this, this! All the stimuli work against them because they need slow and quiet environments to prosper. In my house we know not to yell or bother him. He's spoiled in a way, but he has a safe environment to come home to. He loves to come home! He gets excited and runs up to his room where all his things are. He gets something to eat and makes himself comfortable. That's his solace. And I believe all kids with autism need that.

Support

One of the steps we took was to form FACT, a support and advocacy group. By all means, if you can find a knowledgeable group of parents or just one parent, go and make contact. A support group should be able to help you through issues. Ask members questions when you join. 'What do you do for your son?' If they start listing specific therapies and programs, have knowledge of educational law, know the professionals in the area and beyond and know where to get a diagnosis then you know you're in good hands. But when it's a group of moms taking this as an opportunity to get out of the house and leave their kids, you're in the wrong place. That may be needed, but don't call it a support group. Call it a social group.

If there's no support group in your area either for siblings or yourself, why don't you start one on your own? You can go to the local paper and have them write a human interest story. You can take an ad out. You can put up flyers. The worst that can happen is nobody shows up. So if you want to have a support group, start one.

Early intervention

We're strong believers in early intervention. If we knew sooner that Chris suffered from autism, we absolutely would have started therapy then. The first therapy program we tried and the one I recommend to start with is ABA, Applied Behavioral Analysis. ABA includes programs like Discrete Trial, Lovaas, TEACCH or a combination of them. It simply works by analyzing behavior and breaking down tasks. To work well it has to be intense so it requires a lot of hours and trained therapists. We started our program with forty hours a week of Discrete Trial Instruction!

Socialization

The initial teaching of ABA is very matter-of-fact, where the child sits at the table and instruction doesn't vary. It's very important, but I think that socialization and communication skills are also necessary. After ten minutes of ABA go over and do art. Then go back to ten more minutes of ABA. Singing in another location might be your next activity. Alternate ABA with play and group activities. Don't just match colors. Take the crayon and color a picture. The child has to socialize and do what other kids do. Learn language. Communicate. If we had realized the importance of teaching socialization skills early, we would have originally incorporated more socialization and less Discrete Trial in Chris' program. The more you get your child to communicate, the more he's in touch with the world and the better off he is.

Exercise

I'm also a firm believer in exercise for these children. When you exercise your neurons fire. It helps improve physical health and is great for self-esteem, pride and coordination. Gymnastics has been a wonderful activity for Chris because it requires him to pay attention, learn about safety, and is taught in little steps, much like Discrete Trial Instruction. They have to watch, listen, imitate you and actually interpret verbal commands. What a great way to train their brains! Physical exercise is very important for brain and body development.

Participate

When you take your child to gym class be sure to stay and watch. I hate drop-off parents. I always make it a point to attend all of Chris' activities. Even if I can't participate, I can observe. Being there helps to communicate with my son and build on the activities at home. 'I saw you hang from a bar today so we're going to hang from the bar on the playground.' It's important that you stay and participate or observe your child's activities as much as possible.

Hearing test

What other steps have we taken for Chris? Originally we had him put through a series of doctor recommended tests. They always want you to have a hearing test done because children with autism do appear deaf and it has to be ruled out. Chris also had an MRI and EEG but they showed nothing. Seizure activity is sometimes seen, but if there's already a very strong diagnosis of autism I wouldn't put my child through an MRI again just to rule out other things. I certainly would stay away from psychiatrists. The child doesn't have a psychological problem.

Skilled therapists

A step you should definitely take is to find a trained group of established professionals who don't stick to one philosophy, have their degrees with an emphasis on autism and trained in an autism center. Get away from anybody who tells you they only believe in one philosophy or only use one therapeutic program, or are not interested in literature you read. The person to gravitate to is the one who says, 'Let's see what your child responds to. Let's use everything that helps your child. I use different approaches to reach different children.' Be intuitive about who you hire to work with your child.

Sometimes attending a conference is a waste of time if they talk about theory rather than applying it. It's only worthwhile if you hear a PhD talk about imitative skills and describe how she actually gets kids to imitate. But to talk about theory and not apply it to children is, to me, a waste of time. As a parent I don't want to be invited to that seminar. Invite me to something with practical application instead.

Secretin

Don't waste your time with so-called miracles like adobe bricks or taking your child to Disneyland. You need to discern what's useful and what's not. Do try new theories with medical supervision. For instance, we have had success with the new treatment, secretin. Since taking the hormone, we've seen Chris improve, especially in language.

In the beginning you feel like you're bombarded by everything. Did you give him vitamin A and did you try vitamin B and did you give him a massage with a brush? And you're saying, 'If I don't do all this, I'm failing. I have to do everything for him.'

We went through a period where we said to ourselves, 'Calm down. You have to pick and choose your priorities.' People would ask me if we had Chris on the gluten-free diet and I'd say, 'You know what? Right now I'm glad he's eating and that's not one of our priorities. Our priority is three hours of therapy at home.' So everybody does their own thing.

There are new theories and better schools built everyday. Sometimes you sit there and say, if I had a million dollars I could move to South Carolina and put him in that new program. It can make you feel pretty inadequate. So you try and do the best you can, but you're constantly checking yourself. Does he have the best speech program? Is he getting the best physical therapy? But then you have to rein your emotions in and realize you're taking all the right steps and trying everything you can. There's very little you can try that's a waste of time.

Engage

As long as you are constantly engaging your child, you can't go wrong. That's the key. When school is over, don't stop working with him. Don't just leave him in the corner. Help him join in. Talk and point things out when you go to the mall. If you see your child going off, bring him back.

What you're trying to do on a sophisticated level is get these kids to enter life. They're scared to participate and I don't blame them. My son has trouble opening a door that closes after he walks through. He opens it and backs away because he's afraid the door is going to hit him. So I show him, 'Put your hand here. Now hold it. Now we're walking. See? See, you can hold it like this. Good job!' It's such a simple concept, but so hard for him to grasp.

Love

I used to think my job was to always be there and open the door for him, but now I realize it's to *show* him how to open the door. And then show him how to open the door bravely, and then show him how to walk through every door. And that's what I do with him. When he comes to a door and gets afraid I say, 'Chris, we can do this. You be strong. You and Daddy, we can do this. Come on. I'm going to show you. Walk over here.' And he walks. I hope one day he will walk through all kinds of doors that life puts in front of him.

But no matter what steps we take, he will never walk through those doors without one critical ingredient – love. Unconditional love is really the foundation for all of the other steps you take to help your child succeed.

10

Sibling Impact

Chris laid another twig down on the sidewalk, making sure it was facing exactly the right direction. Then he started to meticulously examine the next twig, making sure its dimensions were correct before allowing it to join the line. Jessica watched as her brother engrossingly worked on his usual summer afternoon project. A bus pulled up and a group of neighborhood kids got off. 'What's he doing?' they asked Jesse.

'This is my brother, Chris. He has autism and likes to line twigs up because of his disorder.'

'Can we help?'

'Yeah! But sometimes he acts like he doesn't hear you. If he does that, just get in his face like this and say here Chris.'

And that's exactly what they did. I'll never forget that! I came home and found a brigade of kids finding twigs and handing them down the line as Chris examined each one. Those twigs spanned the length of the parking lot!

Getting kids to join in with Chris was typical of Jessica. She has never once shown embarrassment for her brother. In fact, my house is like the social center. Jessica is always asking friends over. When I come home it's not unusual for me to find five kids in the house. They all know her brother and she is happy to explain his disorder to them.

It wasn't always this easy for Jessica. When she first learned of her brother's disorder at age seven she had all kinds of difficult questions and emotions. 'Is he going to die?' 'What is this thing that he has?' 'How did he get it?' 'Is he going to be sick physically?' 'Will he get better?' It was very scary for her.

We tried our best to explain what was happening to Chris. We first told Jesse that Chris had autism when we were all at an outdoor market strolling him around. At that point he was rejecting most food and we had plans to get a formal diagnosis. We told Jessica that we thought he had autism and we were getting him help. She was quiet. Then she asked the big question, 'Is he going to die?' We told her no, but from what we read it would continue for life and we weren't quite sure how things would progress, but she could help.

There were two major guilt trips she experienced. The first brought her to us in tears. 'How come I'm normal and he's not? How come I'm the one that is OK? It's not fair.'

'Yes. It's not fair that he has autism.'

'No. It's not fair that I didn't get it.'

We explained to her, 'This is a genetic disorder that mostly affects boys. We don't know if it had to do with heredity or bad luck, but you didn't do anything wrong. There are families where one person has cerebral palsy and the others don't. It just happens. You could not have taken it on for him and have nothing to feel guilty about.'

Everyday she cried for something. She was guilty. She wanted a regular brother. She thought he would die.

The second big guilt trip was not wanting to play with him. Jessica didn't really have that much active play with Chris, even before he displayed obvious symptoms. He wasn't interested in toys or typical toddler play when he was little. Not knowing any better we almost laughed at it and labeled him as a loner. But as he got older and symptoms progressed, Jessica began to feel hurt that she couldn't play with him like a 'normal brother.' Everybody was playing outside with their brothers or sisters and he wasn't going. He had no attention span, no interests, and would go into his own world of spinning objects. It was very hard for her.

When Chris' symptoms were really extreme we were afraid he'd slip away from us at any moment. Life was not easy and Jessica caught the brunt of a lot of our stress. If she'd do something we thought would upset him we'd yell, 'Don't raise your voice, don't touch him! Why are you touching him?! I told you not to touch him!' It was very difficult for her.

I remember an evening where she absolutely broke down crying. We could see something was bothering her for a while, and finally she just broke down. 'It isn't fair that my brother has this.' Jae went to hold her and started to cry too. It was easy to see how devastating this disorder could be to members of a family. Both of them cried for hours. It was a deep sobbing that came from within. I heard my daughter say how bad she felt that he had this and had to go through everything without even understanding. It hurt her to see how hard it was for him. And she just cried in my wife's arms for hours. My wife later said that she cried for her daughter as well as her son.

Right from the start, we took Jesse everywhere we went with Chris. It was our way of building a strong, involved family. I feel it's good for siblings to be included unless there's something they really can't handle. That way they feel a part of things rather than on the outside of things. She came with us to Baltimore for his diagnosis. She was there holding him in his gown while he giggled from the sedative for oral surgery. She took her brother the first few times to summer school at Kennedy Krieger.

We always tried to have something to look forward to after we finished the difficult tasks. That way we'd have something hard to

Jessica and Chris

do first, but have something fun to do after. When we took Chris to Kennedy, for instance, we went to Hard Rock Café and took a boat ride.

Of course, as we got more and more involved and Chris sunk deeper, our whole house changed. Conversation always centered around her brother and therapy. I'm sure that was a very hard time for my daughter. As hard as it was for us, it was harder for her. Her entire world was turned upside down. So we were very careful to sit down with her and explain everything that was happening.

A lot of times the only explanation was, 'We don't have a choice. I know it's harsh. Unfortunately, he has something that requires hours and hours of dedication. I can't even explain to you what we're doing. But there's going to be a point where you're going to feel cut out or even yelled at, and it's not fair.' I think she understood.

She also came to us a lot with issues. Jessica has always been very good at talking with us. That certainly has helped her deal with her topsy-turvy world.

As Jessica's guilt declined, her involvement with Chris increased. In fact, she was the one who did a lot of work in the beginning. She attended every Rutgers workshop and went to conferences. She learned how to do therapy and was put on the therapist schedule. But most of all, she did things on her own with him.

At first when she tried to work with Chris things did not go well. She was a bit pushy so every time she walked in the room, he would move her away or start to cry. Autistics think in pictures and every time he saw his sister he pictured her coming aggressively at him. He wanted to get away before she got to him. He would get aggressive with her and she would say that he didn't love her.

So I said if she was serious about this, she had to get to work and start all over again. She had to let him know that she was going to be quiet and gentle. Finally he started seeing a different picture. She made up her mind and worked with him the way he could accept. It was either that or not having any relationship with him at all.

If he didn't know how to do something she'd say, 'Hey, Chris, let me show you. Come here.' And she'd show him how to open the door or something like that. It was great to be able to tell her how much she helped, how much she's sacrificed and how supportive she's been.

I think she was inspired by the love for her brother. As an older sister she wanted to do things with him. Instead of sitting and saying it's not possible, she looked for ways and worked with him. I remember very vividly the time when he wasn't speaking or responding and she brought us to him and said, 'Watch this. I've been teaching him something.' And Chris started singing and performing a finger play song! 'In a rabbit in the woods...'

'Jessica, how'd you do that?'

'Well, I got behind him, and taught him by moving his hands.' That happens to be a therapy called hand-over-hand. Out of a child's easy mind, almost a naïveté, she was one of the first ones to get a response out of Chris. It was clear she wanted to work with him. 'This is my brother. I want to teach him the song. He's not responding or looking at me so I'll try something else instead.'

Jessica has actually devised several therapy programs for Chris. She would watch the therapies, come up with better ways to teach him, and explain to her mom how to implement her ideas. She knew to take into account his limitations and work with them. Or sometimes she just wanted to figure out ways to teach him something new herself. She helped design a spelling program. We had a program with blocks that she changed entirely. Knowing his limitation with falling backwards, she helped him with that. She'd go up on the bed, stand behind him and then bring him down. Gradually she'd walk away a little bit. I didn't even know they were doing this until one day she said, 'Come on up, Dad. I've been working on something. Watch this.' And the boy flipped in the air and fell down!

'How'd you do that?' I exclaimed.

'We've been working on it.'

Jessica was also a master at running existing programs like sound discrimination with instruments. She was even able to keep the data and did it in front of professionals from Rutgers. They were duly impressed. Helping her brother has been a wonderful way for Jessica to show him her love.

A very dramatic moment for me was when Jessica won the Making A Difference Award. Once a month someone would be chosen by an eastern Pennsylvania news station to win the award and then there'd be a big news segment on the winner. For the remainder of the month one or two minute segments ran about the winner at various times of the day. I was so proud of how much

Jessica was doing that I wrote a four-page letter nominating her. One day I got a phone call telling me she'd won – the youngest person ever to win. I almost fell down! I ran to school and pulled her out of class to tell her. Her school flew a special flag signifying her achievement. She was the first one they flew it for and have only flown it for one other student since. The news people followed her around, interviewed her, and watched her do therapy with her brother. The reporters asked her things like, 'How'd you teach him to turn on the radio?'

She'd answer, 'I told him do this. And I did it again and again with him.'

'Tell us how you've changed your brother's life and what will he remember about you?' They were looking for something extraordinary.

'I wrestle with him and I play with him,' she replied. She was a kid and answered like a kid. And that probably was the most important thing because she related to him like a sibling, not an adult or therapist.

To help my daughter feel that life did not only revolve around her brother, I tried making as much time for her as possible. Of course, it wasn't as if I'd never spent a lot of time with her before. I was very involved in bringing up Jessica before Chris was born. My parenting was always very, very involved. We talked, read and wrote. We wrestled around a lot, took walks, played ball and went to movies. I was very, very involved. In fact, I was probably more involved with Jessica in the beginning than I was with Chris. She was this little miracle baby, the first child in our marriage. And she was a beautiful, loving girl. Just a joy to be around!

So to regain some of that time lost with her after Chris became ill, we started making special days. There was Mommy-Daughter Day, Daddy-Daughter Night and Movie Night. Any time I was free I'd jump up and say, 'Wait a minute! Let's do something with

Jessica… Jessica, come on I'll take you to Fridays for dinner. It's a special night out. You deserve it.'

We also reserved Sunday for family-oriented activities, even if I was working – just simple activities like going out to eat, taking a ride or taking a walk. We did our best to prevent her from feeling neglected. As a matter of fact, Jessica's probably spoiled. I say to myself, 'I'll give her anything she wants.' I'm sure I overcompensate, but I can't help myself. I said I was going to learn my lesson this Christmas and not buy so much, but I ended up getting her nine million gifts.

I've always gone out of my way to get things for Jessica. I took her to see NSync and to a Backstreet Boys concert in Philadelphia. We were seventh row from the stage. Just the two of us. I had to pay tons of money and jump through all kinds of hoops to get tickets from a guy who did sound and stage for them. But it was worth it to see her so happy.

I've tried really hard to be an equally good father to Jessica as I've been to Chris. But it's not always easy to find the time I'd like to spend with her. Recently she wrote a composition entitled, 'My Dad is my hero.' It just picked me up so! Now I had the verification that I've done OK as a father. The feeling from reading that composition will last for twenty-five years.

I really don't believe Jessica was shortchanged all that much over the years. Naturally, time to do things was drastically cut, especially at first. We couldn't go anywhere because we didn't know how to take Chris out. And our house was turned into an open season for therapists so she certainly lost her privacy. But I think she's a pretty well adjusted kid. She has straight As in school, she's in accelerated classes and is a leader with an outgoing personality.

Jessica was always naturally independent, which I'm sure has helped her through our family ordeals. But we also brought her up to be independent. We always took her everywhere and showed her everything. She stood up for herself even when she was very young.

I can remember her not being more than five or six when two little black boys moved in from Kenya. We were walking by and the two little girls next door were yelling, 'Ooh! Black boys. Get away! You're dirty!'

Jessica walked over. She was livid. 'Don't you ever say anything like that to them! They didn't do anything to you!'

'Well, they're black. And our father says they're dirty.' It was like a movie.

'They are not! You leave them alone!'

I was impressed. I didn't tell her to go over. She knew to do it on her own. She always stood up for the underdog. She was so incensed.

I think being part of a family with a disabled child has given her more strength and sensitivity. She sees her parents get up everyday and working constantly for her brother and for all kids with autism. I'm sure it's added some strength and fortitude and understanding of what it is to face adversity.

Jessica's never been embarrassed by Chris when we go out in public. She helps him through the mall and even likes to bring friends along when we're all going to eat. Embarrassment is certainly not a problem for her. In a restaurant he might stand in a booth and yell and flap; she's fine. We even laugh sometimes about how outrageous it all is.

When he was quite young Jessica and I decided to go out for breakfast with Chris. It was not easy taking him out because he had to have his own food and would only sit in a booth with a window. I was always a frantic mess trying to make sure we got the proper seating. So we got a booth by a window that morning and brought Chris' peanut butter and jelly. While Jesse and I ate, Chris lined up the silverware. To keep him happy we kept taking more silver off the other tables for him to use. So he lined up utensils, ate a little bit and looked out the window. 'Jessica,' I said, 'you see? This wasn't so terrible.'

'Dad, I really enjoyed it.' And with that remark, he took each piece of silver and threw it. Forks and spoons were hitting people and bouncing off the tables! Just as he hit a server on the tray, Jessica, without missing a beat called out, 'Check please.' And we couldn't help but break out in laughter.

Jessica has by no means been left to fend for herself. She gets a lot of guidance and love from us. But there's also an understanding that unfortunately, her time and privacy are cut down. We're sorry, but other things often have to take precedence.

Am I unfair to her by only caring about Chris' needs first? Probably. And it's not fair that I play with her less, but it's also not fair that my wife and I have no time for each other. It's unfair that we don't get to go away.

We could change the path we've chosen to care for Chris, but we choose not to. I feel that my son has special needs that must be constantly attended. In order for him to function, be happy, not to hurt, not to hit himself, communicate and laugh he needs constant attention, love and teaching. I cannot step away from that.

If I'm collapsed on the couch and hear Chris cry, I run to him. I just feel he needs me all the time and that I have to be there for him. If Jessica asks me to play a game I can tell her I'm too tired. I know if my son said it to me, though, I would play with him. It's tough for me to admit, but it's true. It's just that I know Jessica will understand and Chris will not.

There's an attitude in this country that I've always hated. Let's say your husband is suddenly injured and becomes a paraplegic or your wife comes home with cancer. Do you tell them to go live somewhere else so your lifestyle is not inconvenienced? No. And what happens to the rest of the family when you care for the sick member? They're put out. 'Dad's going to stay in the family room, and when you come home you watch him from four to six. He needs medication at seven and a nurse is going to be here. We also have to learn how to give him injections.'

I don't see the difference with a disabled child. People always ask me, 'What about the rest of your family? What about your free time?'

I respond, 'How many children do you have?'

'Two.'

'And if one was stricken with bone marrow disease, would you not care for her? Would you be an outstanding parent because you did care for her, or are you just doing your job? Wouldn't you insist that your other child adjust to the situation?'

Obviously, there's going to be an effect on the family. Guilt, resentment and unhappiness are only a few of the emotions experienced when someone in your family has a disorder. But more than likely, siblings will love and protect their disabled brother or sister. Jesse got into two major fights trying to protect Chris. Once a kid on the bus made fun of her brother by mimicking him and saying he was retarded. But one of Chris' splinter skills was spelling, and Jesse asked the boy, 'Can you spell incorporated?'

So the kid went, 'Umm. No.'

And she responded, 'So my *brother's* retarded? He can spell that word and you can't! Now who's retarded?'

Another time a boy in the pool made fun of her brother. I caught her chasing him around the water with a rock in her hand. She almost killed him. It bothered her that he made fun of Chris. So I told her, 'I feel like chasing people sometimes, but you can't hit them even though they make fun of your brother.'

There were a couple other little episodes too. One kid teased, 'Your brother's an idiot. He can't talk and look how old he is.' She responded by pushing him.

These kids are usually about her age so I told her, 'You know what? If your brother was fat, they'd make fun of him being fat. If he was deaf, they'd make fun of him being deaf. Kids are cruel. And they'd make fun of you too. They'd pick on your hairstyle. Kids pick on anything.'

I would absolutely recommend that all siblings of disabled children join a support group at first. It helped Jessica realize, 'Here are ten, twelve other kids in the same position I'm in. It's not just me. They have the same problems, the same questions, and the same household situations.' Support groups show kids they are not alone. It's good for them to talk. They talk about their problems, their joys and their triumphs. I absolutely recommend it. If there is no sibling support group in your area, invite your child's friends to the house and give them a talk yourself.

Jessica belonged to a monthly sibling group from ARC, Association of Retarded Citizens. They had a siblings with disabled children group. She was very active in it. However, she felt it wasn't serious enough. Occasionally she heard a speaker, but she found it was a little too babyish after a while and dropped out. She was talking about it recently and is toying with the idea of starting her own sibling group specifically for people with autistic siblings or for older siblings from age nine and up.

My daughter has also been very actively involved in advocacy work for autism. Every Awareness Day we held, Jessica had a special job like handing out flyers. For one benefit she came up with the idea to sell lemonade. At another benefit a popular, local group performed and she played the tambourine with them. When we had a DJ she picked the songs. We did a live auction once and her job was to collect the money from everybody.

When she was about eight years old she went to the state legislature to stand in for her brother. She was also called to help another girl with high-functioning autism in her school. The mother phoned and said, 'I read about you and I know your daughter goes to East Pete. Could she keep an eye on Kate?' Jesse also helped some of the kids with autism who came to our home for therapy. She's really developed an interest.

As long as the siblings lead normal lives, participating in advocacy work should not overburden them. If your kid comes home Friday night and says I'm going to work on an autism report, I think you better take a look. But if the kid comes home and says I want to go roller-skating with my friends, I think you're OK. That doesn't mean-there's anything wrong with your child doing a report on autism. Jessica once chose to write a school report on why emergency service people should be trained in autism. But that's not all her life is about. Her normal routine is to come home and go on-line with her NSync club, not the autism website.

Jessica still takes a lot of time with her brother and sometimes I hear them laugh for hours. He very much cares for her. But she's a young teenage girl now. Boys and music are becoming her priorities and you can't blame her for that. Jessica sometimes will say, I don't want to deal with him now. I want to be on-line with my friends. If she'd rather watch MTV than help us with Chris we don't force her or make an issue of it.

I really try not to be harsh with Jesse about her responsibilities to Chris. For example, I'll say to her, 'Would you do me a favor? Could you go upstairs and watch your brother for a half-hour?' And she'll say to me, 'I don't want to. I was going to ride my bike.' So I tell her go ahead. I don't make it a requirement. It's not like other households where she could take him along with her to help us. It's not right to expect a young girl to sacrifice her social life.

We try very hard to give Jesse her space. We drive her and all her friends to the roller-skating rink every Friday and Saturday she does things with friends. In fact, she has her friends over all the time. We're the house everybody comes to. She plugs in music and they sit outside, talk and do sidewalk chalk.

Chris loves to spend time with Jessica. He comes right over and hugs and kisses her. He loves her music. She's taught him all the latest songs and he loves to sing along with her. He also loves to flirt with her girlfriends. Chris copies Jessica more than she knows, much like a typical sibling. She's been very influential in his life.

There are times when she plays with him for six hours. They laugh, kiss and hug, and she teaches him. She dug down deep and worked hard for that relationship with her brother. But he's not going to be a normal brother who can join his sister outside and play ball or ride bikes. She can't really include him that way. There's a lot of explaining to do when she's around friends and she's got to keep her eye on him every minute.

Jessica does know that she will be responsible for her brother one day when she is older. I said to her one time, 'There's going to come a time you'll be in care of your brother. We don't know if he's going to make it on his own. That means if we're old and sick or we die you will have to take him in. And that's a fact of life.'

And she said, 'Fine.' Then I went on to explain about the trust fund. I've only mentioned it once or twice to her.

My other daughter, Danielle, unfortunately hasn't seen Chris a lot over the years because she lived with her mother and now is an adult living in New York. She's very proud of him and knows him as well as she can from a distance. He loves her, but I feel Jessica knows Chris in a way that would make her more suitable to be his guardian.

A couple people have told me that I'm putting an unnecessary burden on Jessica at a young age. I disagree. It's not as if I tell her every day that she has to take care of her brother when she grows up. But if I don't tell her now I think I'm lacking in my duty to both her and Chris.

I'm sure that there are times she says, 'There's going to come a day when I might be married and I'm going to have to have my brother in the house,' or, 'I want to go on a date and I'm going to have to stay with him.' I'm sure she must think of that as a burden. But I cannot skip over it. I cannot make this a fairy tale for her.

I'm sure there are times she resents her situation. But we choose not to put Chris in a group home when he is older. Sure, that would alleviate Jesse's responsibility of future care. However, this is the route we choose and this is the way we are teaching our daughter. I believe it is a moral obligation, and insist on teaching my daughter a mode of living that I feel is correct. I feel deep conviction about our moral responsibility to siblings and parents.

Keeping your children in the dark about their disabled sibling is not good. You must empower them with knowledge. They have to know about the future. These are questions I'm sure are floating around in their heads anyway. The sooner you tackle them, the better off you are.

Parents should help siblings of children with disabilities by talking about the disorder honestly. I don't think you have to be brutal, but be honest. Tell the sibling how they can help without being insistent. Teach them how to communicate with their brother or sister. You can't pretend that life goes on normally. And I don't know why that should be the goal either.

People always say they have to keep their home normal. But it's not anymore. It's just not. So why pretend? Be honest with your children about the family situation. Include them in both fun and difficult activities with their disabled sibling and spend special time alone with them. You will probably end up with a strong, loving family that brings your life great joy.

11

Jessica's Own Story

Jessica, aged 12

I was about five when Chris was born. Now I'm eleven and in the sixth grade. I think I was kind of happy when my mother was pregnant because I wanted a brother. I imagined this little boy running around talking to me and playing. But when he was about two-and-a-half everything started getting difficult and my parents told me that Chris had autism. I started finding out all kinds of hard things like he wasn't able to talk and would act differently. I wanted it to be me instead of him. I felt so bad for him.

I like being with Chris. Being with him is not that much different than being with any of my friends. I can hang out with him and play with him. Even though he doesn't talk or play around it's still pretty much the same. We'll either wrestle each other or sit there and watch a movie. I usually talk to him about growing up and what it's going to be like; how it is for me and what he should he expect. I tell him he'll start going to school, and that he'll start going places with other kids and make lots of friends. He'll sit there and not say much, but it seems like he's listening.

I was seven when my family had its first therapy workshop. There were twenty-five people in the house all down the hallway from my room. It was so many people at one time! It was kind of like a party, but really they all just sat down and watched Chris. Imagine how he felt! The first workshop we had, I sat in my room. I wasn't allowed to go in the therapy room or anywhere near there. I couldn't go outside, and if I went downstairs I wasn't allowed to watch TV because they put the therapy session on the monitor. There wasn't anything to do. It was kind of like being punished and I just wanted it to be over.

Chris started getting worse when I was about eight or nine. It was a lot to take. He had pica and was chewing on rocks and eating staples. Basically he ate everything but real food. We had to take him to surgery for his teeth. His talking got less too. I was scared for him. I thought it was weird not to eat or talk. But it was also difficult and made me angry when I'd talk to him and he'd just turn away like he wasn't listening.

I was never angry at Chris for having autism. He couldn't help that. It was really the things he did that got me mad. It'd be the same with any of my friends.

Chris used to stim by hitting himself or hitting other people. I have scars on my arms and legs from him scratching me. All of a sudden I'd be talking to him and he'd get mad and scratch and dig his nails in me. I didn't know what to do. I couldn't hit him so I just walked away and started to cry because it hurt so much. It was hard to deal with. After a while if I saw him getting mad, I learned to walk away. My parents started putting him in time-outs and now he's stopped.

His hand flapping still gets bad sometimes, though. Once he was watching a video and took off his shirt and was stimming by hitting himself. His whole chest was red. It scared me, but not as much as when he would hit me. I try to stop the stimming if I can. At first, if it looks like he's hurting himself I'll say 'hands quiet.' Then he puts his hands down or I'll take his hands and put them down. He'll stop for a little while, but then it's hard for him not to start again so there's not much I can do. If he gets mad in the car sometimes he'll bang his head against the seat. Then I try to stop him by putting pressure on his head.

I don't know what sets him off. Things just get overwhelming for him. He used to have these highs and lows when he'd start crying out of nowhere and then he'd start laughing. A lot of times when he watches his videos he gets overwhelmed and starts laughing. He also can't take everybody around him like other people can, and I guess it just gets too much and he can't keep it in any longer. I don't really know what sets him off. Mostly it's probably being overwhelmed.

It makes me sad that Chris misses out on things like talking and playing with people. He'll go outside but he misses out on playing games with kids. I'll go out and play a game of football with my friends, but Chris can't do that. In the summer, kids will be playing soccer and I'll ask them if Chris can play. Some of the kids are nice about it and they'll say yes and let him kick the ball around. We used to play baseball with him too. My best friend, Corrine, really understands about Chris and loves him. He kisses her all the time.

Other kids in my neighborhood are really rude to Chris. They'll either make fun of him or ignore him. There was this one kid who made fun of Chris and I remember sitting there screaming at him.

When kids ask what's wrong with my brother they think he has mental retardation. Basically all I explain is that he can't talk and doesn't go to school much. I tell them he learns differently and I don't get much more into the specifics. My friends from school understand it, though, and don't make fun of him because my dad comes to class and talks about everything.

I never felt embarrassed or ashamed of the way Chris behaves in public. Usually if he's laughing I'll start laughing with him. And if he's stimming I'll just let it go. I don't really pay much attention to the people around us. It never bothers me. Sometimes if I see somebody staring at him, I'll get mad and I'll stare back just to get them to look away. But really I don't mind. If they would say something about it I would probably get mad and say something back.

When I was about nine or ten I would go upstairs and do programs with Chris. I started watching his classes and got kind of interested. I thought it was kind of cool. The therapists would ask me if I wanted to help because a lot of the programs needed an assistant. They had a flashcard and it would say something like 'clap hands.' They would do it and then I would have to clap. Then he would clap. I liked doing it. I remembered when I wasn't allowed to go near there, and now I felt like I was a part of it. I also felt like I was helping my brother.

I also helped to make up some programs. They wanted him to spell more and I was watching them figure out a program to add in with another one. But I combined the two programs together and it worked out.

When the therapists and my mother reviewed programs with the videos I would sit down with them and take it all in. After the meetings were over, I'd tell my mom my ideas. She thought some of them were good and started doing them!

I was the one who taught Chris how to give people hugs. When he was three and not talking to anyone I decided to try and teach him. So I said, 'Chrissie, we're going to wait five seconds and I'm going to give you a hug.' I wrapped his arms around me and I put my arms around him. 'One, two, three, four, five. See, that was a hug. Chrissie, can I have another hug?' And he put his arms around me. He didn't push me away or anything. In fact, I felt really special because he wouldn't give a hug to anybody else but me for a while.

Only sometimes was I ever jealous of Chris. I remember watching TV when I was about six and my mom and dad were sitting on the floor playing with him and not talking to me. I just got really jealous thinking they weren't doing anything for me. I even started fighting a lot with my mom because I felt they weren't giving me any attention. Now I realize that Chris doesn't get more attention than I do, but when I was little it was different. Everybody was talking to him, and I was over there watching TV and nobody was talking to me. Once the news reporters interviewed me, I started to feel better. In a way, Chris was helping me get attention too with all the TV and newspaper reports.

I even won the Making A Difference Award. I remember they called me down to the school office and my dad was there crying. And I asked, 'What happened?'

He said, 'We had this award we signed you up for and you won.' I remember watching a big commercial about me on the TV for about a month. It was kind of special at my school too because they raise a flag for kids who do something special and I was the first one who had it raised.

My parents also made me feel good by setting aside special times just for me. I really looked forward to them. My mom and I would go bowling every Wednesday and my dad and I would go golfing every Friday. They were always there for Chrissie, but now they were talking only with me and having fun. Every once in a while we'd also have a family day.

I like being with my dad. We're not the most typical people in this world and my dad will see something weird and make fun of it and I'll sit there laughing. We'll go out to eat and just start laughing in front of the whole restaurant.

Actually, because of the attention Chris gets I'm really kind of spoiled. My parents always get me stuff. I'm into bands, especially 'NSync and my dad got me and Corrine tickets to the 'NSync concert last year. He also got tickets to Savage Garden. When my dad told me he got backstage tickets to the Savage Garden concert I was in the car crying, I was so happy!

I would tell other parents who have a child with autism to be there for their other kids too. If your kids ask you to go out one day and you can't, try to go out another day. Don't just completely say no or not do anything for them. Stay with them.

I respect my dad for standing up for himself and Chris. It makes me feel proud of him and teaches me to stand up for myself. I remember at his IEP he'd come home all happy because he told off half the people in the place. He was not taking anything anymore. He's also helped a lot of families. People read about us in the paper and come up to my dad all the time. It feels good to help people. And it feels good to know there's somebody out there like yourself.

There was one family my father helped which was about to throw their kid in an institution. I'm just glad my dad didn't do that to Chris. As long as he's there for my brother, I'm glad about anything he does. He's definitely done a lot more than most parents would. I remember when they first found out Chris had autism, my dad was reading books day in and day out. He even goes to Baltimore every day which is really tiring. I know because I used to do it.

I don't wish Chris was different. I just wish he was more verbal. It's hard sometimes to talk to him when he doesn't say anything.

He's starting to talk a little bit more now, especially with the secretin, but when it wears off he completely breaks down.

Sometimes I worry about being his guardian with the trust fund because it's hard to understand what to use it for. I'm not bothered, though, to think that he would live with me when I'm older and married. I'd rather have him live with me than be somewhere lost, not knowing what to do, or being on his own. It doesn't really bother me at all because I like being with him.

My favorite thoughts of Chris are when he acknowledges me verbally or with affection. When I walk into the room and say 'Hi, Chris' and he says hi back, that really makes me feel special. Hugs make me feel even more special. Just today I was sitting on a chair and he came over and gave me a hug. He doesn't do that every single day. Sometimes he'll push me out of the way or he'll want to wrestle. But if I get a hug or kiss it really makes me feel like something happened just between the two of us.

If I had one wish it would be to have known what I know now when I was five. I could have helped more when Chrissie was younger and it might have made a difference. There's nothing much we can do about it now, but I just wish I understood more when I was younger so I could have been more of a help.

There's nothing much different about having a brother with autism. It's just having a normal family except for Chris not talking. That's about it. Now that I'm older it's easier to play with him. I'm friends with him and I hope we'll stay friends even when we're adults. It's hard to stay away from him because I love him so much and he's so much fun to be with.

Great!
(I'm sure to show your dad!)
10/10

My Dad (Bill Davis)

We're supposed to write about someone
we look up to. I think I look up to a
lot of people. So, I pick my favorite
person out of everyone. My father.

The reason I picked him is because, well,
he's just always been there. When brother
was born he was always there. Then
we found Chris had autism. Most
people would give up and leave kids
like that. Not my dad. The first thing
he did was hit the books. Now he's
giving Chris everything he needs.

I know, he does stuff for Chris
so why should I look up to him.
He dose stuff for me too.

I really look up to him because
he helps other people who need help.
My dad now gives speeches, does police
training, helps my mom, my brother, and
I, keeps a steady job, and has Rutgers
meetings. If that's not helping I
don't know what is.

He's been on 12:30 live twice.
Also he's been on the news and in
the newpaper several times.

He has accomplished a lot during
the passed six years. He has helped
out then anyone I know. The
person I look up to My father.

'My Dad' by Jessica, aged 9

12

Vacations?

Imagine being rescued by the Coast Guard! That's what happened to us while on a ferry in Ocean City, Maryland. Chris, eyes filled with panic, jumped up from his seat and started to move toward the nearest exit of the boat. He wanted off the ferry! He spotted the little door and was going to jump off! I tackled him and tried holding and singing to him, but his eyes were rolling in his head as he fought me. He was about to have a seizure. I called the captain over. 'Listen, my son has autism and you've got to pull the boat over!'

'Sir, we don't stop. But let me assure you. I am an EMT.'

'Listen to me, I will jump off the boat if I have to. Pull the fucking boat over! You're not listening to me. I'm going to give you a choice. I'm either going to jump off this boat with my son because he's going into seizure or I'm going to punch you so hard that you're never going to recover. So make your decision now.'

Due to my gracious powers of persuasion, they pulled the ferry over to an island and radioed the Coast Guard 'child in distress.' My whole family walked off the gangplank onto the island. Chris was still a little distressed, but he was walking around when a motorized dinghy pulled up. 'Sir! Come this way.' They ran and quickly boarded Chris and me. This little dinghy was so small that there was no room for my wife and daughter and there were no seats. Grabbing a bar while holding Chris, these guys took off at sixty-five knots! The spray was coming up and now Chris was laughing! For some reason this little boat was OK with him.

When we reached the dock, police and ambulance were waiting for us. Chris was laughing and singing as the emergency workers quickly approached him. 'Everybody hold on,' I yelled. 'Let me explain to you.'

'Are you refusing service?'

'Absolutely. I don't want you to touch him. He's fine.'

'You have to sign.'

I signed a million waivers, thanked the Coast Guard guys for all their understanding, and apologized for stopping the boat.

So there Chris and I were on the boardwalk and he immediately ran to push his way through a family of about fifteen people to sit on a bench. He loved the feel of wood and had a way of remembering certain benches and what they felt like. Right now this particular bench was very important to him. The family was nice about it and kind of laughed. I apologized and explained to them what happened.

'Oh, son,' they said to Chris. 'We're sorry for you. Are you OK?'

'Chrissie doesn't talk.'

'Ohhh.'

'No. He's fine.' And I went on to explain the whole story to them and how he doesn't speak. This was about the time he was learning to say bye-bye.

Afterwards they got up. 'You're a wonderful man. God bless your son. Bye-bye, honey,' they said to Chris.

'Bye-bye!' he responded.

They started jumping and clapping, 'Oh, Lord! He spoke!' Suddenly I was in the middle of a gospel revival with fifteen people dancing around, thanking God my son spoke.

Welcome to the world of autism and vacations.

We've taken about four vacations, each about three nights long. There were three stays in Ocean City and one in Virginia Beach. Packing was always an arduous task, especially when Chris was eating nothing but formula. We couldn't rely on getting the formula where we went so we had to bring cases of it. Then we had to make sure there was a refrigerator in the room, proper sleeping arrangements and a safe room set-up. We couldn't turn our backs. If there was a window we had to block it off. 'Where are the electric plugs? Where are the window bars? How's the door lock?'

We bought suntan lotion for Chris, but first he had an aversion to it and was constantly wiping it off. Finally he got used to it. I think it was the way my wife told him, 'You need to do this and it's going to make you feel better. You were hot yesterday.' So he stood there and let her put it on.

We were determined to include Chris in everything. He played miniature golf for the first time while we were vacationing. Jae decided to teach him to play using hand-over-hand. 'Honey, you have to put the ball in the hole,' she instructed. So he picked the ball up in his hand, walked over to the hole, and placed the ball in it! Well, he *was* doing just what she said!

Unfortunately, when we went out we usually split up because Chris wasn't interested or able to participate. So one of us took Jessica and the other stayed with Chris. One night, for instance, Chris and I strolled and played miniature golf together while Jae and Jessica went to do other things that would be hard for him.

One July we saw the fireworks on the beach. We were prepared to walk off thinking Chris would be frightened, but he loves to throw sand and was throwing it the whole night. I ended up running around apologizing to everybody while trying to stop him. But he loved the fireworks. A lot of anxiety! A lot of anxiety!

Last summer when we were in Virginia Beach, Chris had an aversion to outdoor pools. Where he developed it from, I don't know. He would go in an indoor pool, but wouldn't go in an outdoor pool. I thought maybe it was because of the dirt so I picked the pool clean. He still wouldn't go in. Then I thought it was the temperature. So I had them heat it, but that didn't work either. So we went into the indoor pool where he was still a little hesitant, but did eventually go in.

There we were at this beachfront hotel with a beautiful outdoor pool and we were stuck inside this noisy indoor pool. So I said, 'Jessica, you know what? Let's just run with him and jump into the pool outside.' And we did. We didn't throw him. It was more like we took his hands and said, 'Come on! We're going in! Here we go! Jump!' He started pulling back on us, but then he went into the pool and happily swam.

Next we decided to go to the ocean. Jessica loves the ocean. Chris just played in the sand, ran on the beach and played ball. And then I said to him, 'Chris, we're going in the water.' He looked at us. You have to realize there are so many tactile things going on in the ocean. You have the current pulling you, the different tastes of the water, the temperature of the water, the waves, the tide, the sand. It's tough. But just like before, we took him and ran. We got into the surf and he stood there. When the tide pulled him, he got a little nervous, but he adjusted.

This turned out to be a wonderful time of realization for us because we saw that Chris was more pliable. He'd become somebody that you could throw in the water and the worst that would happen was that he'd cry and get upset. But it wasn't going to knock him back two years.

Now we knew we could ease up a bit when we went away. It was a very pleasant feeling to know that whatever happened he could adjust. We are now able to go to little shops, grab a snack, watch a movie or go to a little amusement park. Chris will play a game at an arcade and he'll bowl. He may not do things exactly the way everybody else does, but he enjoys himself. It's just a pleasure for him and for us!

There are people who say, 'I have a family with one child who has special needs. I take him to class and when he comes home we tend to him, but we have to lead our lives. We have other children, we have our jobs, a house, and a boat. Sometimes we have to take a family vacation without him. He stays with Grandma because we need a break.'

Well, I'm not going on vacation and leaving my kid because he's difficult, even though that's what other people do! I find it almost offensive when parents say this child who needs their help so much is a burden, and they have to get away.

I will consider leaving my son and daughter with an extremely trustworthy person when Chris can communicate better. He needs to first have the ability to speak up for himself and say when he wants to call his parents or doesn't feel well. When he can understand where I'm going and that I will come back, then I will take my wife away for a night. Until that time I'm not going. I need to know that he understands and won't worry about what's happened. In the meantime, we'll continue taking family vacations and day trips.

Our therapists once offered to send Jae and I away for a couple days while they babysat. They even wanted to pay for it as a Christmas present, but we wouldn't go. It's not that I didn't trust them. I can explain where I'm going to my daughter. 'Mommy and Daddy are going away. We're taking a small vacation. We want to be alone and be romantic. We'll be back and bring you a present. You listen to Kim and do your work.'

But I can't tell that to my son because he wouldn't understand. He could be thinking, 'Where's my mother and father? Why is this girl staying here? I like her, but what's going on?' It worries me what he's thinking.

I also worry about disrupting our daily routine of working with him. I don't really know if it would be that terrible to break the routine for a few days, but in my mind the key is constant, constant work! I'm probably being obsessive, but it's an obsessive disorder. Maybe you have to be obsessive to defeat it.

I worry about a lot of things when someone else is caring for him. I can see when he starts to get aggressive and see what upsets him, but will someone else? For example, one summer the therapists asked if they could take Chris for a walk. I was running to work and Jae was not due home for an hour. I said, 'If you are willing to sit down and listen to me, yes. You can take him. But you must pay attention to what I'm telling you.'

I knew this child. If you turned for a minute at that time he was gone. Gone! Ran! Ran through the streets, through the woods. He took his clothes off. He ate anything. He'd pick up a piece of glass and put it in his mouth. He used to chew rocks and break off his teeth. You could glance at something for just a few seconds and BANG, he'd be gone! He had a terrible fear of dogs so if I heard a dog I'd immediately turn away and say, 'Come on. Let's walk this way.' What if I forgot to tell them and they walked him toward the dog and he went into seizure?

I ended up letting the therapists take him for a walk, and I let them take him swimming too. My stomach was queasy all day, but it worked out. And it would probably work out if we went away. However, I'm not prepared for that yet.

Right now we have the luxury to occasionally use our therapists to babysit for a few hours. They are absolutely his best friends and he loves them and they love him. Jae and I certainly have gone out to the mall alone and stuff like that. But we prefer to be close by. Going out is not a priority for us. There are not enough hours in the day anyway. Our time is precious. I also feel the more I'm with my son and the more we talk and interact, the more he grows. So going out for dinner or going away alone can wait. Anyway, I enjoy being with my kids!

I guess you might conclude that I'm holding Chris back in a way. But after a lot of years being right by his side, worrying and sitting with him, going through MRIs and operations and hospitals and seeing him shake and cry when we started school, it's hard to separate. We're doing it slowly, though. It's like the first time you let your kid go down the sliding pond. You're nervous and they're not, but you have to let them do it. Otherwise they'll never be playing with the kids on the playground. With Chris it's just a little more pronounced. Advancing to new levels with him is more delayed so our separation from him is also naturally more delayed.

13

Friends And Family Support

Around the time Chris was first diagnosed with autism my cousin invited us to a family gathering. Chris' behavior was really extreme and the day was a disaster. He was screaming and flapping and spinning around and eating mud. Nobody would go near him. When he went over to the swing a cousin was frantically yelling at the other kids to let him use it. She wasn't being mean, but there was such nervousness in the air. They all watched me chase my son around and scoop out mud from his mouth until finally we went home.

Of all the cousins and aunts who were there that day, not one of them ever called me. Not one of them picked up the phone to give a small word of support. 'It looked like you had a tough time that day. Hope I don't offend you, but it must be hard. Is there anything you need or want me to do?' That would have been nice.

After I told my mother about Chris' diagnosis she informed everybody in the family. Jae called her family and told all her relatives. The most amazing thing to me was that nobody ever called for years! Jae talked a lot in the beginning about money, not with the intention of asking for financial help, but to explain what we were dealing with. Perhaps that turned them off, but I still can't understand the complete silence from everyone but my mother. My mother, God bless her, offered both emotional and financial support. She paid for Chris' medical tests, bought Jae a car so she could drive around safely, helped pay for secretin and even paid for much of our in-home program set-up.

But support from other family and friends when we learned Chris had autism was practically nil. It was much like what happens when someone gets cancer. Everybody's afraid they're going to catch it. They don't know what to say and they stay away. All of a sudden they're not sure how to treat you. So they don't treat you at all. This attitude is especially true with autism.

People are afraid. Maybe they're ashamed. Most just stay away. If they hear we're having money problems they probably say to themselves, 'I'm not giving them any money. If I call I might be trapped into lending some.' The disorder might make them very uncomfortable. People love the status quo. 'I get up in the morning, go to my job, have my little house. I'm not going to upset my life for this.' So when something terrible hits, your whole life changes, including relationships with family and friends.

One of Chris' classmates has a grandmother my mother's age who drives them around, sits with the kids, learns how to communicate with the kids, takes him to gym class, makes suggestions and even goes in on meetings. I don't have that. It would be a dream to have somebody hook up and help me. We always do everything ourselves. It's very tiring.

How about an occasional call from a friend or family member asking, 'How's your son? Anything we can do for you?' Nothing. From anybody. Not one family member. I certainly don't expect anybody to call up and say, 'By the way, I put aside six thousand dollars for you the other day.' That I can understand. But how about volunteering to babysit? I wouldn't let them sit anyway, but it's the offer, the show of caring that I miss.

We never really had a great circle of friends when we got married, but even those few friends backed off. I guess it's understandable. We became completely different people. We were very busy doing our research and therapy so there was no time for socializing. When you have two people running around like nuts, how can you possibly continue your relationships as they were?

People at the bar, strangers, have treated us with more concern than family and friends. They often say to me, 'I don't know how you do it.' And that makes me feel better. At least somebody is saying, 'Great job.'

Our therapists, the college girls, have also been very supportive in recognizing our work. They even offer their time to take Jesse to the movies so we can go out to dinner. Recognition from other parents of children with autism in the area has also been very heartening. Dr. Landa, a renowned PhD from Johns Hopkins, has certainly been a bright light. Telling us she needed our involvement with her at Hopkins was very uplifting. Other than my wife, kids, and mother, Dr. Landa and her staff are the most supportive people in my life.

We currently see one family socially. Their son is Chris' best friend from school. It's great. I really enjoy the chance to socialize. We actually pack up and go to somebody's house. But opportunities for friendly relationships like these are seldom found.

The public needs to learn about autism because it's such an unknown, misunderstood disorder. I would love for people to call and visit us in order to learn. It would be great if they took the time to ask me, 'How do I greet him?'

When Chris' prospective kindergarten teacher came over she asked us, 'I don't want to be embarrassed, but how do I do this?' Great! Ask me! I was happy that she asked and wanted to know what to do. I prefer that instead of pretending you know what to do and then ending up doing things improperly.

I'm sure it's frightening to come across a person with autism if you don't know what it is. I guess people think the best thing to do is not look. But it would be nice if they caught the parent's eye and gave a nice smile, maybe asked a question. I welcome questions. Once we went to the Hard Rock Café after going to Kennedy Krieger. Chris could not wait on line and could only sit in a booth at that time. So I explained our situation to the manager who got us a booth. Chris was dancing in the booth and flapping his hands, but the manager went to the gift shop and gave him a t-shirt and kept checking on us to make sure we were all right. It's wonderful when people are so kind and understanding.

People often forget to show that kindness and compassion. Unfortunately, we need to be reminded not to abandon those who are sick and in pain. These are the moments that are most important in life. I remember my now deceased father had a girlfriend who was dying from multiple sclerosis. Not one person visited her. She was horribly ill with blindness and dementia. No question it was tough to go over and see her, but didn't she deserve some concern? Didn't she deserve some companionship in her final days? It was unconscionable that she was abandoned in these last tortuous weeks. I could not allow that and was the only one who ever visited her.

I believe that when you're finally measured, it's the time you go up to that little person in the street and give them a nice greeting or that last five dollars that's important. It's when you befriend someone even though he has dirty clothes. It's when you offer help to someone in need that matters in your life. People like these are heaven-sent, and certainly heaven-bound.

14

Institutionalization

While I was at a Temple University seminar, a 1950s film of an institution was shown. What I saw was kids, most of them naked or in big diapers, playing in their own filth. One was eating the mop strings. The walls were gray; the cribs were metal. You didn't see one picture, toy, or color, and there was some kind of trough from which they ate. Orderlies came in at one point and washed the children down with a hose, letting the water pour down a drain in the middle of the floor. Most of the kids just continued rocking and flapping for hours. A man wearing a starched, white uniform came in, looked at them, and went away. There was no therapy. There were no hugs, no social life, nothing. It was storage, just plain storage.

I could not get this picture out of my head for a year. Every time I saw my son under his blankets, my knees would go weak. Here was this comfortable guy, happily asleep and warm with his covers pulled up. In a few hours he'd wake and watch TV. Can you imagine him in an institution? It makes me shiver. I haven't visited a modern day institution, and I'm sure there are different types and degrees of institutional care, but you never know what's going on when you're not there.

Think of the typical child with autism who feels, but can't express himself. Now think of that child living in an institution saying to himself, 'Where are my parents? Where's my room? I want a hug.' And he goes to bed every night in a steel bed and can't tell anybody and learns to live with it. 'This is my life.'

And the untrained, unaware aide looks at this guy who plays with his fingers and eats the mop, and says, 'What an animal! He doesn't want to be hugged.'

It's very easy for me to sit and say I would never institutionalize Chris, but from the depths of my soul, I know I wouldn't. I realize not all people can cope the same way. Not all people can do everything. What if I didn't have the life I have? What if I didn't have the wonderful wife and daughter I have? What if we couldn't scrape up money all the time? I truly feel bad for people who have to send their kids away. I do.

Unless you're there for them full-time, especially the aggressive children, many end up either institutionalized or just completely out of sync with the world. If you're not on top of them right from the beginning these kids often develop more and more self-stimulatory and injurious behavior and eventually they're lost. They may never speak or communicate in any way.

There are kids with autism who have thrown teachers through glass doors, broken classmates' jaws, beat up their parents and jumped from the back seat of the car and taken the wheel. How do you control situations like these?

Parents will tell you, 'I can't care for him anymore. He breaks his head open every two minutes. He needs to be medicated and I can't deal with it.' I know parents who had nervous breakdowns and parents who were beaten up. They couldn't deal with it any longer. They had intelligence, money and time, but they just couldn't take it any more! So they eventually institutionalized their child.

Fathers I know who have sent their children away seem to have eyes that are always without feeling. I think if I had a son in an institution I would probably look like that too. How horrendous it must be going to bed every night knowing that your kid is medicated and being taken care of by strangers. So you take him home every weekend for a visit and ask, 'What's happening?' Some weeks you may get an answer, but many weeks you probably won't.

One family I know worked with their daughter, but there wasn't a lot out there in Lancaster at the time. She became so self-injurious it was ridiculous, and they put her in an institution. She had no speech then, but now the father tells me, 'Suddenly she has speech and I wish she wouldn't. She learned two things, "more cookie," and curse words'.

They worry about her a lot, especially because there seems to be more risk for a teenage female. How can you trust the person who's with her at four o'clock in the morning?

It is very harsh of me to say never, never, never institutionalize. I have friends who sent their children to institutions and to group homes because the children became so self-injurious it was uncontrollable. It may sound egotistical, but I said this to my wife and I mean it: 'If I have to strap this child on my back, he is not going anywhere. He is not being medicated. He's not being dulled and he's not living anywhere else.'

If Chris' behavior escalated I still would not institutionalize him. I'll always make sure I'm there for him. We would have to restrain him as much as we could and work with him as hard as we could and stay with him twenty-four hours a day. It's as simple as that. There's no decision to be made as far as I'm concerned. I would never send that boy away! Even if it meant tying him up and saying, sorry, buddy, you're going to have to sit here for a while.

Some parents feel group homes are another alternative to institutions, but my immediate reaction to group homes is that they are still an excuse to send your child away. What child belongs in a group home? They already have a family. To me it seems like the group home parents are spending time with your child instead of you. To me it says the parents don't want to do the time.

The old philosophy is out of sight, out of mind. You don't have to deal with him. You don't have to think about him. My philosophy is this. It's too bad that your child's disorder drastically changes the family. Yes, you will suffer financially, time-wise, and relationship-wise. But that's too bad. He's also suffering. It's your responsibility as a parent to make the sacrifice.

PART VI
Inspiration

1

Feeling Sorry For Yourself

A diagnosis of autism is not a death sentence. I hate to sound trite, but there are many other horrendous physical disorders out there. I've seen a lot while living in the world of disabilities. There are kids born with their intestines outside their bodies and there are kids who continually go into the hospital for surgery because their brains swell. It's hard to imagine the degree of physically horrifying moments parents and children experience. Parents are forced to become medical experts. I know some who go through the day giving injections to children on breathing apparatus. When I attended the Temple University advocacy class for parents of the disabled, I would sit and listen to the mothers talk at lunch. 'The machine failed so his heart stopped.' 'Well, it was clogged so I had to go into his lung.' Incredible stuff! And they talked as matter of factly as I talked about Chris' Discrete Trial therapy.

So an autism diagnosis is not the end of the world. If you pay attention to your kid and learn how he operates, you'll have a wonderful life. Just give him a chance to be the best he can be.

The best that he can be may be taking walks with you every day or only sitting in the corner stimming. That may not be the nicest feeling in the world for you, but still you love and take care of him; and *keep trying.* The point is if you get an autism diagnosis, then you must continue your life and help your child. Read, learn, travel. Get your child a computer. Teach him to sign and use sentence strips. If the right therapy is not in your means, get it any way you can. Sell your house if you must.

Your child has an intense learning disability. Everything you know about life, forget! The hug, the joke, the playtime – he's not going to give it back to you. He's not going to do it. So you have to re-adjust your whole thinking.

You may even find your child with autism teaches *you* how to see things differently. Chris has taught me a lot about myself. I've become much more non-judgmental and appreciate differences more. It's very easy to look at a child and think here's this little stranger doing all these weird behaviors. Then you start to learn why he's doing them. If you try to think a little like he thinks, you realize that he is capable of living a rich, full life. All he needs is for you to accept him rather than judge him. Work with him, not against him.

Accept your children's differences. In order to put my daughter to sleep I cuddle or sing to her. In order to put my son to sleep I give pressure to his forehead, let him whip around the bed and turn on certain music. Then I rub his back. It's just different.

I'm not disputing that autism is a very tough disorder to handle. But if it's tough for you, imagine how tough it is for him. Imagine coming to a room and you can't walk in. You're a smart boy and your brain knows there's no reason you can't walk in that room, but your body's not letting you. You think to yourself, 'I want a hug from my mother and when I do, it hurts me.' Don't you think that kid who's constantly hitting himself and stimming doesn't realize he's hitting himself in the chest a million times? He can't stop himself! These are tough things. So I would really get over the fact quickly that you might have to sell that boat of yours or you might not have enough free time.

It's absolutely abominable to me that somebody sits back and says, 'Gee, we used to go to the baseball game every Sunday and now we can't.' OK, you can't go to the baseball game. But your son can't go to the bathroom properly! Your son wants to speak – he can't; he can't get it out. Imagine what *that* feels like. Your son wants to date a girl. He knows what's going on, but he can't even get the words out. He knows he's socially inept. You know how much that must hurt, especially to a smart child?

Autism is like a trap. Here this kid is saying to himself, 'I'm watching all these people and I know what to do so I'm going to join in. But I can't do it; I can't say the words. I want to play, but I can't play. Now I'm retreating. This hurts me; I'm hitting myself and I can't help it. Nobody else is doing it. Why can't I stop this?'

I was at a meeting once when a mother asked, 'I can't even make dinner at night. How do you all sit here and be so positive? How do you do all this? I want to make dinner and I have to go over to my child constantly.'

I responded, 'What is your problem? You want to know how to get free time? First of all, who has free time? We don't have free time. If you want to make dinner then set up something that he likes to play with, and cook and watch him at the same time. But your days of making gourmet meals for two hours are over. What are you getting upset about?'

Her big thing was how to normalize her life and get back to what she missed. Well, parents of children with autism are not going to do that, and if we do there's something missing. Then we're not giving enough attention to our children.

I also think people use excuses when they say, 'But I have other family to consider. We have to go on with life. I have to go to work.' I believe that's another way of saying, I don't want to devote as much time to my disabled child. It's another way of saying, I'm glad I got out of the house and spent eight hours away from this kid.

I'm the first to admit it's been difficult caring for my son, and there were times I felt like giving up. We often worked so hard and got no results. After let-downs like those I would sit there and say, 'This is it. I have to face facts that he is regressing. Stop hoping because you're killing yourself.' But then I'd look at my child and know I had to keep fighting for him. And the fighting's paid off. Chris has not regressed. In fact, he's overcome many obstacles.

Don't ever listen to anyone who tells you there's no hope for your child. What does no hope mean? That he's not going to be president of IBM? OK. I know I'm not going to be president of IBM either. My hope is that my son has a fulfilled life. Maybe that means writing some poetry, designing some things and taking a walk with his dad.

So when I say he's going to be the best he can be, that doesn't mean he's going to win the Olympics. When he finishes that section in a workbook and is so proud of himself, that's being the best he can be. When he colors a bunch of pictures and stays within the lines, that's another big thing. I tell him, 'I saw you coloring your pictures. They're so beautiful!' And he yells with delight. He's so excited. He's so proud. So isn't that a fulfilled life?

Listen to nobody. If somebody told me there's no hope, I would get away from her. If somebody told me my son can only do very limited activity or it's too late to teach him language, it's time to get away.

Last summer we were invited to participate in a symposium at Sheppard Pratt Health System in Baltimore. There were PhDs and an audience of educators. The PhDs presented some things about autism. Then Jae and I presented a synopsis of Chris and our program along with Dr. Landa's film of him. Everything these PhDs presented, even new theories, we had done. Chris was a shining example of theories in actual practice.

Following the presentations, we sat on a panel with the experts and answered questions. Every question was directed to Jae and me.

'What is your philosophy? How did you make these marvelous strides?' Lynn Medley was sitting off to the side and I said, 'About two, three years ago, Lynn Medley from Kennedy Krieger came to my home, and she and I agreed on the most important philosophy of all. Lynn verbalized what I always felt, "Whatever's good for the child."'

That brought the house down. Lynn started to cry, and you could feel the audience's enthusiasm. Dr. Landa stood up and said, 'This is what we need here.' And everybody applauded.

It was a really good day for us. Here were these PhDs describing what's necessary for successfully working with kids who have autism, and we were already doing it. And it was working! One PhD even came over and said, 'You people are brilliant! I'd love to work with you.'

We felt so good about all our efforts. All this time, we had been going out on a limb, second-guessing, yelling at each other and worrying we were doing things wrong. And all these experts were saying we did it right; that our work was exemplary!

I believe that any parent will be successful if they keep plugging at it. What is success? If your child even stops hitting himself, that's a success. Feel sorry for yourself? Never. Feel sorry for your child? No. Help him to feel proud of the accomplishments he is capable of, and feel proud of yourself for helping him.

2

Jae's Ingenious Programs

My wife, Jae, and I have always said, 'She sees what Chris sees and I feel what he feels. And that's why we make a good team.' I feel his emotion all the time, and can look at situations and instinctively know how he'll react. But if he has a learning problem, Jae goes right to the computer and comes back with a method that works. She can figure out a way to teach Chris anything *and* she can do it with any child. She's aided many families with programs that have helped their children. Expert professionals have looked in awe at what she's created and accomplished with her autism programs. Hopefully she will find more time in the near future to do consultant work and offer her programs on our Internet site.

The latest program she developed is absolutely phenomenal! I feel very strongly that it needs to be publicly introduced. She created a school day that we implement at home combining incidental play, incidental teaching, Discrete Trial and picture programming. It's just a phenomenal program that she developed from years of running our own in-home program. In a short time we have seen Chris eagerly respond and do very well with it.

Safety programs have always been a wonderful specialty of Jae's. When Chris discovered he could turn on the bath water we were presented with a big problem because he kept turning on the hot tap. We caught him most every time, but once he stuck his foot in the hot tub. While teaching him to test the water first, Jae also put a sign on the hot water tap with a line across it denoting 'no.' A lot of times you can't explain the concept so you do it in words with the aid of a visual cue and a sign. The labeling helped a lot, and Chris learned not to touch the hot water knob.

I'm embarrassed to admit it, but we've had two incidents where we locked Chris in the car accidentally. I did it at the mall when my key broke, and Jae did it recently at a car wash. While she went to get change, Jessica and her girlfriend excitedly jumped out and locked the door with Chris inside. Jae had to try and get him to push the window button to lower the window so she could open the door and get inside the running car.

So after this incident she decided now was the time for him to learn to unlock the door, how to open the door and when to open the door in an emergency situation. He knew he had to wear his seat belt. In fact, if you don't belt him in he gets upset and hands it to you. But he also needed to know how to open the window if told. So she's creating an emergency car program outlining how to escape and how to open the car if locked in.

Traveling in the car with Chris was always a great source of frustration for everybody. When we first started driving Chris around he enjoyed the motion so much that he didn't want to stop. He only wanted to go! So when we reached a red light he threw a fit. Jae decided to devise a way to relieve some of the stress for him.

Chris knew all his colors so she decided to use shiny red and green color blocks from a program he already knew and liked. Jae stuck Velcro to the car dashboard and the bottoms of the blocks. Every time she had to stop for a red light she stuck the red block to the Velcro on the dashboard where Chris could see it. Then she'd point to the red block and the light and say, 'Chris, RED means stop! We're going to stop now. See, it's red. Now look up there. It's red too.' When the light turned green she would point to the green light and the green block and say, 'OK, GREEN, it's time to go!' The first couple of times Jae did this he screamed in anger. But she continued to do this absolutely every time she had to stop the car for a light. Gradually all the stress subsided. About six months later she forgot to point to the green light and block. 'Go!' exclaimed Chris.

'Mom, I think he's got it!' Jessica remarked. And that was the day we decided to stop using the blocks.

Chris also got upset if the route varied when running errands. He either had a destination in mind or wanted to avoid going some-place like the doctor's office. So Jae devised a program to let him know where he was going before we left the house. She went on a photo-taking expedition to all the places we normally drove to both day and night. Every building and every activity was included. For example, picking up dad from work was a night photo and taking dad to work was a day photo. Ideally the photo would include the person he was going to see. She had a picture of Julie, the speech and language teacher, standing in front of the building where she worked. There was a picture of Mel, the hair stylist, in front of the salon. There were doctors' offices, Jesse's school, gasoline stations, the car wash, A–Z Video, Zany Brainy, Toys R Us® and supermarkets. We even had a photo of Jae's car to represent going for a ride when there was no other photo to represent where he was going. You name it, there was a picture of it. Jae carried the camera in her car for months.

Next she labeled all the photos and put Velcro on their backs. She rigged a piece of sponge with Velcro that slipped snugly in the passenger seat visor, and displayed the photos there so that Chris could easily see them. Every time they got in the car Jae would say, 'OK, Chris, we're going to…' If it was speech time she would show him the picture of Julie at speech class. The photo would stay there until they returned to the car and changed destinations. Time to go home? She would put the picture of home on the visor and say, 'OK, Chris, it's time to go home.'

It didn't take him long to catch on and that removed most of the stress when we drove around. As long as he understood where he was going, even if it was the doctor's office, he would sit back and go along quietly. Well, maybe there was a little whining for the doctor's office. Just having the information relieved his anxiety. She could say, 'Chris, we're going to Zany Brainy,' and he could say to himself, 'Oh, OK. I'm going to Zany Brainy and I don't have to get nervous. I wanted to go to the mall, but that's OK.'

This system only works if you go to the destinations pictured. He gets very upset if you don't tell him where he's going or if he doesn't go to the destinations displayed in the photos. Consistency is key. Otherwise the whole program loses its importance to him.

Jae's larger goal with this picture destination program was that someday Chris would tell us where *he* would like to go. She would always get in the car and ask, 'Where do you want to go today?' Finally the day came when he answered! He undid his seat belt, took the 'ride' photo down, flipped through the auto book, pulled out the 'mall' picture, and placed it on the visor. No question where Chris went that day!

The picture destination system for our car has become a vital communication tool for us. Chris now lines up photos on the visor in the order in which he would like to visit them. Sometimes we scuffle about the order, but Chris always wins on the where.

Another travel program Jae created was a backseat communication board because it was hard for Chris to get her attention while she drove. Going down the highway at sixty miles per hour made it too dangerous to keep turning around to see what he wanted. So she attached Velcro to the seatback next to Chris and to the backs of all the PECS icons related to travel. Now they could be attached to the seat in a sentence strip. All kinds of icons were used including bathroom, open soda and I'm sick. So Jae would get a gentle tap and look over her shoulder to see three little icons saying 'Open soda please.'

The backseat communication board saved us all a lot of frustration, but as Chris gained more language he decided one day he didn't want to use it anymore. While driving to school he suddenly tossed the sentence strip out the window. 'Open soda please,' he said. Jae told him that since he threw the board out, he would have to ask for things verbally from then on. We've never needed to replace it.

These are just a few examples of Jae's creativity and expertise in dealing with autism. You will never hear her say, 'My God, this is frustrating. How do I tell this kid? He doesn't understand anything.' Instead she says, 'OK, back off. How does he see things? OK, I know. I can draw this little thing, and put this object here.' And she'll reach Chris every time. She's an incredible woman who has designed a great number of incredible programs! Chris has come a long way because of her intelligence and ingenuity.

We recently put up a picture of his school in Baltimore before going there for the day. As we moved away, Chris sneaked over and replaced it with Zany Brainy Toy Store. He then sat back as if he didn't do anything and acted as if that was where we really were supposed to go. 'Christopher,' Jae said, 'we can't go to Zany Brainy. We have to go to school.'

'Awwww.'

He tried to trick her! He knew just what to do and was trying to be funny. Thanks to Jae's programs, our son no longer sits there frustrated. Instead he is able to communicate and even display a great sense of humor.

Jae used to do only Discrete Trial, but she is trying now to implement naturalistic teaching. I think that's good because Discrete Trial can be a little bit too strict, especially for small children. Little ones seem to burn out on it really quickly. So

I think it's great that she's intertwining all these different therapies. Jae's always on the cutting edge with programs for autism. I don't even think the leading therapists in the area are doing what she's doing now. She really should have her PhD with all she's done and knows. So many times 'experts' told her not to implement ideas she had, but she tried them anyway and they always worked. If nothing else, she's certainly the best judge of her own child and his abilities.

Kim Egger, therapist

Bill and Jae were excellent teachers. Jae does more of the hands-on classroom training. It is wonderful. She knows her stuff inside and out. She always has wonderful ideas. If there's something that's not working she'll tell you, 'Why don't we try it this way?' You can always go to her with questions and she always has an answer for you. Even if she has to think for a couple of minutes she'll come up with something.

Melissa Bennett, therapist

3

The Human Spirit

I know a boy who was institutionalized with a whole host of physical disabilities including autism, blindness and an inability to walk. He never spoke a word and never had a single visitor. At one point he was hospitalized and while there his therapist came to see him. She lay down in bed with him and gave him a hug. This boy who never before spoke a word looked at her and said, 'Mama.' This one act of kindness changed his life. The woman ended up adopting him, and he evolved into a happy, social human being.

His miraculous change seems pretty simple to me. Here was a boy to whom nobody would pay attention when all he wanted was somebody to hug him. You may have a shunt, spastic muscles, mental retardation, an inability to eat except by tube and screwed up genes, but you know what? You still want what most people want deep down. It's a very simple equation. You want some friends and love. You want your parents and a warm home. You want to be included. The human spirit can rise above the most horrid of circumstances with just a little show of love. Look how one hug brought this boy's spirit out from hiding!

If a child's in a wheelchair he understands that he can't run around with the other kids. But he's also thinking, 'Just put me by the group. I'll laugh and watch.' He still has human desires and needs. My son knows that he's different; he doesn't expect to play baseball. Maybe he will someday, but right now I'm sure he's thinking, 'Play with me. Take me out! Let me run around or maybe I'll just look at the grass.'

When we go to an amusement park Chris doesn't go on the rides. That's OK. We go anyway. He still has as much fun as my daughter. He walks around and looks at the people. We go in the water and shoot a gun together. We eat. We laugh. What's wrong with that?

You have to appreciate human beings at their purest when you see a child with autism who has no social awareness. Their souls are really angelic. If you watch, you see these loving little souls just floating through life who probably have all the answers. They're so bright. They contain so much. As a father I have to remove myself a little bit, but what a fascinating disorder!

Unfortunately, you also see how cruel people can be and how much misunderstanding there can be. With most babies, the daddy says goo-goo and they say goo-goo back. They learn to communicate right away and it draws them right into the social frame of life. But with autism, kids are without that. What a way to be born! What a way to get through life! They are stripped of everything we take for granted. People with autism have none of the tools we use to get through our days. What a hard life it must be! So I just admire them. I think they're absolutely phenomenal.

I read a nice story once about a dad and his teenage son with autism. The boy came home one day and said, 'Dad, I want to go to the prom.'

The dad almost fell on the floor. His son did not function that well socially and certainly never dated. But the father didn't want to discourage his son and replied, 'OK.'

The boy proceeded to try and plan for his prom. There was a pretty girl in the neighborhood who was always very kind to him so he asked her to be his date and she agreed. The boy, who didn't speak that well, wanted to get her a corsage and rehearsed what he would say before going to the florist. But when he and his Dad went to buy the flowers the boy's words all came out wrong. Instead of the father taking over and making the request for his son, he just told his boy to try again until he said it right. Upon completing the transaction, the florist said to the father, 'You're so patient. I really admire you.'

The father got mad. 'Don't admire me. I'm not patient. It's my son who works hard. I can say "give me the purple corsage." I'm not a blessed person. It's my son who deserves the credit!'

And that's the truth. It's what I say all the time about my own son. What makes me particularly proud of Chris is how he evolved from a child refusing to do anything but sit in the corner of a room to what he is today. Nobody can tell me he didn't do that by himself! Sure, he had help with programs. But it was his heroic spirit that got him through his personal hell. Now my son plays on the computer, sings, spells, reads, has friends, jumps around, dresses himself, eats and watches movies. He goes everywhere, does everything and is not afraid. That's triumphant!

Chris used to markedly toe walk, a very common trait of autism perhaps because the pressure on the feet did not feel good. While walking through the mall one time, Jesse turned to me and said, 'Let me take him. I want to walk with him.' Chris looked over and watched her walk. Probably noticing that he was different than his sister, he started to make himself put his feet down just like her. You could see the determination on his face. He made himself walk and feel that pressure on the heels of his feet! After that day he practiced walking on his heels all the time. It was as if he was desensitizing himself. Whenever he started to toe walk he'd force himself to put his foot down. He was determined to walk just like his big sister. It was absolutely heroic.

There is tremendous power in this child, tremendous fight. I can't imagine another child this brave. He gets up in the morning and goes through six, seven hours of school, speech and gym while constantly dealing with the frustrations of his disorder.

I believe he works very hard, not to be normal but to be included in life. I used to watch him go to the mirror and pretend he was talking. He would gesticulate and mouth, making expressions as if he was practicing for the day when he would join in with the rest of the world and speak. He was saying to himself, 'These people do this and one day I'm going to do it. I'm going to practice.' And he'd have pretend conversations.

He tries so hard. Now he runs over to a huge slide, climbs up and slides down! He got on a swing the other day. These are activities he had to struggle to do. Spatial things, climbing and going backwards were all very hard for him. I just admire his courage. Every time I saw my son do things like practice talking or walking flat-footed or trying to put his own shoes on, I knew I had a very strong son. But even if you don't easily see that strength in a child, he should still be given as much power and confidence as possible.

I believe it's the parent's job to help your disabled child do the things that you take for granted with other kids. Especially with autism, teach them what funny is. If humor is not part of their lives, don't let them be content to sit in a corner and finger flap. It's your job to bring them out and find their spirit. I always say, 'That is so funny! You are funny. Good laughing!' We joke. If he makes a face to be funny, I make a big deal out of it. In a way I'm rewarding him for being fun loving, for enjoying life and the world around him.

Chris has taught me the power of the human spirit. It's phenomenal. My son fights all the time. I know that he knows he's different. I'm sure of it. I'm sure he knows that he's lacking a few things that other people have. I'm sure he knows he doesn't quite fit in. Yet that doesn't stop him from enjoying his life. He loves going to the mall and looking in his favorite stores. He goes to a school for little autistic guys and he loves it. He paints, makes us valentine cards and sings. He loves his friends. He's having a good time going through life.

So what is he really saying to me? 'Maybe I don't do the things you do. That doesn't mean I'm not happy and it doesn't mean I can't get enjoyment. Do I have to be like you to get enjoyment out of things? No.'

As his father should I introduce him to life as much as I can? Yes. In a way we're introducing each other to life.

Bill and Chris

I hate when people say they don't understand how I can do all I've done for my son. I hate that! Please don't put me on a pedestal. Chris is the one who's worked hard. *He's* the hero. It's his strength that should be admired. He's the one who did not allow himself to be trapped in this disorder. He's the one who is strong. I hope a little bit of his determination came from me, but I know that most of it comes from his amazing human spirit. He and all the others fighting to get out of this disorder's trap are my heroes.

4

The Future Of Autism

I once listened to an advocate for children of special needs give a talk. She had two children with cerebral palsy in the 1950s, an era when there were no rights for kids. She called the institution where one child was and said, 'I'd like to visit my daughter.'

'Oh, we moved her upstate,' they told her.

'Well, why didn't you call me?'

'We don't have to call you.'

When she arrived at the facility she found her daughter lying naked and dehydrated in a crunched up position. She was dying! And the mother said, 'My God! I'll call the nurse.'

The daughter replied, 'Don't! They get mad when I bother them.'

This is a child who had learned in an institution to shut her mouth because she would get yelled at or slapped and pushed around! So she stayed like that.

The woman covered her child, gave her fluids, and telephoned her doctor who said, 'I agree with you. This is an emergency situation and I'm coming down.' The mother saved her child's life.

'That's what advocacy for your child is all about,' she said in this speech. 'I can't tell you what to do. I can't give you specifics. There's no book. But you should know to just do something! Never stop doing something. Make the call. Go somewhere. Call the doctor. If that doctor doesn't answer you, call the next doctor. Knowledge is wonderful. But there's no book that's going to say "Call the Governor's aide." Just think to call the Governor's aide on your own. If he doesn't do anything, call someone else. Keep demanding something.'

That's what I believe in. I believe you cannot settle ever. There are times when Chris is doing beautifully and I think life is absolutely easy at this point. But we can never stop working. Never stop demanding services and research.

I've recently been invited to attend a special state committee meeting to determine if special education has done its job. The committee for this was formed after we wrote letter after letter demanding programs for autism and after Jae spoke before the state legislative body. Of course I don't need a committee to tell me necessary services aren't being provided. I'm now involved in a class action suit filed by the Philadelphia Law Center that I used for Chris. It is against the state of Pennsylvania for not providing services, and I will be called to testify.

All these memories come flooding back when I prepare for my testimony. One official actually wrote that a good thing to do for my child's socialization was to take him to Chuck E. Cheese. My child was eating the wall and this was the social therapy she recommended! Finally, these officials are being brought to task.

Government officials in charge of special education in Pennsylvania should hit themselves on the head. How do they go out and make a speech about what a great job they're doing? When they go back to the office they have to know they're not giving services. It angers me when politicians or educators speak and go out in the community and try to placate everybody but the very recipients of those services.

They always start their work by appointing a committee which appoints another committee which does a seminar. And at these seminars they all have lunch. I said to one of the heads of Special Education at one of these seminars, 'Gee, just think of all the services you could buy with the food you put out for this conference.' He walked away. That was enough for him.

But it's true. So they had this conference and two hundred and fifty people were fed. That money could have bought speech for my kid. And what did they prove at this conference? Nothing at all was said there that was going to make any difference to my son's services. They probably could have communicated the same information just as effectively through the mail.

Instead of conferences they need to revise their budget policy. They need to pour money into qualified speech and language pathologists, not charts, meetings and dinners. Instead of saying we're budgeting for twenty years, budget for the first two years of treatment for autism. That's when it's most needed. Pour money into early intervention. Find out what services are really needed by first asking the kids and the parents. What is he lacking? Speech? Are we in agreement that they all need a lot of speech and language? Then that's where we'll put the money.

There are six hundred thousand kids in the United States with autism, but the educational system is much quicker to acquiesce to the needs of those with physical disabilities than to the needs of those with disorders like autism. It's been a battle for us all along.

When my school district told me they will work with us and help set up a program appropriate for Chris, they really had no interest in following through. Why not? I was told that there were only two kids coming into the district who had autism, and a special program just for them would not be cost-effective. Why should they have all these special things for only two kids?

'If there was one kid in a wheelchair you'd build a ramp and pay for the highest grade of wheelchair technology,' I responded. 'There always seems to be funding for that. God forbid, you didn't build a ramp. But what about my son? Why is there never funding for him?' I hate their attitude. This disorder is not a passing thing.

The school systems' other way of thinking is to hire their own group of specialists and refuse to fund any other therapists better able to work with special needs children.

'The district has so-and-so for a speech teacher. We'll send her to you.'

'Well, I don't like her. I like another one. We found a teacher three blocks away who has experience with kids with autism and she's very good with my son. Pay for this teacher instead. This one works.'

'Well we don't want to pay for that one too.'

I understand their viewpoint, but if I find a speech teacher that reaches my son, then I think they should pay for her. These kids with autism are so particular. If you reach them, if that's what works, then you should go with that and the officials should understand.

There's now a movement for children with disabilities requesting non-traditional services be funded. 'Please don't send me an occupational therapist. I found that swimming everyday works much better for my son. Pay for the pool instead;' or 'Please pay for gymnastics rather than an OT. He's made far better progress with the gym class.' But for funding policies like these to take effect autism needs a much stronger advocacy movement. A centralized organization is needed to coordinate fundraising and lobbying efforts.

Most disorders have centralized places for information that are backed by big money and lobbies. An individual can go to them and get all the information he needs. Autism doesn't have that. The disorder is still a big question mark. Where did it start? Can it be cured? What's involved? Well, everything's involved from hormones to neurons. So there are a bunch of scientists arguing with one another and a bunch of splinter groups each looking at something different.

They've got to get together and say, 'We've got x amount of dollars and we're going to use it to bring the best results.' When the funds are spread too thin, they can barely pay for test tubes. What we need is a centralized group that raises a large lump sum of money to attract the best scientists and the best research for autism. Right now the few scientists involved are begging for money.

Autism needs a centralized information center to promote awareness. Pediatricians need to be educated to recognize early symptoms. The general public needs to understand that autism is the third largest disorder in this country. People need to realize that these children may look normal, but they have a severe debilitating disorder that's life-long and can result in horrible outcomes.

So if you really want to conquer autism you have to get to work and raise money. But getting funds raised is difficult, especially for autism. Most people are used to seeing more tangible results. One lobbying group for another disorder might say, 'See Tommy? He was in a wheelchair a year ago? Tommy, walk across the stage! More money, let's give money!'

But what would they say for autism? 'OK, Chris, what can you do?' Chris has come so far, but how do you explain that to a person? Chris used to sit in the corner and eat rocks. Now he doesn't. That's a big deal, but people expect to see something more dramatic like in the telethons.

Autism needs a big mover and shaker. It needs to become the in vogue thing. Some big celebrities have children with autism, but you never hear them talk about it. Ball players seem to be the most vocal. There's Doug Flutie who has probably done the most for awareness. And Dan Marino has donated a lot of money to build. BJ Surhoff is now getting more vocal and is a member of Pathfinders. But that's about it. Autism needs more spokespeople, big fundraisers, research and coordinated services. Thankfully, celebrities who don't have children with autism like Anthony Edwards and Renee Russo are now becoming active spokespersons.

The disorder also needs to hear more from skilled therapists. We were told early on that if Chris doesn't speak by age four he's not going to speak. Well, he's now age six and does speak. So-called experts are too full of theory. They don't spend enough time with the kids. When you're an expert it usually means you've either been researching or writing, but you're not in the field with the families. Experts collect data and make guidelines, and next year they find a new theory. But it's the therapists and teachers who are with the kids that know more than anybody.

The bureaucrats, geneticists and scientists all have to be involved with the therapists and the parents. You can do all the clinical work, but if you're not in the classroom observing the children you don't really know the disorder. The ones with money and power are not always close enough to see what's going on. I think it's important that these people step down and come observe a classroom and talk to parents.

A big danger is when programs claim they can fix everything. Beware of somebody who says they have the cure. The good majority of these kids can do wonderfully. I think my son's going to get very far. But don't expect everything to disappear. So far there is no cure, and much more research is needed. That's not being pessimistic; it's realistic.

Sure, there are those isolated miracle stories, but those are not the rule. Sometimes something will just hit that works. A diet, a word, you never know what. Often when these kids get a little language the frustration lessens and they zoom off and lose a lot of the stimming. So a lot of the characteristics of autism are lost, but not all of them.

People have to know that a good ninety-three per cent of people with autism don't get married and don't leave home. Not everybody becomes a PhD, not everybody does artwork and not everybody conquers the world. Look, I'm not saying I want my son to have autism. If tomorrow you said let him take this pill and he'll be cured, that would be great. I just think people have to be realists.

I have gotten very political, demanding and outspoken over the years. I'm sure there are some politicians and administrators who stay away from me. No doubt a lot of my letters to the editor lambasting the system turned them against me. I certainly wasn't helping their political careers. I've made a lot of enemies over the years, but I'm not scared of making enemies because I know I'm fighting for what's right. I'm simply saying, 'I know what works for my child. I also know that you know. Now I want you to give him what he needs.' Why should I compromise?

5

Loving Your Child

I was sitting in the mall one day with Chris when he was about four years old. His behavior was very extreme in these days. People would stare all the time because he screamed and jumped and flapped his hands. Well, I was sitting on a bench with my arm around him while he drank formula from his bottle. While we were sitting I noticed another little guy about his age walking with his dad as they both ate ice-cream. The boy looked up at his dad and asked, 'Daddy, can we go play video games?' And he said, 'Sure, son.'

You might imagine I felt great envy and sadness at the realization that my son and I could never do that together. But actually I felt quite the opposite, 'I have this too,' I thought. 'It's a little different, but I have a great relationship with my son.' I was never depressed over what my son could or could not do. Who cares if he doesn't score the touchdown? The other boy can score all the touchdowns he wants.

My boy performs equally amazing feats. When he said his first sound it was one of the greatest moments in my life. I just love my son. He's very easy to fall in love with. I don't love him any less because he's disabled.

That's the point I always try to get across. Why should I feel jealous of other, 'normal' children? OK, we don't play ball, but we do other things, and we're together all the time. I absolutely adore every minute with Chris. It might not be a typical father–son relationship, but it's as fulfilling as any could be. When I come home and he hears the door opening he squeals with delight. He actually refuses to go to sleep because he waits for me. The door opens and you hear this big, loud, happy squeal. I run upstairs and he laughs and we roll around together. What more do you want?

Jealousy has never found an entryway into my heart when I look at typical boys. I feel I have so much with my own son. It's a little different than the other dads, but I don't miss anything. I really don't. Of course I'd like it to be a little easier. When we take a family trip I would gladly welcome less planning. And I'd like to know he's able to participate in whatever he wants, but I certainly don't miss the fact that he won't be a football player.

I never grieved for the loss of a 'normal' son. The only time I ever remember crying or feeling sad was when I couldn't get a handle on what to do for Chris. When I made those calls for eight hours a day unsure of what we were doing, it was the most awful time of my life. I was willing to do anything for my son to help him, but I couldn't find where to get started. I cried night after night worrying that I wasn't doing enough.

I once saw a documentary on a father with a disabled child. The kid had cerebral palsy, couldn't talk, could hardly walk and crawled most of the time. The father said over and over how he grieved for the loss of his son's normal life, and thought about playing football with him. I began to get so angry. There was a moment when this man was looking out into the horizon from his porch being reflective. His voice was in the background saying, 'I accept him. I take care of him. He's still my son.'

While hearing these words you saw the boy crawl from inside the house to the porch and climb up on his father to hug him. I thought, 'Here comes the moment I've been waiting for.' But the man barely responded! Then I thought, 'You ass! Here's this idiot talking about the fact that his son is not going to play football, and look what he missed!' This kid wanted a hug from his father and crawled all that way on the wood to get it! The next natural thing would have been to turn around and hug him, but instead the father stood there looking out in the distance with a far-away glaze in his eyes. How stupid. What a beautiful moment he lost.

Who cares if your son is the quarterback? I would rather he was bright and sensitive and loving. I never grieved at the loss of a 'normal' child. I was actually relieved when we found out what was wrong with Chris. For months we were so scared for him and kept asking, 'What's wrong with our son?' Once we got a diagnosis of autism I took a sigh of relief. 'Good! Now we can get him help!'

Now that we knew what we were dealing with, we could roll up our sleeves and get to work. It certainly wasn't the time to sit and feel sorry for ourselves. Parents of children with autism can't afford to worry about themselves. They have a child who desperately needs them.

My child has a disability. He's simply different. Whether it's physical, mental, neurobiological or hormonal he's a little different than what we're used to. That's all. He deserves our full love and attention.

Believe me, having a child with autism is hard work and it's financially draining. It is very difficult to reach these children, and parents want immediate feedback just like everybody else. But here's a child who sits in the corner and everything you've learned about loving doesn't work. He doesn't want to kiss you. He doesn't want to hold you. He doesn't want to talk to you. Whatever you do for him you get no feedback. I can remember being up till five in the morning because Chris wouldn't go to sleep. We dealt with feces smearing and aggression. But it didn't matter. That was my child.

I'm sure other parents feel a lot of anger and frustration. So often there's a tendency to say OK, he went to his little class. Now we can leave him in the corner and let him flap his hands; he's comfortable. But I cannot and will not condone that in any way. That's your baby! Too bad. That's the lot you got dealt with in life. Now do the right thing and love and care for your child.

I think you have to let these children know you appreciate what they do and love them for who they are, not despite who they are. I don't love Chris because he has autism or because he's disabled. I love *everything* about him and he knows that. When he makes up a string of sounds for me to imitate, I laugh. When he flaps his hands I get joy. When he spins around the room and jumps on me I don't pity him. And he HAS to know that. I think that's important.

I'm sure Chris knows that he's different. But I'm sure he also knows that I love him as he is, not out of pity or because he's changed or going to change. That's not why I love him at all. When he takes a bath and splashes water on me, I laugh and he laughs. He performs in the mirror for us. When he fixes himself I'll say, 'Look how handsome you are! You look in that mirror and look how handsome you are!' We enjoy each other's company, and our close relationship allows me to communicate with my child just as well as anybody else does with their typical child.

My wife always said wherever he goes he has to look good. It's not that he has to be dressed in his best clothes, but you see a lot of disabled who look disheveled. The attitude of a lot of parents is, 'What difference does it make?' But it does make a difference. If you don't think they're worth the trouble to dress nice, then their self-image is destroyed. My son will always hear me say, 'You are the best looking guy. Comb your hair. You are the handsomest guy. Look at you. What a great job you did.'

Jae and I make a point to tell each other the details of Chris' day. 'Mommy told me you climbed on the rings at gym? Give me five!' So he knows that I'm keeping track of him and he knows that I appreciate what he does. I work very hard all day at praising him. When he laughs I tell him that's great, that he's funny. I praise him when he plays with a balloon because he's learned to be a kid. In my house when little accomplishments like playing with a balloon happen, we all – literally, therapists and family – leap around the room. We cry and jump around for the damndest things.

He said 'Ah' and you went 'OH!' because he never uttered a sound. Or he repeated a sound and people threw things. It was an amazing time for us. We saved this guy who was a withdrawn shell of a person and was now communicating, eating, playing, taking walks and hugging us.

People say the hardest thing with a child who has autism is you don't get the affection back: 'I'd give anything if he kissed me or hugged me or said Mama.' I've accepted this behavior, but I've also worked a lot on it. Chris is actually quite affectionate now. My God! I remember when he gave me a kiss. It wasn't a real kiss, but he put his mouth out and I was in shock. What a wonderful moment. He was learning to give love!

I can't tell parents how to cope with hurt feelings because I never had any. I believe that people who grieve and are hurt and disappointed should get over it. It's a selfish reaction. Think of your child as being betrayed by his neurons. He's lonely inside that shell and wants to hug you, but can't because his brain won't let him. Don't worry about bragging about your child either. There's plenty to be proud about. I brag about my son all the time. His accomplishments took much more work than your next-door neighbor's winning play in the Little League. But even if my son never moved an inch from that corner I would brag about him. He's a wonderful human being.

I went to a picnic once with disabled kids and their families. The kids were all different ages, some even in their thirties, and they all had different disabilities. One boy in a wheelchair was laughingly playing tag with another boy. A father and his very ill son were playing ball. I heard these parents saying how their children had been with them always, and how they liked to read and take walks together. They were just happy to be with their kids. All these people were very uplifting to me. They talked about fathers who deserted them and professionals who told them to institutionalize their children. But they didn't care. Instead they stayed with their children and loved them and loved being with them. They had a good life.

If tomorrow I were told that Chris could be typical, it wouldn't change my love for him. He is just a marvelous guy. When we go out and hold hands or roll in the grass I'm in heaven. I just love this guy. I love our relationship. I love the way he smiles at me and comes through the door and runs up to me. We sing together. We lay in bed together. We hold hands. What I feel for this guy has nothing to do with his disability. He's just the sweetest person I've ever met. So wouldn't it be idiotic of me to say, 'We want to teach him how to play soccer so he can play on the team?' Well, maybe he doesn't want to play on the team. I just appreciate everything he does. And he loves that I appreciate his accomplishments. But that's my job. You have to take an active role as a father and as a parent.

This is the lot we were given in life. So what? My son's a marvelous human being. Disabled or not, he deserves all my love, unconditionally.

6

Chris Today

Today Chris woke up laughing. Jae and I both jumped on him in bed while he laughed hysterically, and then we tickled him. Afterwards he got up, got his drink and bread and watched a movie. I played with him and then went to work. As I left I told him, 'Give me a kiss. You take care of Mommy.' I know he understands.

He'll go to school today with his friends and have therapy when he gets back home. He puts in a long, hard day. Later when I get home I'll take him for a walk and we'll run through the fields and fall down together.

One of my favorite times is when we take our walks because we have a lot of fun holding hands and running up hills. We take different routes and sometimes they'll last an hour or two. The walk has been ours even when he didn't want to leave the house. That first step and that first walk up the block I'll never forget. He wouldn't venture out of the house so I said to him, 'Come on. We can step out. You're a strong boy. You can do this.' We got up to the end of the block and I said, 'You are the greatest guy,' and we walked further. Soon he started looking at the trees. He began to enjoy the grass and the sun, and we started going different places. It just became our thing.

When I think how severe Chris' autism was in the beginning, it's hard to believe he's the same boy. My son never had eye contact nor ate a drop of food. He wouldn't sleep, wouldn't use the bathroom, wouldn't talk. Everything was as base level as if he was an infant. He was just so severe. I think in a way we saved his life. If we didn't give all that constant, constant attention he surely would have been one of the lost ones.

Without even realizing it, I gave Chris occupational therapy and desensitized him whenever I rubbed him or played physically with him. Anytime I got a response, I went with it. It took a lot of good intuition, a lot of love and a lot of dedication.

I'll meet parents of children with autism who'll say, 'My child is doing real well. He took the Discrete Trial program and he's beginning to speak.' But these are kids who originally were lucid, eating, playing with others, or had some language ability. I'm not belittling their accomplishments, but they were often high functioning. Chris displayed a total lack of normalcy. He wasn't eating or talking and showed aggressiveness and the possibility of self-injurious behavior. That's what makes his change so dramatic.

I defy any six-year-old to have the day Chris has. He begins with speech and language therapy. Then he has an hour-and-a-half ride to Kennedy Krieger for afternoon kindergarten, goes back home and does three, four hours of ABA therapy at night. But he never tires and never complains. We go to gymnastics twice a week and swim at F&M university. He recognizes sounds and pictures, works from a task book and is beginning to develop good language skills. He knows his numbers and letters, counts, writes, spells, reads and uses the computer. Chris' imitative skills are tremendous. He works the VCR like a pro and freeze-frames everything so he can draw or design what he sees. He's a very independent little guy who goes everywhere – restaurants, stores, school and amusement parks. His days are enriching and full. Remember, this was a boy who wouldn't leave the house.

I'll get in the car now and say, 'Come on, Chris. We're going shopping.' And he gets in and we go shop. There's not one place he won't go or one activity in which he won't participate. The only difference is we have to bring his own food when we go to a restaurant. He's not going to eat menu items like fried chicken so we bring his specially prepared peanut butter sandwiches and rolls instead. No big deal. We can still go to the pizza place. He just has something else.

We still have to teach about life; that's the tough part. Little things in life that we take for granted, you have to teach and reteach. If I were to open the door when Chris was naked he would walk right out onto the street. But we've made headway. For example, Chris loves these little rubbery lizards, and he goes to a special store in the mall to get them. He used to run in, grab them and run out like a madman! So we taught him that you have to stand on line and pay. The first time he waited on line it was very hard for him to stand there. Now he stands on line, sorts them on the counter, and puts down his money. He's rewarded with lizards and a 'Good job, Chris!' from the cashier.

He also used to insist on going directly to certain stores in the mall. Now I tell him, 'We'll go into your store for the Honkers, but Daddy has to go to the bank first. You'll wait with me on line... Good job! You're doing a great job... Let's go over here and sign the check... Would you like to go now? What store? Do you want to go get the Honkers? OK. Let's go get the Honkers.'

But he understands that he has to go to the bank, perhaps stop to eat lunch with me and maybe later take a break. I'll say, 'Let's sit down. I'm tired.' He might not want to sit down, though, so I'll continue. 'Come on, Chris. Sit down.' He sits down. 'You want something to eat? What do you want?'

'Roll.'

'Roll? OK. Here's your roll. Let's eat.' Originally this scene would have been impossible. I remember the first time I took him to

the mall he was hit by a million lights and people, and didn't want
to go in. Now it's one of his favorite places to visit.

One night recently in his gym class he was the damndest thing.
A newspaper photographer was snapping pictures of him on the
balance beam, and he was posing and laughing. There were girls
jumping, guys on the apparatus next to him, music, cheerleaders
screaming. And here was a news reporter talking to him and his instructor, and he was fine! Two years ago I struggled to get him just
to walk out on the floor.

He does all kinds of things that continually amaze me when I
think how far he's come. The other day he cleaned his VCR. He
picked out the cleaning tape from the all the movie tapes, put it in,
let it run; it clicked and rewound, he took it out, and put in his
movie. Such a complex task for a boy who could barely do
anything not long ago!

I believe I have a happy well-adjusted child. He plays with his
sister and her friends and he plays with boys at school. They give
high fives, wrestle and play around like regular little guys. Of

Bill and Chris

course he's not like a 'typical' child, but I don't believe it's bad just because he's not what we normally expect.

I really enjoy my time with Chris. I meet him in the hallway at school and he has the biggest smile when he sees me! He jumps on me and hugs me and pulls me into the room so I'll throw him up and down. All the while he's laughing so heartily. We rough house and wrestle at home. He knocks me down and I knock him down. I love the humor in our relationship. He laughs all the time.

We do a lot together. We walk and talk. We sing together, color together, and watch movies together. There's a song 'Fuzzy and Blue and Orange.' It's about the monsters from Sesame Street that he loves. Out of the blue, he'll start to sing for me and I can't do anything but kiss him. It took a long time to build this relationship with my son.

I firmly believe that in most situations Chris now takes care of himself. He's able to tell you what he wants and doesn't want. But he's also learned to comply to the rules. In school if he's not following directions, the teacher will say, 'I'm sorry, Chris, but your schedule says art,' and he will snap to it.

The greatest pleasure for me is to see the way Chris recovers from stressful situations. I once startled him when I came up from behind and he got all teary-eyed. So I took him over and apologized, 'Honey, I'm so sorry. Daddy wanted to tickle you and I really apologize. I'm sorry.' He turned and looked at me so I knew he understood what I said. With something like that a few years ago, I could have lost him for three days. He could have gone off.

When something goes wrong, he recovers so quickly now. I don't have to watch every little thing anymore. When I watch him on the monitor it's only to keep up with what he's doing so I can use it too. There's no more tiptoeing for fear that he'll never speak if things don't go his way. I actually hear myself saying to the therapists in our home, 'I'm going out to get a pizza and will be right back.' I remember I wouldn't even take a phone call, never mind going out for pizza.

Chris was drawing at a party recently and someone took his crayons as a way to tease him. But he got mad and grabbed the crayons back! It was great to see that he can handle himself. I now know that he can stick up for himself in difficult situations. It's so important to know he'll be OK if I'm not around to protect him.

In gym class he can fall off the balance beam and it won't ruin his day. He may cry a little or flap his hands, but then he gets back up. It's the most marvelous thing. Another time a classmate pushed him at school. Two years ago he would have either thrown a tantrum, cried or refused to go to school. It was horrible. I read stories about kids who threw tantrums for forty-eight hours because a TV news program wasn't turned on at a certain time. Something so seemingly trivial could just throw everything off.

Before Jae's skills became so professional we used to hire the therapist Ruth Donlin just to figure out what was happening. Chris would sometimes refuse to work, forget everything or stop talking and we never knew if he really forgot everything or just refused to use what he knew. Now he likes his home classes and develops different relationships with different therapists. He does his work and has ways of showing that he's tired so the therapists respond.

We used to be afraid to leave Chris alone in his room during the day. Now we know it's OK. We're not as frantic about constantly working with him or worrying that he'll go off into a daze and be lost to us. We don't worry anymore if he wants to watch cartoons or go upstairs to his room. He's so resilient that anything can happen and he doesn't shut down. He's able to go with the flow.

I'm very close to my son. And it's not because I feel sorry for him. Chris is my best bud. Being with him is an absolute joy. He is a loving, loving son and we have developed the best relationship. I treasure every minute with him. 'Don't put him to sleep before I get home,' I tell my wife all the time.

And she'll tell him, 'Daddy's going to be home soon,' and he gets all excited. We've just become the best of friends, a real dad–son thing. We have a routine we go through whenever he goes to Baltimore. 'Bye-bye,' I say to him.

And he goes, 'Bye-bye.'

And I'll say, 'See ya.'

'See ya.'

'Love ya.'

'Lva.'

'You take care of Mommy. You're the man. You take care of her.'

If he was the most normal, typical child in the whole world I couldn't have a better relationship. We may be broke, pushed and overscheduled, but this is still the most delightful time of my life.

When people say I've worked so hard, *he's* worked so hard. I've just done what I'm supposed to do. If your child was sick and vomiting in his bed, you would stay home from work to clean it up. Too bad it's disgusting. You're the parent and it's your job.

I'm not afraid of Chris' autism and don't dread it anymore. I think I know the disorder well enough where I can cope with it and help my son to cope with it. I understand that it will probably never completely disappear for him, but that's OK.

I once read a story about a woman professor who taught children with autism in a camp. She was on a public bus and recognized a young man in his twenties walking past her with a briefcase and a suit. He stopped, turned to her, and said, 'Mrs. Stewart, I'm so-and-so. I was in your autism class at camp and now I'm in college.' She said she remembered him and was really pleased by his success. What she didn't tell him was that one of the reasons she recognized him was because he was walking on his toes. Here he was a law student with his briefcase and his suit, yet he never stopped toe walking.

Autism is a lifetime disorder. You don't lose it. You simply do well with it. If you get taught a lot about life you can cope with it. I think that is paramount in my job as parent. I have to teach Chris what anger and jealousy mean, what a relationship is, how to sit in a group, and how to make friends. So we just keep plugging away, hoping he will learn to cope well with the world. But whatever he attains is fine for me. I will never be disappointed, even if it's just going to the mall or to the grocery store himself. He will probably always have some social issues and most likely live with us as an adult.

Last night he was a wonder. We went to the mall and shopped. Chris bought things, we went to eat and we laughed. Later that night he wanted to wrestle and he was the funniest thing, jumping and leaping on me.

When I put him to sleep we went through our usual routine. We listened to music, laughed, got kind of naughty and then Jae as always yelled, 'He has to get to sleep. Calm him down.' And we started tickling each other. So he was laughing hysterically and up for another hour, but I couldn't help myself.

I get a big joy out of the love he has for us. How ironic, considering that the main thing you're told about autism is that people affected are cold, don't love, don't have friends and don't have relationships. Supposedly they can't differentiate between people. Not true. Chris has a different relationship with every one of us. He adores his family, his therapists and his daily activities.

Sometimes I'll look around while I'm writing at my desk. There's Jesse watching TV, Chris is upstairs playing, and my wife is on the computer. I think how this is really nice. I just like when everybody's home and we're all comfortable. A lot of times we'll all climb into the bed and we play and laugh and watch TV. I could not ask for anything more. I have no desire to go out and no desire to own a big house or a yacht. We were always a close family, but certainly autism has made us closer and very aware of what life's all about.

I think of the old Jewish grandmother telling me, 'If you have your health and your family, you're OK. When you grow up, you'll understand.' Well, Chris' disorder has certainly helped me grow up and I definitely understand.

7

Chris' Future

I was in the bank and met a woman with her wheelchair-bound son. He was in his forties and had Down Syndrome. 'You know,' the mother said, 'He was born forty-four years ago and they immediately told me to get rid of him. There's something wrong with him. Put him in an institution.' Then she straightened up and said to me with proud indignation, 'That's my son. I'm not giving him away. Only now my husband has passed away and I'm pretty sick. I've been looking into what to do with him, but none of his brothers and sisters will take him so I'm trying to find out about group homes. I don't have a lot of money.'

Can you imagine forty-five years ago how bad things were for the disabled? There was no education, no services. But she made it and now after all that she's sick, he's in a wheelchair, and they face an uncertain future. He's probably thinking to himself, 'My dad is dead and none of my brothers and sisters want me. I'm talking to my mom about where I go after she dies, but I'm used to living in my home and eating dinner.' How sad. How hopeless.

Right now I foresee Chris living with me as an adult, and that's not my protective ego talking. I would happily change my view if Chris becomes capable of earning a living and really dealing well with life. I'm not in favor of group homes. I think that's the stupidest concept. What step is it to take if he lives with five others and aides that care for them? So what if he can wash the pots? That makes them feel better? I don't understand that. I don't get it. Why would a person get a sense of independence if he lives segregated with five people who all have autism? He's still not a part of the outside world. *I'd* rather watch him. Who better than his parents if he needs somebody to help him?

To me, a group home is necessary when you don't have Mommy and Daddy, you don't want to live in an institution and you need some help with daily living. It's great for a person with cerebral palsy in a wheelchair who doesn't want to live with her parents and needs somebody to help cook. It's great if you have no family and don't want to live in an institution, but can function quite well in the world.

If Chris isn't capable of going out on his own, if he just can't cope with the street, then he'll live with us. And it'll be fine. And I think it'll be great.

I would hope if Chris does continue living with us that he at least reaches a point where he's able to stay alone for a day or two at a time. That would give him independence, make me very happy, and I think it would make him very happy. But if that's not possible, who cares? On the other hand, he might be able to maintain his own place and become a person who says, 'Dad, I have a job and I need to move out.' Great!

I think people always set their expectations to normalize the person as much as possible because that's what *they* wish for them. I don't see any harm in recognizing the person's disability. Recognize their strengths, but you have to recognize their disabilities. A person in a wheelchair couldn't function outside if they didn't have ramps. My son may not be able to function outside because of certain social or language disabilities.

People always say to be successful you have to live on your own, be married and hold down a good job. Well, maybe my kid just can't do that. They're nice goals, but I don't understand the big deal. I would like him to be able to communicate. I would like him to be happy. I love the guy. I don't want to see him scared. I don't want to see him hurt. Those are the things I'm really concerned about, not if he lives in a group home.

All I really wish is that my son leads a very happy life; that he's able to take care of himself to the extent where he doesn't need constant assistance. I don't care if he lives on his own. It would be wonderful, but the things people put emphasis on to me are unimportant. If he needs some help from his parents or sister that's fine.

People always say he's got to be trained to do a job. Well, OK, if he can't do a job, he can't do a job. That's the least of my worries. Leading a fulfilling life is my priority for Chris. A lot of kids with autism can't fit into the workplace because they can't deal with people that well. OK, fine. We can accept that. Does he really have to pull his weight money-wise?

If this guy can go to the store, do some design work or draw that would be enough. If he's satisfied, has a few friends and goes to the movies with his dad, I think he'll be leading a great life. Of course I'd love to see him turn his creativity into higher planes. That doesn't mean he has to earn a living by it or get paid for it, but I'd love to see him draw a blueprint rather than just design with buttons. I think he's capable of great things. I say this not because that's what I want for him, but I see he has great talent in that area. He's got some great imitative skills. They're just not mature yet.

Hopefully new computer technology will offer opportunities for people with autism like Chris who can't work well in a traditional office setting. That's why I always say he will probably do well in design or art or computers. He just loves it and the computer will enable him to pursue that talent if he needs to work at home.

The thing people don't realize is that ninety-three, ninety-four per cent of these kids never leave the house. They don't have savant skills. They have a decent life, but probably live with mom and dad, and usually don't get married. They have very poor social lives and are very inept at tries for romance.

In fact, the only twinge I ever get is when I hopefully dream about him with a girlfriend. I think it'll be a hard time for him when he gets older. They say children with autism have a terrible time during puberty and the teenage years. Here you have children whose hormones are already imbalanced and are now raging even more out of control. The hormones even tend to bring on seizure disorders. A lot of these kids who typically crave order are disgusted with the changes in their bodies. They can't cope with them. Their sexuality is awakening and they have no social skills. Imagine a kid trying to approach a girl because he has sexual urges and has no social cues. It's bound to be an almost impossible situation. I'm sure it will happen to my own son and I feel sad about that for him.

Soon there's going to come a time when he's really cognitive of the world and painfully aware that he is very different. Even now I'm sure he realizes, 'There's a whole population out there doing a lot of stuff that I'm not doing. They're different from me.' He's not an idiot. He walks by, sees seven kids playing, and he's either not interested or can't approach them. He must know. Later he'll see kids his age dating the pretty blonde girl in the neighborhood who he can't even say hello to. That's going to hurt.

So helping him get along without being made fun of will be an important role for me when my son is a teen. I've already watched kids make fun of him as a toddler. I've heard the name 'retarded' thrown at him and his sister. 'Your brother can't even talk. He's a dummy.' I've seen them make fun of him physically. I've seen them make fun of his voice. I've heard it in the background. 'What about the retard? Ha. Ha.' So if this guy, three, four, five years old is getting taunted, just think. Who can be the meanest people in the world? Teenagers. He's my kid. I don't want him to be the butt of jokes. Naturally, I'd love to see him have friends and go dating. I'd love to see him married. I see great things for my son, but I also see hard, social things for him. His sociability is a much bigger concern than his work skills. I'm not going to fool myself. We don't even know how his language will progress. I sadly envision him looking at me one day and saying, 'Dad, why am I like this? Why am I different? How come I can't talk to that girl?' That's going to be tough.

I think it's a possibility that he might have a relationship with a woman, but the worst feeling for me is the thought of him standing on the side. Knowing that he's thinking, 'I would like to have a girl-friend. I would like to have a dance. But I can't make myself do it. I don't fit in. I'm different.' That's got to be a sad moment for a guy. Companionship is a part of life he's probably going to miss.

A lot of our questions we ask professionals are about teenage years. My wife even questioned Temple Grandin. Things were happening to her body that absolutely disgusted her, she told us. And she didn't think she could have gotten through her teens without medication. If Chris starts getting out of control during ad-olescence it may be the one time we consider medication; but only to get him through that period. We're preparing for that period right now by reading as much as possible.

I know one thing. The work and preparation never stops. There's not a time where you sit down and say, 'I did my job.'

A woman I know in Harrisburg who has a twenty-three-year-old with autism once warned me, 'Wait. Wait till you look into needs for adults with autism. It's terrible what's out there job-wise, and there are very few people or organizations who want to deal with them.'

Right now we just bought a bunch of books on different therapies and IEPs. Five years from now we'll be buying books on jobs and living. If we feel that he's going to be living on his own and he's going to have a little job, then we'll start preparing for that.

If we feel he's going to be with us, we'll start preparing that direction. It's too soon to know now, but it's always in the back of our minds.

Of course we've taken care of the legal basics to protect Chris as he grows into adulthood. We drew up a will and we are also slowly but surely trying to build a trust fund. Hopefully Jessica will be around and willing to provide for him when they are older and I am gone.

One of the jobs I've chosen for myself is to explain things to Chris and help him fit in as much as possible. If there are times when he's terribly hurt or somebody makes fun of him I really want to be there. I think that's important.

Hopefully in the next few years Chris will do well and we'll be able to send him to a regular public school. I know kids that function very well in the outside world. They know that they're different and understand they may only be able to talk to a limited number of people, but they have happy relationships.

Worries about the future for Chris seem endless. I worry about having enough money for now and for his adulthood. Hopefully we will always make do and come up with our heads above water, but it's a concern that weighs heavily on me. I also worry about lack of services for Chris now and in the future. Will he experience seizures, great hormonal rushes or violence during his teenage years? Is he going to be terribly frustrated sexually and be upset by his bodily changes? These things I always think about.

And of course, I'm concerned about later years when Jae and I are older or gone. If we go suddenly, where is he going to live? How is he going to earn a living? I pray that he will be self-sufficient enough or that his sister will care for him so that he continues leading the life to which he's accustomed.

When I dream of the future for Chris, I dream of a miracle cure. If that can't happen, I still dream of him being fully independent. But mostly, I just picture the two of us together having the same close relationship we've always had. In my mind I see us walking in the woods side by side, enveloped in the love of a father and son.

Epilogue

Since the writing of this book, my son and family have grown dramatically. Chris has been interacting beautifully – singing, speaking and playing. He has had a joyous summer filled with day camp, swimming and gymnastics. He watches movies, learns new songs and wrestles with his dad. We have begun to treat Chris bio-medically and teach him about safety, socialization and independence.

My wife continues to forge ahead, creating ground-breaking new therapy and has even designed a 2001 calendar for the Autism Society of America. My daughters grow stronger and more beautiful each day.

I wanted to write a brilliant epilogue – a fitting conclusion. But Chris finished the book for me the other day when we were playing. I was leaving for a conference at Penn State and wanted to soak up all the love I could because it was the first time I would be away from home for more than just a few hours. We wrestled and tickled and laughed and I started explaining that I was going off to 'work' and would be gone for almost two days when suddenly Chrissy grabbed my neck, looked up at me knowingly, smiled, and with great grace and passion, kissed me lovingly. I knew then that we had broken down autism's barriers.